Officer Ken Hubbs, San Diego Police Department:

"The scene inside the bathroom was one of horror. . . . Beard had forced both women down into the bathtub, and was standing over them with a large knife in one hand, and in the other, a .45 automatic pistol. Both victims were terrified at the look on Beard's face. It was obvious that he would carry out his threat and within seconds they would die. . . . The words that came over the radio took away my unsteadiness and fatigue. The crosshairs locked onto the target's head as if the rifle was held in a vise.

"PRT 1 to Sniper 1 . . .

"I held my breath and tightened my finger on the trigger.

". . . ready, ready . . . FIRE! Entry, GO!"

PRAISE FOR CRAIG ROBERTS'S *COMBAT MEDIC: VIETNAM*

"Awe-inspiring stories. . . ."
—*Proceedings*

PRAISE FOR *ONE SHOT—ONE KILL*

"The . . . reality of sniping is achieved superbly by personal accounts. The effect is both shocking and brutal."
—*Marine Corps Gazette*

Books by Craig Roberts

Police Sniper
Combat Medic: Vietnam
One Shot—One Kill (with Charles W. Sasser)
The Walking Dead (with Charles W. Sasser)

Published by POCKET BOOKS

For orders other than by individual consumers, Pocket Books grants a discount on the purchase of **10 or more** copies of single titles for special markets or premium use. For further details, please write to the Vice-President of Special Markets, Pocket Books, 1230 Avenue of the Americas, New York, NY 10020.

For information on how individual consumers can place orders, please write to Mail Order Department, Paramount Publishing, 200 Old Tappan Road, Old Tappan, NJ 07675.

POLICE SNIPER

CRAIG ROBERTS

POCKET BOOKS

New York   London   Toronto   Sydney   Tokyo   Singapore

An *Original* Publication of POCKET BOOKS

POCKET BOOKS, a division of Simon & Schuster Inc.
1230 Avenue of the Americas, New York, NY 10020

ISBN: 0-671-79459-0

First Pocket Books printing November 1993

10 9 8 7 6 5 4 3 2

POCKET and colophon are registered trademarks of Simon & Schuster Inc.

Cover art by Tim Tanner

Printed in the U.S.A.

This book is dedicated to all of the fine law enforcement officers who daily risk their lives to protect ours.

And—

To my agent, Ethan Ellenberg, for showing me the way; and Paul McCarthy, Senior Editor, Pocket Books, for his loyal support and constant encouragement through the years.

Acknowledgments

The author wishes to thank those who made this work possible:

To the National Tactical Officers Association, and in particular, to Mr. John Kolman, Director, for his invaluable assistance and support in this project. Mr. Kolman retired after twenty-six years of service with the Los Angeles County Sheriff's Department, nine of which were spent within the tactical section where he served as a SWAT team leader and SWAT commander.

To Major James Land, USMC (Ret). Major Land, a former competitive shooter with the Marine Corps rifle and pistol teams, established the 1st Marine Division Sniper School in Vietnam in 1966. He now shares his knowledge with law enforcement agencies around the country, and has been an invaluable source of information regarding the mental discipline and mind-set of the police precision rifle shooter.

To Lieutenant Burney York and Sergeants Jim Clark and Rob Cartner of the Tulsa Police Department's Special Operations Team who were willing to assist in any manner requested.

To Sergeant Robert Giban, Indianapolis Police Department, for providing information regarding SWAT operations in rural areas.

To the members of the Houston Police Department SWAT

ACKNOWLEDGMENTS

team for taking me under their wing for a day of familiarization with equipment and tactics.

To all of the fine men who shared their experiences with me: Sergeants Charles "Chuck" Foster, Ken Hubbs, and Garry Evans of the San Diego Police Department; Officer Mike LaVigne, Newport Beach Police Department; Lieutenant Lance Young, Ventura County Sheriff's Department; Officers John Gutmann, Ron Lindsey, and Robert Connolly of the Milwaukee Police Department; Public Safety Officer Al Morris, Kalamazoo Department of Public Safety; Trooper Jim White, Kentucky State Police; Master Officer Rick Phillips, Tulsa Police Department; Sergeant Rodney Hill, Houston Police Department; and Sergeant Ben Fravel, Prince William County Police.

And finally, to my friend Gunnery Sergeant Carlos N. Hathcock II, USMC (Ret), for sharing his unlimited knowledge and personal contacts with the author.

Author's Note

The information contained in this book came from sources ranging from official police reports, transcripts, and other official government documents and publications to actual taped interviews with the men whose stories appear on these pages.

The book is based upon the personal recollections of the participants and includes dialogue that was reconstructed as accurately as possible. Often, the actual dialogue between two people was taken directly from written reports or other documented accounts written at the time of the incident. However, in a few places, due to the passage of time and the participant's not remembering the exact words, minor dialogue was inserted to match the situation, the action, and the personalities involved.

"The first time you pull that trigger as a sniper and take a man's life, *your* life changes forever. Everyone changes. I don't care who you are. You will never be the same man that you were the instant before you squeezed that trigger. You have to learn to live with the fact that you were the instrument of death. If you can't, you're in the wrong business."

—Major E. James Land, Jr., USMC (Ret)
Commanding Officer
1st Marine Division Sniper School
Vietnam (1966)

Contents

CONTENTS

Preface

This book began not on the streets of an American city, but in a lonely jungle tree line overlooking a wide expanse of rice paddies south of the Song Cau Do River, near Da Nang, South Vietnam. The year was 1966. I was a Marine sniper. And it was my first time out.

As I scanned a wide expanse of steaming rice paddies through my scope, watching intently for any movement that might give away the enemy's presence—and a target—I felt that I had total control over my own fate and the fate of whoever fell within range of my Winchester. It was a feeling of anticipation—and question. When the time came, would I pull the trigger? Could I? Could I line up the figure of a human being in my crosshairs and squeeze the trigger, knowing that to do so would send a .30 caliber bullet slamming into an unsuspecting man, ending his life in a split second? It's one thing to shoot at paper targets and quite another to shoot at a living, breathing human being.

These are questions asked by everyone who has ever held a precision rifle in their hands and waited patiently for a "target" to present itself. They are questions that are only answered when the time comes to make the final decision. And when the time comes, not everyone can do it.

When my time came to answer "the question," I acquired my first target, lined up his black-clad figure in the fine lines of my crosshairs, hesitated only long enough to make sure he was armed—a prerequisite to taking a shot in those days—and squeezed the trigger of the Winchester.

In the following years, I have relived this shot and many others a thousand times. Not because of any vestige of remorse, but because they were turning points in my life. It's now been almost a quarter of a century since those days of waiting patiently in the sweltering jungles of Vietnam to take that single well-aimed shot. I harbor no bad memories from the experience gained in Southeast Asia. I was there to do a job and I did what I was trained to do. And the "targets" were my enemy. They were the people who would kill me or my buddies if given the opportunity. It was war.

Today there is another war being fought. It's not a conflict between governments or countries, fought by soldiers of an organized force who are defending a nation or advancing a cause. It's a battle of the most basic kind: between good and evil. And it's being fought right here in the United States.

It's a guerrilla war between criminals and the law enforcement officers who man that "thin blue line" between order and chaos, right and wrong, peace and anarchy.

It is a one-sided conflict. Like Vietnam, there are "Rules of Engagement." But the only ones who have to abide by the rules are the good guys. The criminals can arm themselves with anything they wish, ignore jurisdictional boundaries, attack whomever they want, hide within the population, and use their constitutional rights to defend themselves when they finally do get caught. But the police must strictly mind the laws, abide by departmental rules and regulations, policies and procedures, and every conceivable court decision and legal precedent.

For hardware, the cop on the street is normally armed with only a service pistol, and if he's lucky, a pump shotgun. Any force needed beyond what can be provided by these weapons requires outside assistance.

That assistance normally arrives in the form of SWAT. Most large law enforcement agencies, and many smaller ones, have their version of a Special Weapons and Tactics

Team. Each team is made up of specially equipped officers trained to handle extremely violent situations beyond the scope of the street patrol force. Often when the situation dictates it, the key member of the team is the police sniper.

As a former military sniper with combat experience, and now a twenty-five-year veteran police officer, I've been privileged to live in two worlds: that of the warrior, and that of the soldier of the streets. By melding my past experiences, I've been able to recognize many parallels between the two worlds—particularly that of the sniper. The one man who, even though he is part of a team, is singular in his final action.

On the following pages are the stories of many of the dedicated law enforcement officers who have served as police marksmen. From California to Virginia, the Great Lakes to the Gulf of Mexico, twelve police snipers relate what it is to become the final solution. For when all else fails, the one man that even SWAT turns to is the *police sniper*.

Introduction

By
GySgt Carlos N. Hathcock II, USMC (Ret)

Carlos Hathcock is a legend in Marine Corps history. As a U.S. Marine sniper in Vietnam, he is credited with 93 confirmed kills—and over 200 others that were not confirmed. He now spends his time traveling around the country conducting SWAT sniper schools for law enforcement agencies. For further reading about this legendary marksman, read One Shot—One Kill *by Charles W. Sasser and Craig Roberts (Pocket Books, NY).*

It is said that the most deadly and cost-effective weapon in the world is "the single well-aimed shot." For as Teddy Roosevelt once said, "In battle, the only shots that count are those that hit." This is doubly true in police work.

By taking Roosevelt's line of thinking one step further, one could say that "only the shot that hits the proper target counts." Though these statements are similar, there is a decided difference. To understand the difference, one must also understand the variation in roles between the military sniper and the police marksman.

The military sniper has one basic mission: to kill the enemy. Every shot taken is fired with a threefold purpose: eliminate an enemy soldier with surgical precision; deny the opponent freedom of movement in critical areas; and finally, reduce his morale by instilling an ominous feeling that out there, somewhere, is an undetectable and deadly threat.

The mission of the police marksman is just the opposite. Even though the final result may be the same, the motivation is different. For the police sniper, any shot taken is fired with one purpose in mind: to *save* lives. It is a shot that is taken when time has run out and no alternative remains.

When that time comes, and "Rule .308" is invoked, it becomes the responsibility of a very special person to end the confrontation. And do it without hesitation.

What kind of police officer can fill this role? It goes against the very grain of most law enforcement officers, men and women who are trained to save lives, not to end them.

Cops are the good guys. They consider themselves the guardians of civilization. Even though they realize there will be times when they must use deadly force, it is usually to protect themselves or someone else. And it is an unusal case when even that happens. Many officers spend entire careers without having to resort to gunplay.

Even after years on the job, as officers become hardened and cynical from witnessing injustices on a daily basis, they are still reluctant to use deadly force in an encounter. But for the police sniper, these feelings of reluctance must be overcome. He must be ready, at a moment's notice, to fire the shot that kills.

It is not a job for the meek. There is no room for hesitation when the time comes to squeeze the trigger. It must be an almost automatic reaction based on mental preparation and training that has taken place long before the fact.

In the classes I teach to SWAT snipers around the country, I ask my students: "If you had to, could you shoot your next-door neighbor? Your buddy down the street?" They had better be able to. If they can't, or are not sure, they are in the wrong business. If their next-door neighbor goes nuts, grabs a gun, and begins shooting the house up—maybe taking his own family hostage—and they get the call, they'd better be ready to take him out if that's the only thing that can end the situation.

"Think about this for a minute," I say to my students. "Here's a guy you've gone fishing with, drunk beer with, maybe spent weekends at his house watching ball games. Then, for whatever reason, he loses it and becomes a deadly threat. You get the call and realize that it is right next door to your house. Then when you arrive you find that he's holding a hostage. You take a position and wait while the negotiators try to talk him out. As the hours go by you have time to think. What do you think about? The fishing trips? The ball games? No. You think about sight alignment and trigger squeeze. That's all that matters at this point. Because when you get the green light, when you have the clear, unobstructed shot, and there is no other solution available, you no longer see the face of your buddy next door. What you must see is a target. A threat that has to be neutralized.

"If you can do this, then you can consider yourself a professional."

In Vietnam, when I taught at the sniper school for the 1st Marine Division, I had several sniper candidates I had to wash out. They simply didn't fit the mold. They may have been fine marksmen and good Marines, but when they looked through the scope, when they lined up a human face in the crosshairs and saw the eyes, they simply couldn't squeeze the trigger. Even combat experienced Marines sometimes couldn't do it. They found that being a sniper was a lot different from being a grunt in a firefight. In a firefight you shoot at muzzle flashes, distant forms, shadows. As a sniper you see the eyes. You see a person. And you know that in a microsecond you are going to kill him.

And that is the way a police sniper *has* to look at his job. His single well-aimed shot is the shot that saves. It has to be.

INTRODUCTION

To understand the function of the police sniper, one must understand how a SWAT team works.

A call for SWAT is normally initiated when a situation cannot be handled by the personnel who originally received the call. The situation may range from a holdup that has gone bad, trapping the robbers inside with innocent bystanders, to some psycho who has barricaded himself into a defensible position and opens fire on anyone and everyone in the area. Whatever the situation, specialists trained and equipped to handle such a confrontation must be utilized to bring it to a successful conclusion.

The first thing that must happen is containment of the area. The first officers to arrive on the scene, and the backup units who respond soon thereafter, set up a perimeter to contain the suspect or suspects and keep other bystanders at a safe distance. This is not an easy task. Usually the perimeter is ragged, and due to the small number of personnel that are available on short notice, often plagued with gaps. But because it must be tight enough to contain the immediate scene, the perimeter is often too close to keep bystanders at a safe distance from gunfire.

Because of this, a delegation of responsibility occurs as soon as the SWAT units arrive. The personnel of the Special Weapons and Tactics Team take over the scene from the first officers and readjust the perimeter as necessary to provide the most tactically advantageous positions. The primary officers, now relieved from this "inner" perimeter, take up positions farther away to form the "outer" perimeter. The inner perimeter personnel now are free to concentrate on the bad guys.

As soon as sufficent numbers of SWAT personnel arrive things begin happening fast. While every situation will have its peculiarities, in a typical SWAT senario the most likely pattern of events occurs as follows: a command post (CP) is established nearby, but out of any line of fire or vision of the suspects; the inner perimeter is established, manned, and shifted as necessary to give the best coverage and tactical advantage to the police; selected officers (often the snipers and their observers) scout the area and report back to the command post; anyone connected with the structure where the suspects are holed up is contacted if possible to provide information to the interior layout; maps and diagrams are drawn; and specially trained hostage negotiators attempt to establish communication with the villains.

Inside the command post several things are occurring simultaneously: the hostage negotiation team, if contact is established, records and writes down everything that is said between them and the suspects; an officer is assigned to be a "recorder" to write down in a log everything else that transpires; command is divided between an overall commander and the SWAT commander; an entry team is formed, and as soon as possible, briefed on the interior layout of the structure; communications specialists set up and man radios on various frequencies; medical support is established and put on standby; a press-release officer is delegated to deal with the media; and logistical support in the form of food, beverages, and other items is arranged in case the situation drags on for several hours—or days.

And the SWAT snipers are deployed.

By examining the initial reconnaissance reports, the SWAT commander designates areas of responsibility to the sniper teams. Ideal coverage will include all sides of the scene. However, this cannot always be done. Obstructions may make some areas useless, or there may not be a sufficient number of sniper teams to cover a large or many-faceted area. The final selection of positions is normally left to the snipers themselves. As soon as they deploy and establish a satisfactory observation and firing point, they report over the radio to the CP exactly where they are and what they can see. They are now the eyes and ears of the command post.

The range-to-target distance of these positions varies, but in an urban environment is normally less than one hundred yards. This differs dramatically from military snipers, who often shoot at ranges in excess of five hundred yards.[1]

If the position is ideal it will have certain key elements. First, it will have good cover and concealment. Cover is something that the marksman can use as a barrier against his opponent's fire. Concealment is something the sniper can hide under or behind that conceals him from the suspect's vision. Cover often offers concealment, but concealment does not necessarily offer cover. Next, our sniper will have a good kill zone between himself and the target's location. Should the suspect step outside—even with a hostage as a shield—the sniper should be able to cover the area without endangering others and without having to shoot around or too close to obstacles that might interfere.

His next step is to note everything he can see in front of him in his TAOR—tactical area of responsiblity. With his observer's aid, they draw a range card. On the card is every key feature in the TAOR. The card diagram, which resembles a fanshaped wedge that expands from his point to the target area, is then divided into sections and each section labeled by either number or letter. Later, when time is crucial, the observer can say "target . . . sector two, seventy-five yards," or "target . . . bravo, range fifty-five." Inside the sectors individual obstacles or key features can further be broken down and numbered.

In the case of a building, the windows and doors are numbered—usually left to right. This simple system puts

---

[1]Author's note: Carlos Hathcock, while a Marine sniper in Vietnam, made one kill at one and one-half miles by firing a single shot with a .50 caliber machine gun mounted with a Unertl scope. The shot was taken from the crest line of a hill down to a trail intersection that he had previously sighted in. Other sniper incidents have been recorded at ranges of 750 to 1,000 meters. These shots were fired from bolt-action Model 70 Winchesters (.30-06) and Remington 700s (.308).

both the sniper and observer on the same sheet of music. The observer can simply say "second floor, window three."

During this "setup" phase, which normally takes place in a matter of minutes, the marksman is also evaluating several factors that will influence his shot. The time of day and weather conditions play a key role in this evaluation. If it is night, what kind of lighting is available? Will he have to shoot into shadows? Into a lighted room? If it is raining or snowing, will the visibility decrease? Temperature will also affect his shot. A cold barrel behaves differently from a hot barrel. Even the muzzle velocity is affected between a barrel that has just spent several hours outside in subzero temperatures in the winter of the north or one hundred degree days in the summer of the south. A cold barrel squeezes the bullet more, creating more pressure and therefore more velocity. This means the bullet will drop less over the same range on a cold day. This is an extremely important consideration when a half-inch error at the point of impact might mean the difference between life and death for a hostage.

The marksman then analyzes the wind. If it is calm, his shot will be straight on. If the wind is blowing, he must adjust his angle accordingly. This done, if he is using a variable power telescopic sight, he adjusts his scope power. Most departments use a 3×9 variable. Nine power is for the most extreme ranges, three for close ranges. Most shots average a power setting of between four and six.

Finally, he checks the angle. There is a difference in ballistics between an "up" shot and a "down" shot. In the countersniper role, when our marksman's mission is to take out another sniper, this may be critical information. Because of the effects of gravity, a bullet fired up—say to the rooftop of a ten-story building—drops more than one fired on a flat trajectory. A bullet fired down—such as from the same rooftop—drops much less. At fairly close ranges or steep angles, this latter shot may not drop appreciatively at all. This is an interesting aspect when one considers that on November 22, 1963, Lee Harvey Oswald was supposed to have made a head shot at a moving vehicle at a range of almost a hundred yards, from a six-story high angle to street level, using a crude 6.5mm Carcano carbine with a worn barrel and a defective scope. And I doubt, since he was not a trained sniper, that he knew of the downward trajectory formula. Add to this fact that he supposedly fired three rounds in 5.6 seconds, through the leaves on a tree that partially obscured the car almost half of those 5.6 seconds —dropping the rifle from his eye to work the bolt after each shot. And all of this time the limousine that carried President Kennedy and Governor Connally was moving on a curve. If one is to believe the Warren Commission Report, these were three remarkable shots indeed.

All of these factors must be considered when the sniper team takes its position. But the main thing on the rifleman's mind is the target—and how to neutralize it if called upon to do so. This is another area where military sniper and police marksman differ. The military sniper normally, because of the much longer ranges, shoots at "center mass." This means that he must content himself with striking his target somewhere in the center of his body. Not every center of mass shot is fatal. But even wounding an enemy soldier can be effective, for now he requires stretcher bearers and medical care.

The police sniper, on the other hand, must shoot to kill. In a hostage situation, where a criminal is holding one or more hostages as a shield, possibly gripping a knife to their throat or a gun to their head, the first shot must be instantly fatal. There can be no muscular reflex that can spasmodically jerk and pull a trigger or draw a knife across a throat. To do this, he concentrates his crosshairs on a point within a narrow band (approximately two inches) around the head of his target. This band is basically eye level, and if penetrated with a high-velocity bullet, causes an instant shutdown of physiological systems and motor movements by separating the brain from the rest of the nervous system. Because of its effect when hit, this area is known as the "no-reflex zone."

When the time comes to take the shot, the no-reflex zone is the police marksman's focus of attention.

And because of this, he is also looking directly into the face—directly into the eyes—of someone whose life he is about to extinguish.

Not everyone can do it.

In this book are stories of men who can, and *have* done it. Stories of nerve-wracking hours spent on blistering hot rooftops and in dark, freezing cold rooms watching, waiting, patiently for their services to be utilized.

No matter what they are called, whether it is sniper, rifleman, marksman, or countersniper, the job is the same. But it is a job that few can perform—and a job that is performed only when all else fails. For when the criminals can't be talked into giving up, and the entry team can't perform a rescue, and the clock begins ticking down to the point where an innocent life may be lost, the single well-aimed shot of the police sniper becomes the final option. It is the ultimate instrument that eliminates the threat.

And at this time, it becomes *the shot that saves!*

1
Massacre in San Ysidro

Wednesday, July 18, 1984, was a typical midsummer day for the coastal cities and beach towns of Southern California. The weather was clear, and the morning sea breeze shifted early to bring the hot dry desert air to the city. By afternoon, the sky glared warm and blue as the temperature along the coast soared to ninety-six degrees.

For James Oliver Huberty, a forty-one-year-old unemployed welder from Ohio who had migrated with his family to San Diego eight months before, the day had not begun well. He, along with his wife, Etna, and one of his two daughters, had spent most of the morning in traffic court in answer to a traffic citation. By lunchtime, he had grown sullen and moody.

Still, there was no reason to waste the remainder of the day, especially since they had come all the way in from San Ysidro, a community south of San Diego on the edge of the Mexican border, where the Hubertys lived. Perhaps an outing to the San Diego Zoo would take his mind off the court experience—and the fact that since coming to the Land of Opportunity, he had encountered little luck in finding a job. For a short time he had worked as a security guard for a condominium complex in Chula Vista, but that didn't last. His employer, citing general instability in

Huberty's behavior, had fired him one week earlier. Nothing seemed to be going right and it was beginning to affect his family life. His wife, Etna, began noticing his moodiness. As the days had gone by since moving to San Ysidro, she noted that he became increasingly introverted. He had always been a nervous person, unable to cope with pressure, but lately had become even more withdrawn. She agreed that a visit to the zoo would be nice. Maybe it would cheer him up.

Huberty first took the family to a McDonald's restaurant across the street from the courthouse for lunch, then drove to the San Diego Zoo in Balboa Park. After a few hours of wandering around the asphalt paths that separated the animal enclosures and cages—and mumbling something about "Society had their chance"—Huberty wanted to leave.

Shortly before 4:00 P.M., the Hubertys arrived home. Etna, tired from the excursion, lay down for a nap. But James was restless. He changed clothes, pulling on a black T-shirt and military camouflage trousers. Then started for the door.

"I'll see you later," he said to Etna.

"Where are you going, honey?"

"I'm going hunting humans."

The statement did not register with Etna. She had heard him say many irrational things whenever he was dealing with stress, as he had been this day. She lay back down and closed her eyes.

But this day would be different.

Huberty didn't go far. The San Ysidro McDonald's restaurant at 522 West San Ysidro Boulevard was only two hundred yards from his apartment. It was 4:00 P.M. To a deranged mind, the restaurant must have appeared an excellent target. With its playground in front near the street, parking lots on each side and rear, and Interstate 5 blocking rear access, it was an acceptable urban defensive position to one not concerned with escape. As an added advantage, the building sat slightly above the level of the street and parking lots, giving any defender a commanding view of the frontal and side approaches.

And there were plenty of "humans" inside. At least fifty.

Huberty wheeled his brown Mercury Marquis into the lot and parked. He grabbed a bag containing a portable AM-FM radio/cassette player and ammunition of various calibers, jammed a 9mm Browning Highpower semiautomatic pistol into his waistband, picked up a 9mm Uzi semiautomatic carbine,[1] and a Winchester twelve-gauge pump shotgun, and went inside.

"I've killed thousands and I'll kill thousands more," he screamed as he stormed through the door. The patrons sat frozen in shock as he opened fire.

All units, 245 just occurred at West San Ysidro. Got about four calls on it.[2]

A 245 alert was a shooting. To a police officer responding to such a call, the numbers squawking from the radio always sent a surge of adrenaline racing into one's system. Someone had been shot, and until more information became available, the gunman might still be there—and still shooting.

Two officers picked up their microphones, keyed the transmit buttons, and volunteered. *712 William. 714 William.*

The dispatcher continued: *It's supposed to be at McDonald's at 425 West San Ysidro.*[3] *It's a 245 shooting. Anyone else enroute besides 712 and 714 William?*

Four more cars answered the call. It was now 1603 hours—4:03 P.M.—and more information was beginning to

---

[1] The Uzi carbine is a semiauto version of the Uzi submachine gun. But to meet federal law it is fitted with a 16.1-inch barrel. Two magazines are available: twenty-five and thirty-two rounds.

[2] All italics are from actual radio transcription of incident.

[3] The first address to come into dispatch was the address where the complainant found a telephone, not that of the McDonald's.

flood into dispatch. Immediately it was passed to the responding units. *The shots were coming from inside the McDonald's pointed out across toward the post office across the street. The little girl that was shot is being brought into the post office now.*

More cars volunteered and accelerated toward San Ysidro. Finally a description was broadcast. *They've got a description—reportedly the suspect is a white male, about forty years old, with a light blue shirt and dark pants . . . and shooting is with a rifle.*[4]

The first officer to arrive at the scene, Officer Miguel "Mike" Rosario in 712 Nora, came under fire as soon as he pulled up in front of the post office across the parking lot east of the restaurant, three hundred feet from the side door. Bullets slammed into his car, one shattering the windshield, causing him to lurch to a stop and grab his mike. "I'm taking rounds. We're taking rounds here!"

10-4. Where are you, 712 Nora?

"I'm east of McDonald's!"

It wasn't an advantageous location. Other units would arrive shortly to block the street, but there was no one in the back of the restaurant to cover that quadrant. Now that Rosario's police car had been seen, the gunman might try to escape from the back door. Rosario dropped the mike, slammed the car into reverse, and drove behind the post office. From there, he exited the vehicle and raced to a Dumpster in the northwest corner of the McDonald's parking lot that commanded an angled view of the back door. Rosario, a member of the Primary Response Team (PRT),[5] would have to hold this position until the remaining team members could arrive and get into position.

Behind Rosario, on Interstate 5, another marked unit pulled up and screeched to a stop on the shoulder of the

---

[4] This is the first of four separate descriptions that would be received that day.

[5] San Diego Police Department's on-duty portion of SWAT.

4

freeway. The back of the restaurant was now effectively covered.

But other responding units had more difficulty in getting into position. The traffic was building and jamming the streets nearby, and those patrol cars trying to get to San Ysidro on the freeway found the going almost impossible due to the rush hour traffic. For them, frustration started to build quickly as the radio began passing even more morbid information.

211 Baker . . . we need someone near the Yum Yum Doughnuts. There we have three children [that] have been shot, plus apparently . . . the suspects are inside the McDonald's restaurant.

More suspect descriptions began to flow in. It appeared that there was more than one assailant inside the building. Was it an armed robbery that had gone bad? Were the suspects using the customers as hostages? Every minute created more confusion.

715 William, I've got two victims on the north side of McDonald's. That was two that 715W could see. Actually, three eleven-year-old boys had ridden their bikes to the restaurant to buy soft drinks and play on the playground equipment. But as soon as they arrived, they were gunned down. Two died instantly. Another, Joshua Coleman, played dead until officers could finally get to him much later.

The number of shots coming from within the McDonald's kept any officer from getting close enough to see the carnage inside. Huberty ordered everyone inside the restaurant to lie on the floor, then as soon as all had complied, he began shooting at random. Anyone that moved was shot immediately, others he killed as he took a notion. As he walked up and down the aisles, shooting into his victims, furniture, and even light fixtures, he paused occasionally to release a fusillade through the windows toward the officers manning the perimeter. The windows, now spiderwebbed and cracked, were almost impossible to see through from the outside.

Still, officers began to size up the situation.

710 Sam, [are the] two victims on the north side of the McDonald's . . . is that in the clear where paramedics can get to them?

Negative. It's in the line of fire.

712 Nora [to dispatch], better make this a code 11 also, we're getting shots fired. We have numerous people inside who are shot!

It is now 4:10 P.M., seven minutes after the first call was transmitted by dispatch, and a full SWAT mobilization has been requested by a "code 11" sent by 712N.

711 John . . . I have a victim on the freeway with a couple of shots in the leg . . . north on I-5 just about a hundred yards south of McDonald's. . . .

Then, the call that turns one's blood to ice water: *I need an ambulance at Smith and San Ysidro—baby shot.*

As the bloodbath continued, a dozen things seemed to happen at once: reports of victims being struck by gunfire outside the McDonald's began trickling in; a command post was established at the Bank of Coronado one block away by the first supervisor to arrive;[6] a fire truck responding to the scene was taken under fire and disabled, the firemen abandoning the vehicle pinned down behind the truck; Medevac ambulances were summoned but told to stay back until the area could be secured; news helicopters appeared overhead adding to the confusion; more shots sporadically being fired inside—and from—the restaurant; two victims who had been dragged into the post office died; and the officers on the perimeter, due to the difference in sounds of the three weapons used by Huberty and the conflicting clothing descriptions, still could not tell how many suspects were involved. Attempts to locate and identify the assailants were made doubly difficult by now—the sun, angled in the western horizon, painted the shattered window glass of the

---

[6]Sergeant Ken Hargrove of Southern Division.

restaurant almost opaque, making it nearly impossible to see through from the outside.

All of this in just twenty-six minutes.

At 4:30 P.M. the PRT units began to arrive. And within minutes the first sniper team, Sniper One, took its position on the rooftop of the building across the street north of the restaurant. From there, they could cover the front of the building and east and west parking lots in case the gunmen exited. But they could not see well enough into the interior to take action.

For the next fifteen minutes, Huberty had all of the luck. Then at 4:46 P.M., that changed. Two employees of McDonald's managed to escape undetected through the back door and ran into the waiting arms of the officers manning the perimeter. Debriefed within two minutes, a new scenario developed. There was only one gunman, armed with three weapons, and he was wearing a black T-shirt and camouflage trousers. For the first time, the officers had an accurate—and final—description of the suspect.

At 5:02 P.M., SWAT sniper Charles "Chuck" Foster, and his spotter, Officer Barry Bennett, climbed to the roof of the post office overlooking the parking lot and the east side of McDonald's.

For James Oliver Huberty, now sitting on the stainless steel service counter surrounded by bodies, casually reloading magazines for his Uzi as a tape—*Heartbreak City* by The Cars—plays on his portable radio, the situation was about to change.

2

Charles "Chuck" Foster, San Diego Police Department
July 18, 1984

The day that I will remember for the rest of my life started rather routinely. It was a hot, clear July day, and I was participating in advanced officer training in Balboa Park, a lush green expanse of thick lawns punctuated by eucalyptus and palm trees covering almost four square miles in central San Diego just north of downtown. It contains the San Diego Air and Space Museum, several walking and jogging paths—and the San Diego Zoo.

We were working out with the PR-24 baton, a nightstick equipped with a ninety-degree handle at one side that is useful for various defensive and trapping techniques not available to the standard straight baton. For our department, this was a relatively new innovation in equipment in 1984, and I found the training interesting. The class went well, and by early afternoon we finished and were dismissed. With a little time remaining before heading home, I returned to my substation, Western Division, and hit the weight room for a workout.

There was no radio in the workout room, nor in the locker room. I had no way of knowing of the events transpiring in

San Ysidro, nor of the SWAT call-out that had been announced just two minutes before I walked out of the station to head home.

"Hey, Chuck," called one of the officers in a patrol car parked outside the station, listening intently to the radio. "Did you know there's a PRT[1] call-out? Big deal down in San Ysidro. A two-four-five at the McDonald's."

I knelt by the car door and listened to the radio for a few seconds. I could hear the excited voices of officers talking about suspects firing shots at them, people "down," apparently shot, and generally all hell breaking loose.

I had heard enough. You don't stand around and ask a lot of questions when there's a call-out. You just go. I ran back into the substation, grabbed my SWAT gear and rifle—a Steyr SSG Model 69 in .308 mounted with a 4X12 Bushnell scope—and sprinted to my car.

Running Code 3[2] south on the freeway toward San Ysidro, I could hear the situation unfolding on the radio. More casualties were being reported, paramedics couldn't get to them, more shots were being fired, officers were pinned down, everything bad that could happen seemed to be happening. My gut churned with both adrenaline and frustration. It was now rush hour and the traffic was horrendous. In California, the freeways at rush hour often become little more than slow moving masses of cars lurching forward in an enormous accordion stop-and-go routine. And in the worst times, like when there is an accident, they are little more than parking lots.

The address in San Ysidro was only fifteen miles from my substation, but it took thirty minutes to get there. Those minutes, as I fought my way through the traffic, seemed to drag on forever. Officers and citizens needed help, and I

---

[1]San Diego maintains a Primary Response Team normally consisting of one sergeant and five officers. Their job is to respond to and contain a dangerous situation until SWAT can arrive.

[2]Emergency lights and siren on.

could be of little use stuck in traffic miles away. Besides fighting the traffic, I now found myself fighting stress, frustration, and tension. The radio calls kept coming in, and as they did I painted a mental picture of what was developing at the scene. I thought, *Okay, there's a guy there shooting. Must have been an armed robbery that had gone bad and the cops showed up before the robber had a chance to get away. So now it's turned into a standoff and the guy wants to keep shooting instead of talking.* It never did occur to me that this guy was just there to kill everybody he could. We just thought that some people got caught in an exchange of gunfire and maybe a few got hit.

Finally, at 4:40 P.M., I wheeled up to the command post that had been set up in the 300 block of San Ysidro at the Bank of Coronado. Within minutes I had changed into my SWAT uniform, strapped on my equipment, picked up my sniper rifle, and reported in to the SWAT equipment van.

"What's the situation?" I asked Sergeant John Madigan, the SWAT mission leader who was busily reviewing intelligence as it came in.

"It's hard to tell at the moment. All we know so far is that some guy's inside the McDonald's shooting at everything that moves."

"Where do you need me?"

"Take Bennett and get over to the post office next to McDonald's. See if you can establish your position on the roof where you can cover the east side of the restaurant. We've already established one sniper position on the building across the street to the north, so your call sign will be Sniper Two. Let me know when you're in position. And . . . if you can get a shot, take it."

I nodded at Officer Barry Bennett, who would serve as my spotter, and went in search of the post office. I had never been there before, and neither had Barry. We asked directions from some of the officers manning the outer perimeter, but they were obviously as inexperienced in the local geography as we were, as we were misdirected and started off on the wrong side of the street. But we finally managed to spot the McDonald's and changed course accordingly, running as fast as the weight of our gear would allow.

We could hear shooting as we reached the post office, a flat-roofed one-story building of Spanish architecture. Inside, several frightened employees looked at us with wide eyes as we entered with our weapons and SWAT gear. I took in the layout of the building, then quickly got directions to an interior ladder that led to the roof.

We climbed to the roof, opened the trapdoor, and peeked out. The roof was about fifty-by-fifty feet square, surrounded by a short retaining wall that stood between three and four feet high that would offer concealment—and depending on the ammo being used by the bad guy—hopefully cover against any incoming fire. We crawled onto the roof and scurried to the wall nearest the McDonald's.

It was hot, and the combination of heat and the run to the post office had taken its toll. We were drenched with sweat, breathing heavily, and pumped high on adrenaline. I sat down with my back against the wall to catch my breath and compose myself. I pulled my OD cravat[3] from around my neck, wiped my face, then wrapped it around my forehead. I looked at my watch. It was 1702—5:02 P.M.

I picked up the hand-held radio and notified the command post that we had made the roof and were beginning our surveillance. As I did, Barry retrieved a pocket mirror and edged it up over the top of the wall to serve as a crude periscope. No use presenting ourselves as targets to the gunmen if a mirror would do.

It wouldn't.

"Chuck, I can't see a thing with this thing," Barry said disgustedly. "I can't get enough detail at this range." The

---

[3] A cravat is a neckerchief or headband made from a cloth sling found in a first-aid kit.

distance to the target from this position was between thirty-five and forty yards. Too far to use a small hand mirror.

That only left one alternative: the Pop Up routine. This entailed us moving up and down the wall at a crouch and "popping" our heads up, exposing ourselves for just a few seconds to see whatever we could, then changing locations and repeating the routine. We took turns moving, peeking over the edge of the wall to scan the building, then advising each other what we saw. For fourteen minutes we kept this up.

As we did this, ragged and intermittent shots rang out in the vicinity of the restaurant. But none, as of yet, had been directed our way.

Below us, Sergeant Chuck Wallace, the PRT leader, had taken a position at a window in the post office that faced the restaurant. He had been observing the McDonald's from his street-level position for some time. Finally, he spotted Huberty inside. We caught part of his radio transmission.

. . . This guy's sitting on the front counter, an older guy with a balding head. He's got a gun folded across his arm. Sniper One, can you see him?

Negative. Not from our position.

Wallace sounded frustrated as he acknowledged: *10-4. I can see him, but I can't take a shot at him. He's behind a truck. He's just standing there and walking around.*

Barry keyed the mike. "Sniper two, which way is he facing? Which way is he facing?"

He's facing the street where the fire truck is parked, answered Wallace. *He's behind the counter where the cashier would normally be. Appears he's standing in front of the counter. He is moving toward the front of the building now.*

Then we had to ask the question. Though we had been told to take a shot if we could get one, I wanted to make sure that hadn't changed—and I wanted it on the record. *"We got a green light. Was that affirm on the green light?"* A green light meant that we were authorized to shoot if the opportunity presented itself.[4]

502 Lincoln . . . that's affirm.[5] 502L, a patrol lieutenant, had the authority to make the call. That was good enough for us.

The radio traffic continued with updates from Wallace: *. . . male, Mexican, balding, in his forties, wearing glasses, a maroon shirt, and camouflage pants . . .*[6]

What's his 10-20? someone asked, wanting to know the suspect's "location."

PRT leader . . . I've lost him. But he was at the front counter just a second ago.

SWAT commander . . . they don't have the green light if he's inside the building with the hostages!

Damn! I couldn't believe it. We had the green light when I

---

[4]The terminology for permission to shoot varies around the country. In San Diego, a "green light" means that a decision has been reached that the suspect's death is the only means left to resolve the situation. A "red light," on the other hand, does not prohibit shooting. It does, however, permit an officer to use deadly force to protect citizens, themselves, or other officers from death or serious bodily injury.

[5]Unlike military radio protocol, where the sending station calls the receiving station first, then identifies itself second (such as: "Alpha two-niner hotel, *this is* Bravo seven-six delta, over?"), in police radio protocol, the sender identifies himself first using his call sign, then sends message. Example: "Seven-twelve Baker . . . [pause] I need a backer at Second and Main." Unless otherwise identified, the dispatcher is the receiving unit for all calls transmitted blind. However, radio protocol often degenerates to less rigid rules in closed frequency operations such as SWAT operations, sounding more like normal conversation than radio transmissions.

[6]Three separate descriptions conflict on the color of Huberty's shirt. Some reports indicate black, others maroon, and still others light blue.

left the command post—Madigan, the SWAT mission leader, had told me to take a shot if I could get it—which I had just reaffirmed. Now it was withdrawn.

10-4, advising units, you do not have the green light if he's inside the building with hostages, repeated the dispatcher.

PRT leader . . . 10-4. Make sure both sniper positions and all PRT members are 10-4 on that.

I continued to watch what I could see through the door with my scope, which was set on six power. And at that range—just over a hundred feet—I had good clarity and magnification.

SWAT commander . . . if he comes out, tell them they have a green light. If he's inside with the hostages, they have a red light. And also, let me know how many SWAT officers are there so we can form a rescue.

PRT leader . . . we have four officers and one sergeant containing the scene at this time.

Other orders and chatter punctuated the radio traffic as Bennett and I continued to focus our attention on the side entrance of the McDonald's: a nearby shopping center was being evacuated; an entry team was being readied; and people who have gathered on rooftops of nearby buildings to watch the action were being ordered to vacate the area. Then, some idiot who lived in a nearby apartment came out with a gun and had to be taken down by the outer perimeter officers for the safety of everyone in the area.

Then the word came.

502 Lincoln . . . advise the sniper teams that the green light is on.

The dispatcher paused for only a second. *10-4. You want me to advise the sniper teams the green light is on?*

That's affirm!

I heard Team One reply from their position on the roof of the building north, across the street from the front of the McDonald's: *Sniper one . . . confirming, inside or out?*

That's affirm. Acting on the information we have, inside or out, the green light is on for the sniper units.

14

Sniper one . . . 10-4.

"Sniper two . . . ten-four," we acknowledged.

We had the green light, but we didn't have a target.[7] We continued to wait.

Then at sixteen minutes after the hour, a rapid exchange of gunfire erupted between McDonald's and somewhere below our position in the post office building.

Wallace, who was positioned by a window inside the room below to observe the restaurant, had spotted Huberty. He broke out a window in preparation for engagement. He knew that if he had to cover anyone, or defend his spot, he had to break out the glass to get maximum coverage and view—and prevent any blow-back of glass caused by shooting through it. As he was breaking out the glass, Huberty saw him. He took aim at Wallace and fired a shot.

Wallace immediately returned fire, squeezing off one round with his .223 Ruger Mini-14 that struck a window frame. Huberty, not dismayed, shot back, and this was answered with another shot by Wallace. This shot also hit the window frame. Huberty, now enraged, leveled his Uzi at the post office and began jerking the trigger until the magazine ran dry. This done, he retreated farther back into the restaurant.

The bullets ripped into the walls below Bennett and me, many penetrating into the building, driving Wallace back from the window. Miraculously, he wasn't hit.

But Barry and I didn't know of the minifirefight taking place below. To us, it was obvious that the rounds had come in our direction. We thought that we had possibly been seen sticking our heads up and had come under fire. We both dropped as low as we could and looked at each other.

"Is that guy shooting at us?" asked Barry, a look of apprehension on his face.

---

[7] Neither sniper positions had a clear view of Huberty as of yet, so the changes in shooting instructions did not affect the outcome.

15

"I'm not sure," I replied. Then, to lighten the moment, I asked, "Are we having fun yet?"

Barry's face split into a grin and I felt a bit of relief come over me as I mentally regrouped.

Back on the radio, we asked if anyone knew whether the suspect had shot directly at us, or if anyone could advise us of exactly where the guy was. That's when we found out about Wallace and the situation that had taken place below. Now we knew that Huberty still had not seen us.

PRT leader . . . can anybody see this guy now? asked Wallace.

Several people tried to talk at once, each drowning the other out. Finally one voice came through, followed by a more orderly exchange. But the information was confusing and contradictory.

. . . appears to be in front of McDonald's inside, on the San Ysidro side.

Team leader . . . he's at the counter now. He's back by the front counter.

. . . which way is he facing?

. . . facing the street . . . sitting down at the front counter now.

I needed a heads-up on when the gunman might approach my door. I couldn't engage anything with precision beyond the tiny area of entryway inside the door, and even that was reduced in half by the downward angle of our view. My entire engagement area was like a wedge-shaped room, similar to a closet under a staircase. The gunman would have to present himself within that area, and hold his spot long enough for me to react. Split seconds counted and I needed all the warning—all the help—I could get.

"Barry, we need to get some kind of warning when this guy might head toward the door."

Barry keyed the mike. "Sniper two . . . when they give a location, tell us which way he is facing." If he was facing the post office, perhaps he was thinking of coming our way.

He's still facing toward the fire truck.

10-4, he's probably reloading.

The pop-up technique was not working too well. The big problem that surfaced was the fact that it was now late in the afternoon and the sun was angled above the western horizon, in the direction we had to look. The light from the sun was diffusing through the broken and spiderwebbed patterns of glass in the picture windows of the restaurant. Other than being shattered, the tinted safety glass remained in place. This created a visual barrier as the glare of the sun made any observation through the windows extremely difficult. The side doors, on the other hand, had most of their glass shot out. If I could get into position to get an angle view through a door, I might be able to report something.

I eased farther down the roofline and popped up. I checked my breathing, regripped the Steyr's stock, and focused my mind—and the crosshairs—on the doorway. All I needed was a target. Even if it appeared for just a couple of seconds—long enough to acquire, identify, and squeeze the trigger.

The door, void of glass, centered in my view. I immediately saw a pair of legs, wearing camouflage pants, hanging over the stainless steel service counter. I could also see what appeared to be a small rifle or carbine, black in color, resting across his lap. This guy was obviously very calm and unconcerned about the whole situation. From what I could observe, he seemed to be reloading a magazine.

"I see him, Barry. But I want to wait until he is in a more exposed position. All I can see are his legs."

I felt that initial shot of adrenaline that hits you when you realize that you are about to become the center of everything that is happening—and that you might just be the one to take the shot that everyone is depending on. My heart began to race, my pulse pounding in my temples and chest.

I had to stop and get a grip on myself. I began to mentally talk myself down through these sensations and feelings, to calm myself long enough to concentrate on lining up the crosshairs to take the shot. I wanted to make it good. There needed to be only one shot. And if it wasn't good, a shot that took the guy out permanently . . . I didn't even want to think about that.

It was only a few seconds later when he made his next move—and I made mine.

I watched the legs as they approached the door, then saw his torso, and finally his entire body up to his shoulders. Then he stopped. He had casually stepped over bodies, more strolling than stalking, and now stood about ten feet from the doorway—framed perfectly. He stood there, apparently once again checking out Wallace's position below, completely surrounded by bodies. The dead lay in front of him, behind him, and to each side. It was a sight you would expect to see in the movies, but not in real life.

With my view of his head obscured by the top of the door frame, I had to make a decision. I could take the shot now, using a center of mass shot for the heart, or wait and see if he would move closer, exposing his head for a no-reflex zone shot to the head. I decided to take the shot.

I centered the crosshairs over his heart and took up the slack on my trigger.

The recoil of the rifle didn't seem like much. It was almost as if the shot were underpowered. The Steyr, instead of bucking up, only recoiled straight back. The scope stayed centered on him and I could see him fall back. It was unreal, almost surrealistic. My mind, now working in two speeds simultaneously, hyperspeed and slow motion, recorded the scene before me and took notes of the little things, the unusual things, that were happening. First the rifle barrel had not risen with the discharge, then my ears, after the shot, were not ringing. And I had not worn earplugs. They should have been ringing with the loud report of the .308 round, but weren't. Incredible.

I didn't dwell on these thoughts. They just came.

I could see the man down, on his back, with no sign of movement. I immediately worked the bolt, chambering a fresh round, and reacquired the target. Barry, watching with his binoculars, picked up the hand-held radio and keyed the transmit switch.

"Sniper two. The suspect is down."

Advising the suspect is down?

"Sniper two . . . he's on the floor in front of the counter. It doesn't look like he's moving. Don't move in yet, though."

SWAT team leader . . . hold your positions. Units hold your positions at this time.

Then someone came on the radio, evidently reporting the sound of my shot and mistaking it, because of its loud report, to be from the suspect's shotgun.

He just shot off his shotgun.

Barry keyed the radio. "Sniper two . . . negative on the shotgun."

Sniper one . . . has he been hit by one of our men?

"Sniper two . . . that's affirmative," reported Barry. "Have units hold their positions, I'm watching him now. He's on the floor in front of the counter . . . he does not appear to be moving. There are at least three people down with him. They look eleven-forty-four."[8]

PRT leader . . . do we have an ETA for the SWAT team?

SWAT team leader . . . they're moving down now.

We updated the entry team as they moved into position. "Sniper two to SWAT team leader . . . the suspect is in the middle of the ordering area. He's on his back, his head is facing toward the west, we haven't seen any movement since he fell down."

PRT team leader to command post . . . we have absolutely

---

[8]In San Diego, the code "11-44" means "dead." Other departments use various other codes to denote death, such as "10-7" (a slightly twisted meaning since this means "out of service"), and Signal 30 (the DOA code normally used for traffic accidents but applicable to any death including suicide).

no movement from inside the McDonald's. Have at least three or four ambulances standing by. We're going to need them.

Barry and I continued to watch the assailant, now convinced that he was dead and would not prove a threat to the entry team. Barry reported in. "Sniper two . . . I'm watching the suspect. There doesn't appear to be any chest rising at all through my binoculars. He's lying on his back, his head facing west, his hands toward the counter and his feet toward the street. Like I said, there's been no movement since the shot."

SWAT team leader . . . 10-4. SWAT team leader to all perimeter units, the entry team is making their entry. All PRT units, the entry team is moving.

I sat down on the roof with the rifle across my lap and prepared myself for what I expected to be a flood of emotions—the aftershock—that I had heard would follow the act of killing someone. Kind of a cross between guilt feelings mixed with emotional release. Maybe a shaking of nervousness or fear. The questions that would come: Did I do the right thing? Did I follow procedure? What would the investigators, Monday morning quarterbacking the shooting, say? I expected all of this and sat there waiting for it to happen.

Nothing did. I was expecting the worst, but nothing seemed to be happening to me mentally. I gave it a couple of minutes, then said to myself, *Okay, so much for that.*

I got back up to my knees and looked over the retaining wall toward the restaurant. The guy was still there. It definitely was no dream—or nightmare. He was still there . . . dead.

I watched as the entry teams made their move and entered the restaurant. Within seconds, the place was declared secured and a friend of mine on the entry team, Officer Tom Rizzo, came back out into the parking lot.

He looked up at me and pointed. He had a kind of "did you do it?" look on his face.

I nodded and made a slashing motion across my throat to inquire whether the gunman was dead or not. He gave me the "thumbs-up." As he turned to go back inside, ambulances and paramedics began to stream into the parking lot. Remarkably, there were still survivors inside.

I knew that Barry and I would have to be debriefed by the homicide investigators. This is normal procedure, though an unpleasant one, whenever an officer is involved in a shooting where the suspect dies. Lieutenant Bill Becker, the SWAT executive officer, made the arrangements. He would take me to the Southern Division substation for the interview. But first, he came up to the roof to see the layout. When he was ready to leave he asked me, "You want to go inside and look around before we leave?"

"No, thanks, Lieutenant. I saw enough through my scope."

• • •

James Oliver Huberty would never again hunt humans. The Federal 168 grain jacketed soft point bullet entered his chest, tore through his aorta, severed his spine, and exited his back. He was probably dead before he hit the ground. But by the time Chuck Foster could take the single shot that would end the massacre, Huberty had killed twenty-one people and wounded nineteen others. And he did not discriminate. The victims ranged from eight months to seventy-five years.

In one hour and seventeen minutes, Huberty fired 251 9mm rounds from his Uzi and Browning—192 of which were Czech-made military hardball capable of penetrating soft body armor. He also fired 12 twelve-gauge shotgun rounds of both buckshot and bird shot. Ninety of the 9mm rounds were recovered inside the restaurant, giving some idea how many rounds may have been fired through the windows at officers outside.

Had it not been for the single precision shot fired by Chuck Foster, Huberty could have continued his onslaught.

He still had plenty of ammunition left, and there were still people inside who would have died had not Huberty been taken out when he was.[9] Some of the people that he had shot, possibly unknown to him, were still alive. Incredibly, most of these were lying around the serving counter—the same counter where he casually sat reloading magazines and drinking soft drinks. And there were other survivors.

In all, twenty-four people were rescued from the restaurant. Most of these, many of whom were employees, had retreated to the back of the building where they entered an underground basement-type storage area which they locked from the inside. They stayed there, hunkered down in fear, as shots rang out above their heads for over an hour.

It was not totally unexpected when the San Diego Police Department received notice that they were being sued by the estates of the victims alleging negligence in reacting in a timely fashion. The suit alleged that though the police arrived on the scene four minutes after Huberty started shooting, they improperly waited more than an hour before starting an operation to "neutralize" him and rescue the victims. But in a ruling by Judge Mack Lovett of the 4th District Court of Appeal, the suit was dismissed on the grounds that though police are liable for failing to protect victims, it is only when officers have said or done something to cause the victims to rely on them—and then by negligence increase the danger to the victims. At the San Ysidro McDonald's, this was not the case. In summation, Judge Wiener, part of a three member panel that heard the suit, stated, ". . . in view of the sheer horror of the ordeal, it is difficult to imagine anything the police could have done, or

---

[9]In the teletype sent out by the San Diego Police Department to all departments titled *Synopsis of Massacre at 522 West San Ysidro Boulevard*, a statement sums up Huberty's remaining capabilities: "At the time Huberty was shot by police, he still had sufficient ammunition on his person and in his weapons to kill all of them."

failed to do, which would have made the risk any greater than that to which they were exposed before the police arrived."

For Chuck Foster, the anticipated mental aftershock came later that evening. After finding out how many victims actually were involved—he could see only five or six from his position—he became frustrated that he, and the other officers, could not have done more for them sooner. But as for the shooting, in his words, "I had it completely justified in my mind that it was one of the most necessary shootings that I had been a party to."

Rightly so. The worst massacre in the history of American law enforcement was ended with one bullet. A bullet fired by a police sniper.[10]

---

[10]In total, the fire discipline of the San Diego Police Department was exemplary. During the entire incident, they only fired a total of five rounds—including Officer Foster's fatal shot—and every round was accounted for. In all, 175 officers were involved in the incident including ten homicide detectives and four evidence technicians.

3

Ambush on Crandall Drive

San Diego, California, is a beautiful city. It has been described as one of the most, if not *the* most, liveable cities in the world. The climate is almost Mediterranean, with the hottest of summer days cooled by sea breezes that provide a natural air-conditioning, and the coldest of winter nights still comfortable in a light jacket.

It is a clean, well-maintained city of 1,118,300 people that takes pride in providing cultural and scenic attractions to residents and visitors alike. Sea World, the world famous San Diego Zoo, Scripps Institute of Oceanography, and one of the few intact square-rigged sailing ships, *The Star of India,* are just a few of the points of interest. And for those who come to enjoy the Pacific Ocean, miles of scenic coastline stretch from Torrey Pines State Park north of the city to Imperial Beach, two miles from the Mexican border.

The casual traveler will also note a marked military presence here as well. Because of its huge natural harbor, several naval installations lie scattered throughout the area. Miramar Naval Air Station (home of the navy's Top Gun fighter weapons school) and Coronado Island (home of the UDT and SEALs), have both garnered recent Hollywood fame. Other installations and bases include the headquarters of the Eleventh Naval District, North Island Naval Air

Station, and the U.S. Marine Corps Recruit Depot and the U.S. Naval Training Center—the "boot camps" of the sea services. And it is likely that the visitor, if ever in the navy or Marines, lived in San Diego at one time or another during military service.

Besides a history of being a "military town," San Diego has a heritage rich in Spanish history. Discovered by Portuguese navigator Juan Cabrillo in 1542, the settlement established there eventually became known as "The Cradle of California." For it was here that the famous El Camino Real—The Royal Road—began, winding its way from the Mission San Diego de Alcalá up the coast through every mission settlement of importance in Southern California. The Spanish heritage of the city can be seen in much of the local architecture to this day.

But besides the cultural and natural attractions, the sparkling steel blue sea and scenic beaches, the swaying palms and majestic eucalyptus trees, and the laid-back and neighborly people, the city has a more sinister side. For in spite of the city's natural beauty and magnetic personality, San Diego and her suburbs—like any other cities of size—have their problems. Drugs, shootings, thefts, burglaries, robberies, virtually any crime committed by man that demands the attention of the police occurs in the backwaters of the urban—and suburban— areas.

And for the San Diego Police Department, the areas where these crimes occur cover over four hundred square miles of industrial, business, and residential communities. One of these areas is Linda Vista.

Linda Vista is a bedroom community of 3.7 square miles located north of downtown, midway between the San Diego Freeway and the Cabrillo Freeway, and a little over four miles east of Sea World. But other than the Sam Snead All American Golf Course and the Tecolate Canyon Natural Park, Linda Vista is a peacefully boring suburban community.

At least it was until one fateful day in the summer of 1981. For on that day, two police officers, for the first time in San Diego history, would die in the line of duty. Both on the same call. Both within seconds of each other. Both in Linda Vista.

It was the 6th of June 1981.

Thomas Siota, a thirty-nine-year-old electrician whom the neighborhood children nicknamed "Zombie" and "Grinch" for his unfriendly personality, was a bitter man. He had no friends and did not want any. If anything, he was the classic loner. He kept to himself and demanded his neighbors do the same. He did not want them, or anybody else trespassing anywhere on his property, an older one-story stucco home at 2436 Crandall Drive.

On that day, his next-door neighbor, Shannon Rooney, busied herself planting a rosebush in her front yard. To Siota, it was too close to the property line, and if given time, would eventually grow across into his yard. To the Grinch, this was totally unacceptable.

He approached Mrs. Rooney, stopped short of the property line, and began to harangue her. "I don't want that goddamned bush there. It might grow over into my yard. Understand?"

She tried to reason with him, explaining that it would be pruned when needed, but he would have none of it. He wanted the bush taken out and that was that. The confrontation escalated. Siota began to grow more agitated as his temper flared. Finally, he reached the point where he became violent and began to assault Rooney, hitting and kicking her until her face was bloody.

Morgan Rooney, Shannon's teenage daughter, came out of the house to investigate the commotion. Seeing her mother being attacked by "that nut next door," she tried to intervene. Siota then turned on her.

A neighbor, hearing the commotion, came outside to

investigate. Spying the altercation in the Rooneys' yard, he quickly ran back into the house and called the police. This time, Siota would have to answer to the law.

624 John . . . see the woman, 2438 Crandall Drive, reference a neighbor dispute.

It was just another routine call. It held no more threat to the responding officers than a family fight or a drunk disturbance call, and would probably demand no more paperwork than a simple notation on the daily journal denoting time assigned, time arrived, time cleared, address of call, and disposition. Just a single line that would be soon forgotten, replaced by other, more significant, memories of calls. It would be nothing more than spending a few minutes mediating an argument between neighbors until you were satisfied that everyone would calm down and go back to their own business.

This time, it would be different.

624 John, 10-4 from Mission Valley. Officer Ron Ebeltoft acknowledged the call and hinted at the distance he would have to drive from Mission Valley.

626 William will cover. Officer Keith Tiffany volunteered to back up Ebeltoft.

Tiffany was much closer to the Crandall Drive address and arrived first. He located the victims, Shannon and Morgan Rooney, and noted their injuries. He radioed dispatch that a battery had occurred, asked his cover unit, Ebeltoft, to "expedite," then waited for him to arrive.

At approximately 1620 hours—4:20 P.M., Ebeltoft wheeled his cruiser to the curb in front of Siota's house and parked. He met briefly with Tiffany, who explained the circumstances of the assault on the Rooneys, then accompanied him next door to 2436 Crandall Street. They stopped in Siota's driveway long enough to take down the license tag number of his small, dirty, yellow Ford Courier pickup truck to run a "wants and warrants" check on the inquiry frequency[1] on the hand-held radio.

As they waited for a reply and discussed how they would handle the situation, Thomas Siota made his move. From a concealed position behind a fence next to his garage he raised a .30-06 M-1 Garand rifle and drew a bead on the two unsuspecting officers. With no warning, he opened fire.

No one knows exactly what happened next. But by the radio call received at dispatch at 1624 hours, it would appear that Ebeltoft was the last to die. For he shrieked the last words heard from the two officers: *624, I need cover now!*[2]

But the officers in the surrounding districts did not hear the call for help. Ebeltoft's radio was still on the inquiry frequency. Even the dispatcher missed the transmission. It was some minutes later, when citizens in the neighborhood began flooding Communications with calls, that the police department first realized something was drastically wrong.

Finally units were dispatched to the scene. Police officers knew that one of their own was in trouble, and cars raced toward Crandall Drive from every direction. But fortunately, as they arrived, they were flagged down by panicked citizens a block away from the scene of the shooting. Siota, gripping his rifle, could be seen from that distance defiantly parading up and down the street in front of his house. Then, as more officers and supervisors arrived and began trying to put together what was happening, Siota retreated to cover behind a two-foot brick wall on his front porch. After scrutinizing the activity taking place down the street for a few seconds, he opened fire.

Officers, scrambling for cover, managed to quickly ana-

---

[1]The "inquiry" frequency is a frequency used for running various records checks. It is separate from the six normal operating frequencies used by San Diego.

[2]Later discovered on review of the tape recording of the transmission.

lyze the situation. Siota had not only picked a very defensible position, he had armed it well. For by now he had not only the M-1, but a .30 caliber carbine, a .22 semiautomatic rifle, and one of the downed officers' .38 pistol. He was more heavily armed than the responding patrol officers who now crouched behind what cover they could find.

He fired at random, sweeping the street in both directions as targets presented themselves. Officers were pinned down behind shrubbery, trees, vehicles, and anything else that could offer cover or concealment. Siota, commanding the scene with massive firepower and a will to use it indiscriminately, turned Crandall Drive into a wide open kill zone. Even the houses that lined the street offered little protection against the high-velocity M-1 rounds. The heavy bullets could penetrate the light stucco and frame structures like an ice pick through paper. No one inside any of the surrounding homes would be safe.

Two things had to be done immediately: The gunman would have to be contained, and the families in the houses would have to be removed from danger.

Despite the high volume of fire that ripped through the air up and down the street, heroic officers broke from their positions of cover and secured a perimeter. That done, they began evacuating houses. They still did not know what had happened to Ebeltoft or Tiffany as they could not see the two bodies lying in the driveway from their distant positions. The radio continued to ask, to plead, for 624J and 626W to answer. But there was no answer.

Then the decision was made. Only one thing could effectively counter Siota's heavy rifle fire. A police sniper.

4

Agent Garry Evans, Western Division, San Diego Police Department
June 6, 1981

It began as a typical lazy Saturday. I had spent the morning lying around the pool at home with Holly, my fiancée, drinking coffee and reading the newspaper. Even though I would have to go to work later that afternoon, I expected little more excitement in the day than the normal activities encountered by my six-man squad, the Ocean Beach Enforcement Team.

As the acting supervisor with the rank of agent—similar to corporal on most departments—it would just be a day that began with briefing my officers at roll call at the Western Division substation on the crime updates, then heading out to the beach area to see, and be seen, by both the citizens and the criminals who preyed on them. There are a lot of police officers around the country that would change jobs with me any time. After all, how many police beats are populated with young ladies in the skimpiest of bikinis?

But besides the sights, there was plenty of police work to go around. And I loved it. I'm not one to be confined behind a desk on an eight-to-five job. Instead, I've always been drawn to the more exciting occupations. The element of danger, to me, adds spice to life. And the more physically demanding, the better. As soon as I turned seventeen I enlisted in the Marine Corps. Not the army, navy, or air force—the Marines. I figured if you're going to be part of something, be part of the best. After all, why take the easy way out. And it would get me out of New York, my home state, and allow me to see more of the world.

After boot camp at Parris Island, I was sent to Camp Pendleton, California. It was a far cry from New York. The beautiful coastline, the friendly people, the wonderful weather, all combined to make me decide that Southern California would be where I would settle down after the service.

By age twenty-four I had served my hitch and had joined the San Diego Police Department. Police work seems to draw former Marines like a magnet, and I was no exception. And by then I was familiar with the Southern California communities and had especially fallen in love with San Diego.

Like everyone else I spent the first few years in patrol to gain experience and "pay my dues." But, as had been the case when I picked the Marines over the other services, I decided to push myself a bit further and apply for an extra-duty assignment position on the Special Weapons and Tactics Team. SWAT.

I was selected, but SWAT was only a part-time job. The members were trained and equipped, then underwent periodic training on a monthly basis that included tactical exercises and weapons training, but their daily assignment was as patrol officers. My job, at the time, was supervisor of the Ocean Beach Enforcement Team, an enforcement oriented, high-profile[1] patrol unit working out of Western Division.

Today would be just another hot day on the beach. At least that was what I thought by midafternoon when I had to break away from the pool—and Holly—and head for work. Holly had to leave too. She was a police officer herself, working the Linda Vista area. We both worked evening shift, but other than the occasional linkup for coffee or dinner, seldom saw each other during working hours. But the rest of the time was ours and we spent much of it together. I kissed her good-bye and headed for Western. Neither of us knew at that time that this would be the most significant day of our lives.

By 1630 I had arrived at the station and had just begun changing into my uniform in the locker room prior to line-up[2] when one of my officers, Bernie Updike, burst in.

"Garry, I've been monitoring Station 'A' and it appears there's been a shooting in Linda Vista. I think maybe an officer's been shot!"[3]

I felt that sinking feeling that immediately surges through you when you hear the worst possible news. I grabbed a radio. "Six-thirty Sam, my people are suiting up at Western. Where do you want us?"

---

[1]The Ocean Beach Enforcement Team, because of the nature of area of operations and the work, wore tan jumpsuits, bloused boots, and baseball caps. Two of their main concentrations while on the job at Ocean Beach were the bikers and narcotics dealers who frequented the beach community.

[2]In San Diego, "line-up" is the predispersal roll call briefing. In other departments, the meeting is called "squad meeting," "roll call," and other names. It is here the officers are updated on the crimes that have occurred in the past twenty-four hours and told of the new "wanteds."

[3]All dialogue in this chapter is taken from a participants' memory of the event, taped interviews, police reports, and other documents. In a few places, due to the passage of time and lack of records, dialogue has been re-created to match the events, circumstances, and personalities involved.

630 Sam . . . we haven't got a code 11 location yet. Medevac is at Crandall and Fulton. Why don't you make it there?

"Six-thirty Sam, ten-four." I turned to Bernie. "Get the rest of the guys. Tell them to get suited up and to head out to the scene as soon as possible. I'm going to the armory to get my rifle. I'll meet everyone at the scene as soon as I can."

I rushed to the armory and drew my Remington Model 700 .308, mounted with a Bushnell 4X12 variable scope, picked up my SWAT bag, and raced for my car.

As I drove I began to pick up details over the radio. There weren't many. The dispatcher kept calling for the original officers assigned to the call, 624J and 626W, to answer. But no answer came. I prayed it was because they either had radio trouble, or were pinned down away from their radio.

I drove on toward Linda Vista as fast as traffic would allow, and within a relatively short period of time, slid to a stop at the intersection of Crandall and Fulton. I found a suitable spot, parked my car, and within seconds had donned my equipment harness, grabbed my gear bag, and retrieved my rifle from its case. Now ready for action, I looked around for anything resembling a command post.

Crandall Drive was in pandemonium. I could hear shots cracking down the street—some light and some extremely loud, like a .22 rifle and a shotgun being fired alternately. I could see officers huddled behind various spots of meager cover—any cover they could find. And in the direction where the sounds of gunfire seemed to originate, I spotted a group of officers crouched down behind some bushes near a house. That seemed to be the likely location for me. Closer to the action.

I still didn't know the circumstances of what was going on. No one did. All we knew was that we had three elements to comprehend: two officers were missing, some nut was shooting the hell out of the neighborhood, and everyone was pinned down.

We didn't even know for sure that any officers had been shot. No one had been able to get close enough to the suspect's house to see them at this point, and we couldn't even tell exactly where the shooter was. It was utter confusion.

Then I heard Lieutenant Bob Rogers's voice come over the radio. *602 Lincoln . . . I need an officer with a shotgun at this location.*

I squinted down the street and could see that Rogers was alone behind a car parked in the street about three houses north of the suspect's house. I looked around just as an officer, Jesse Morris, came running up carrying a Remington 870 twelve-gauge pump. "You going to cover Rogers's position?" I asked.

"Yeah, if I can get there in one piece."

"I'll go with you. Maybe I can find a spot to set up." Even if I couldn't, at least I could get a bit closer and maybe find out what in the hell was going on.

We sprinted through the yards, dodging between shrubs, trees, and other obstacles that hid us from view, until we came to Rogers's position. I slid to a stop next to him and asked if he had any scoop on the situation yet.

"Yeah, a little," he replied, not taking his eyes from the area where sporadic sounds of gunfire cracked and popped. "We got two guys we can't find, some crazy is shooting up the neighborhood, and we still aren't exactly sure where he is. I've ordered all the houses around here to be evacuated and several of the officers are doing that now. I'm getting ready to pull back and organize a SWAT response as soon as everyone gets here. Right now, I just want to keep this contained and keep the tourists out."

"What do you want me to do?" I asked.

"Find a spot and help maintain the perimeter here on the north end of the suspect's house. Keep Morris and his shotgun with you here." With that, he turned and sprinted away.

Morris and I sat crouched behind the tires of a car and tried our best to see what was happening down the street.

But from where we were, we could see damned little. It just was not a suitable position—especially for a guy with a scope-mounted sniper rifle. We could hear plenty of gunfire, but it may as well have been on the next street.

I was uncomfortable. I couldn't find the bad guys, and therefore my sniper rifle was useless. It just wasn't a good spot. My training dictated that I should try to find the best location where I could employ the rifle—a position of high ground or at least someplace where I could see what was going on so I could bring the rifle to bear.

And the radio traffic didn't help. There was plenty of chatter on the air, but nobody seemed to have a clue to what was happening. And like us, no one had yet seen the suspect or suspects. Whoever it was that was out there blowing the hell out of the block controlled the street and all of the front yards of the houses. Anyone trying to cross that open area would get gunned down without ever seeing who shot them.

I was becoming frustrated at the lack of coordination and information. I had to do something besides sit behind a car's tire while all Crandall Drive turned into a free fire zone for some idiot with an arsenal. I picked up my radio.

"Six-thirty Sam to six-oh-two Lincoln . . . I'd like to leave this location and try and find a position somewhere across the street from the suspect's house. I can't see anything from here."

10-4. Keep me advised.

Leaving Morris to cover the sector, I moved out.

As I rounded the corner to the backyard of a house across the street I ran into some of my Beach Team officers who were busy evacuating residents from their homes. I decided to pick the first one that could break loose from that and draft him as my spotter. Larry Ingraham, who had just finished taking a family to safety, was my pick.

"Larry, I've got to try and find a shooting spot somewhere across the street from the suspect's house. I need a spotter. Want the job?"

Larry, though not in SWAT at the time, agreed to go.[4]

We began climbing the fences that separated the backyards of the houses on Crandall Street and Crandall Court, making our way south as quickly as the obstacles and the bulkiness of our gear would allow. It was hotter than hell, and each fence seemed to be higher and more difficult to climb than the last. By the third yard we were drenched in sweat and puffing and gasping for breath like wounded bulls. Though I was in good shape, between the adrenaline ups and downs, the heat, and the exertion, I was becoming exhausted. But we had to press on.

Between each house we stopped long enough to look across the street, maybe spot whoever was doing the shooting. But it was to no avail. And each time we crossed between houses, large volleys of fire erupted sporadically from somewhere in front. Somewhere that we could not identify.

By the sound of it, some of the shooting was light stuff, maybe a .22. Other discharges were heavier, like a shotgun. On several occasions, as we passed between houses, the air around Larry and me buzzed with ricochets.

When we had progressed to where we estimated the house to be that faced the shooter's position, we stopped. Larry cut the patio screen door to gain entry, then forced the door open. We entered, but once inside, it immediately became apparent that the house would be useless for our purposes. There were no windows that faced the direction of fire. My heart sank.

"Let's try the next house," I said.

Scaling another fence brought us to the back door of 2437 Crandall Drive, the house that we would soon find was exactly across the street from the shooter. As we entered the

---

[4]Ingraham later volunteered and was selected for SWAT. Several years later he retired from the police department because of stress—partly because of this incident.

back door I had a really strange feeling. It was like God said, "Right here, Garry. Here's your spot." It was almost chilling.

We opened the patio glass doors and entered. I followed Larry through the kitchen and dining area into the family room. We were almost as shocked to find a family still there as they were to see us, two heavily armed police officers that appeared out of nowhere. And to cap it off, the father was standing at the front door watching all the action as if it were on TV.

"We've gotta get you people out of here," said Larry. "Come away from the windows and door and get into the kitchen. You could get killed standing there."

The mother and father looked at us like: "Oh, really? Well, if you say so." It was incredible.

As Larry evacuated them back farther into the house away from the street I listened to the radio. I caught a piece of a transmission that said something about an officer that thought he saw a policeman down in a driveway next to a yellow or gold Courier pickup. I thought maybe the shooter had hit someone by now.

When Larry returned we began looking for a spot to set up. From the layout of the house, the room that proved the best tactically was a bedroom in the southeast corner of the home. A bedroom that was absolutely littered with junk. Toys, books, every kind of item imaginable covered the floor. It was almost impossible to walk through there, but we had little choice. As I entered I stepped through a guitar.

Shaking it loose, I crept on, carefully trying to dodge debris, until I made the window and peered out. What I saw was horrendous. Sometime during our mad scramble through the backyards, the suspect had shot up the police car parked at the curb in front of his house that belonged to either Ebeltoft or Tiffany. One or more of his bullets had torn through the trunk and ignited a box of highway flares, setting the car ablaze. Now it burned furiously, black smoke belching into the air in a column that partially obscured his house from my view.

I examined the driveway—then the yellow Courier pickup truck that was parked there. And it dawned on me! . . . *Yellow or gold Courier pickup . . .*

Beside the truck, lying on the concrete, was the prone form of a police officer in uniform. He wasn't moving. And he was covered with blood. The sight made me miss the first radio call from Lieutenant Rogers, but not the second.

602 Lincoln to Evans.

I picked up the radio. "Go ahead."

Where's your visual from right now?

"The house directly across from the suspect's, but my vision's partially obscured by a tree," I replied.

Do you see the officers down there?

"Affirmative," I answered, but I could see only one. "He's right in the driveway. He's on his back. I can't see who it is."

Then another voice joined in. One of the other officers, looking from a different angle, spotted something else. *621 John, I can see two of them there.*

I looked again. Just beyond the first officer lying on the ground I could see the head of the second. "Affirm. There's two. I can see the other one. Ten-four."

I laid the radio down and was amazed that I felt no emotion. My training had taken over and I knew that there was a job to do that required a clear head and unemotional determination. It was too late to help the officers, and the guy that did this had to be taken out before he could hurt someone else. And if I got the chance, I would be the one to do it.

Just then Ingraham locked onto something else. "Garry, I see a white or Mexican male, about forty to fifty years old, wearing a white T-shirt, crouched behind the brick wall on the front porch."

I confirmed his observation. "Yeah, I can see him. I can get him." I could see his head and shoulders behind what looked like a two-and-one-half-foot-tall brick wall. "Range is about fifty meters."

"He's got some type of rifle—.22 maybe—pointing north down the street," Larry added.

After identifying the suspect, I rapidly scanned the area of operations—the area right and left of the suspect's position—to ascertain the layout of the scene and possibly spot other suspects before I gave away our position. Besides the burning police car, other obstacles stood between me and the gunman. A large tree drooped its branches in our front yard, partially blocking my view, and another in his. Several bushes and shrubs seemed to close in on my field of vision to the right and left that tunneled my view to a smaller area than I would have liked. But it would have to do.

"Let's get this window open," I instructed.

Larry tore the drapes down and began working on the stubborn window. As he did this I called Lieutenant Rogers. "Six-thirty Sam to six-oh-two Lincoln."

Go.

"I can see the suspect. I can get a shot if I can get this window open."

602 Lincoln to 630 Sam, if you have a shot, take the shot!

"Ten-nine?"[5] I replied, wanting to make sure I heard the transmission correctly.

If you have a shot, take the shot, Rogers repeated.

"Ten-four," I acknowledged. It was showtime.

Larry crept back from his handiwork at the window. He had managed to slide it to the left, exposing an adequate open area, and had cut a small hole in the screen. "She's all yours."

I raised the Remington, chambered a 158 grain Federal boat-tailed hollow point, then brought the scope to bear on the suspect. He was a bit fuzzy and distorted. I thought maybe it was because my eyes were still burning with sweat.

---

[5]10-9 means to "repeat" or "say again."

I wiped my face and repositioned my cheek on the rifle's stock. No improvement. Then it hit me. Too much magnification. I had been to the range recently and had not reset my scope to an intermediate range. It was still set on twelve-power. Too much for such a close range. But instead of trying to make a last minute adjustment, I decided to try for a shot. This guy was cutting loose with another string of shots and I didn't want him to shoot any more if there was anything I could do about it.

I leveled the crosshairs on the rifleman. "Larry, spot for me. I'm going to take a shot, and the recoil will raise me off target. I won't know for sure if I hit him unless you see the hit."

As I concentrated on the crosshairs, sweat dripped into my eyes, burning like hell. But I held my concentration in spite of the distraction. I settled the center of the crosshair reticles on his head and squeezed the trigger.

The Remington boomed, slamming back into my shoulder as the scope jerked up in recoil. But just as it did, my target moved. I heard Larry say, "He moved. It was a miss. Hit the wall behind him."

Then, "Uh-oh."

I brought the rifle back down just in time to see the killer turn in our direction, shifting the muzzle of his rifle toward us as he did.

Almost instantly, he began firing. Rounds began to pepper the wall near the window, then, as he got the range, began coming through the window itself. I could tell by the sound of the weapon and the tiny buzz of the bullets as they came through the window that it was probably a .22 rifle.

We hit the floor. I looked at Larry, then for some reason, probably to relieve stress, I said, "Fun, isn't it?"

Just as a slight grin began to split his face the wall exploded over our heads. The sound was like that of a cannon going off. In my mind's eye a scene instantly played itself in explanation: The scum bag had assaulted us! He had crossed the street, probably with a shotgun, and was now standing outside our window blasting holes through the wall. In reality, he had exchanged the .22 for the M-1 and had busied himself slamming .30-06 rounds into and through the house in an effort to ferret us out—or kill us. And the thin stucco walls offered absolutely no protection. They may as well have been cardboard.

The bullets came through the wall within inches of my head, crossed the room, zipped through the next two interior walls into the hallway, then the exterior wall at the rear of the house, then carried on out into the backyard somewhere. Other rounds came within a foot of Ingraham. For us, there was not a barrier in the house that would suffice as cover against such artillery.

Since discretion is often the better part of valor, Larry and I immediately elected to low-crawl, as fast as we could, out of the room and into the hallway to regroup and come up with an alternate plan of action. In our haste, we forgot to take our radios.

It was like crawling through an obstacle course. Junk, debris, and toys were everywhere, and we had to compete with all of this garbage for the lowest position on the floor. But after what seemed like an eternity, we made the sanctuary of the hall.

I sat down in the hallway, my back up against the wall and my rifle across my lap, as Larry, wishing that one of us had managed to bring a radio during our "strategic withdrawal," made his way to the kitchen in search of a telephone.

As Ingraham advised Communications what had transpired, I worked the whole thing over in my mind. I thought of the officers that were lying in the driveway, and how close we came to death in the onslaught that just blasted the walls around us to pieces, and came to a conclusion. To no one in particular I stated, "That guy's trying to kill us." And I knew that I had to try to kill him first—before he could get us or anyone else. I also knew that there was only one place I could make that attempt: the bedroom we had just abandoned.

As these thoughts were going through my head I realized that I couldn't tell what was going on outside without my radio. I picked up my rifle and low-crawled back into the room to retrieve it. As I neared the window, I decided to take a quick look to see what the gunman was doing now. I could tell by the sound of the shots that the firing outside had now changed in direction. He was no longer shooting at our house, but had begun firing down the street toward other officers. I took this opportunity to crawl back to the hall to call Larry back into the room.

Once back at the window, I braced myself on the wall and mentally prepared myself. This shot had to be good, nothing left to chance. I took my time.

Larry took his position to my left as before, wiped his eyes on his sleeve, then locked his eyes on target. We were ready.

I brought my cheek to the stock of the Remington, adjusted my head for the proper eye-relief, and once again acquired my prey. As I focused on the crosshairs, my adversary slowly began turning in my direction. Almost as if he knew I was once again sighting in on him.

"Watch out, Garry!" Larry blurted, fearing another volley from the high-powered rifle. But it was too late to move. I had him in my crosshairs, a clear view, one that put his face right where I wanted it. I held my breath, took up the slack, and slowly, evenly, squeezed the trigger.

The Remington cracked and jumped. Shouldering the recoil, I brought the rifle back down on target, worked the bolt to chamber a fresh round, then searched the porch. He wasn't there.

"I think I got him," I said quietly. "I think he's down. Get on the radio and advise Rogers."

Larry keyed the radio and relayed my message. I continued to watch the porch for movement. If he popped back up, I wanted to be ready. We now had all the time in the world.

If he was just hunkered down behind the wall, waiting for us to move next before he opened fire again, I'd put another bullet in him. But I didn't think he'd reappear.

Then, within just a couple of seconds of my shot, I saw Lieutenant Rogers advancing across the front yard toward the porch, a shotgun shouldered and pointing at the brick wall. As he drew close, he fired. And fired again—and again, working the slide each time to eject a smoking shell without taking the weapon from his shoulder—or his eyes from the suspect. Another officer, Steve Sloan, who had been in another position behind some bushes near the house adjacent to the gunman, fired another shot. Other officers rushed up from both sides, and as I watched, they tensed as they closed on the killer, then relaxed when they saw what I couldn't. I knew then, knew for sure, that he was dead.

I had to see the end of this. Larry and I pulled back from the window and ran out of the house, across the street, and over to Rogers.

I looked down at my adversary. He definitely was dead. I found out later that my bullet, because of the angle he was in with his body when I fired, had entered his face, traveled down his neck, and lodged in his chest cavity, killing him instantly. Even if it hadn't, Lieutenant Rogers would have finished him with the shotgun. His shoulder showed where a blast pattern of twelve-gauge .00 buckshot had found its mark.

Rogers picked up his radio. *Hold all fire. Hold all fire. The suspect is down. Get Medevac to the house code 3.*

Medevac was for Ebeltoft and Tiffany. But I already knew, from what I had seen through my scope, that it was too late for that.

After quickly searching the suspect's house with Ingraham and Sloan, I walked out to the driveway. Ambulances, police cars, and a fire truck were converging on the scene en masse, sirens screaming. The whole area just seemed to implode with activity. And it looked like the aftermath of a major battle. Dead bodies, a burning car, men with weapons running around, radios blasting orders and questions, too much happening in too small an area.

I walked by my two brother officers who had paid the extreme price. Paramedics were giving CPR and mouth-to-mouth resuscitation, but I knew it would do no good. It was a futile, but necessary, effort on their part.

I walked over to the middle of Siota's yard—by then I knew his name—and sat down. Before that time I had known him as only a "suspect" and my "target." I looked around. The scene in the driveway was very emotional. I knew both of the officers well. They were friends of mine, and Holly's, which made it very personal. I was saddened, but at the same time I was glad that Siota was dead. He deserved it. Knowing that there is very little justice in the courts these days, I felt a sense of "street justice" having been done. I had absolutely no ill feelings about it. It was a damned good shooting.

I turned and looked at Lieutenant Rogers when a question came over the radio from the command post: . . . *have we accounted for the two officers?*

Rogers replied, "Yes, we have."

Are they all right?

"Negative."

I could imagine the scene at the command post as Rogers's answer hit home, especially when it took a moment for them to come back with the next question. *Do we need Life-Flight?*

Rogers glanced at the driveway, brought the radio to his lips and replied, quietly, somberly, "Everybody's eleven-forty-four."

The police code 11-44 meant one thing. Dead.

Holly Murlin, Garry Evans's fiancée and herself a police officer, had also gone to work that day. She left after Garry and did not find out about the events that were transpiring on

Crandall Drive until she pulled up to a parked police car to check on an officer who, because he had his head down on the steering wheel, she thought had been injured.

As I drove south on Linda Vista Road, approaching Genesee, I spotted a sheriff's helicopter circling to the southeast. It dawned on me that a SWAT mission might be under way. Then, as I approached 6900 Linda Vista Road, I saw a marked unit parked in front of a store. There appeared to be something wrong with the officer. He had his head down on the steering wheel and was not moving. I felt a knot in my stomach and pulled over to check on him.

I walked up to the car, a bottle of Coke in my hand, and looked inside. I could see that he didn't seem to be injured, but I could see tears in his eyes. I asked what was wrong.

"Ron and Keith are dead. And Garry . . ."

Garry?

I dropped my Coke, shattering it on the street. Garry was dead! My God! I felt as if I had been hit with a brick.

". . . Garry shot the bastard. He's okay. He's down at Homicide now giving his report."

I felt weak. Confused. I don't even remember the drive to Western. But when I got there, I knew there were things that had to be done.

I knew that Ron had a very close friend, who would be there and probably by now had just about lost it. She was also a friend of mine, and my sergeant knew it. When I entered the station, he told me to go into the locker room and get her and take her home. For the rest of the evening, I stayed with her.

Garry called me at her house two hours later. The television news programs were broadcasting nonstop coverage of the incident. To the media, it was a sensational bloodbath and they pulled no punches. Garry had caught some of it and was concerned about *my* reactions.

"You okay?" he asked in a very calm voice.

"Me? Sure, I'm okay. What about you?"

"I'm fine. You should know that. I'll pick you up as soon as I finish here at Homicide."

But it was several hours before he "finished up."

After we got home, we sat and watched the news and drank wine. There was very little conversation between us. I didn't know what to say, and thought it best for him to open up first. Finally he did.

"I'm really proud of my guys. They did a fabulous job. All the guys on the Beach Team really proved themselves. I couldn't ask for more."

He didn't say a thing about killing Siota, or about all the other things that went on, only what a great job "his" guys did.

"I told them to go ten-eight and get to the scene and do whatever they could. They just jumped in without any further orders and did whatever needed to be done. They just kind of knew where to go and what to do."

All he could talk about was his team.

Until a few more glasses of wine came and went and he began to loosen up.

"My goddamned scope was too high. I missed the first shot. Then, Jesus, all hell broke loose!"

I listened intently as he related the shots coming through the walls, the pullout to the hallway, then the decision to go back. But I felt like I wasn't getting the whole story. It was like he was minimizing everything for my benefit.

The next morning Garry started clipping newspaper articles for a scrapbook. And as we sat around drinking coffee, the phone started ringing. Call after call. Friends checking on us, concerned relatives, guys from the department, one heck of a lot of support. As if Garry needed it.

He took the whole thing in stride. He was just doing his job. That's all.

But I knew, to Garry, it was one of the most important events of his career. He taped the news broadcasts, collected copies of all the radio log tapes, all the reports incident to the circumstances, and even received the bullet from Siota's body from the medical examiner's office. He keeps it in his nightstand.

As the hours ticked by and the days passed while Garry waited for the word to return to work, I watched for any changes. Then after the investigation of the shooting was over and he went back to work, I watched him carefully for signs of flashbacks, or stress, or any negative reactions one would expect. It almost drove me crazy. But there were none. He had no remorse or pain, guilt or confusion at all. He was actually on a high of sorts. Several backseat would-be psychologist friends warned me to look for signs of traumatic stress, and that it might take a long time to surface. But it's been over ten years now and the only feeling Garry has ever shown is of a person simply doing the job he was trained to do. That's professionalism.

In Garry's mind, a dirt bag had to die and Garry obliged him.

• • •

Though postshooting counseling was offered, Garry Evans decided not to take part. "I didn't feel badly about the situation. Only that two of my friends had been killed. The shooting itself didn't bother me."

Garry Evans is now a sergeant with the San Diego Police Department. Besides SWAT, he has worked narcotics and as a patrol supervisor. And for their actions on Crandall Drive on that fateful day, both Evans and Larry Ingraham were awarded the department's Medal of Valor.

5

Countdown to Death

He seemed like a nice enough man. At least that was what Donna White[1] thought when she met him on the bus that wound its way through the San Diego traffic. He appeared to be a sincere, polite black man who had just—according to him—fallen on hard times. And as they rode through town on that clear, hot San Diego day, he became very friendly indeed. He explained that he was out of work, and was at that very moment riding across town in search of a job.

Donna, remembering that she had recently spoken to her mother about getting some things fixed around their home, thought this chance meeting a stroke of luck.

"I may have some work for you, if you can do a bit of fix-up work and odd jobs around my house," she offered.

"Yes, ma'am. I can do that. I'm pretty good with tools," said the man.

"Fine." Donna smiled, reaching for something to write on in her purse. "I'll give you my address and you can come over tomorrow and we'll see what you can do." She scribbled on the paper and handed it to him. "I live there with my mother. She's getting on in years and can't do much herself, and I'm afraid I'm not much good at do-it-yourself

---

[1]Due to the nature of this incident, both of the victims' names have been changed to protect their identities.

projects. We can use all the help we can get. By the way, what's your name?"

"Tennyson," he said, smiling, "but my friends call me 'Tenny.'"

"Fine, Tenny. So I'll see you tomorrow? Say in the morning?"

"Sure. I'll be there."

"Tenny," or Tennyson Star Beard, was more than an out-of-work fix-up man. At thirty-five years old, he had already accumulated an extensive criminal record, and in fact had just been released from prison. And it hadn't taken long for him to revert to his old ways. His latest escapades involved the use of rock cocaine, known in most parts of the country as "crack." Possibly the most addictive drug known, rock cocaine is the crystalline substance that is formed when powdered cocaine is chemically processed down to its most potent base. Its name is derived from its appearance. Small crystals less than a half inch in diameter, dubbed "rocks" because of their shape, are smoked in special pipes by holding a flame against the "rock" and inhaling the fumes. It has been credited with a potency of one hundred times that of the equivalent amount of powdered cocaine. And crack is one hundred times as addictive. As one crack addict explained, "Crack, crack, crack. That's all you think about. Smoke it once, and you gotta smoke it again, and again. It takes over instantly. You gotta have more. You don't care about anything else in life. Not your mama, your papa, your kids, your old man, nothin'. Just the crack. You'll steal for it, you'll sell your body for it, you'll even kill for it. And you don't care. 'Long as you get the crack."[2]

And that was Tennyson Beard's problem. Crack.

* * *

---

[2]Statement of a rock cocaine addict, twenty-three years old, mother of three, interviewed by author after an arrest.

The next morning, Beard reported to Donna White's house as promised. He met Donna and her eighty-seven-year-old mother and after a bit of chitchat, began the first of several small jobs that the Whites had in mind. He worked well through the day, and late in the afternoon received his first pay. He promised to return the next morning to finish the remainder of the jobs.

His day's pay didn't last long. That night he used every penny to buy crack. And he stayed up all night smoking it. By the next morning he was strung out. He had gone without sleep and without food, but he didn't care. He didn't even notice. He was on a crack binge, and the more crack he smoked, the more he wanted. And now he was out. To get more he needed money. And he knew who had it.

Klauber Street was quiet when he showed up at 6:30 A.M. It was much earlier than he was supposed to arrive, but he didn't care. Performing odd jobs at the Whites' house had nothing to do with his plans—or his needs.

Beard, still high from a night of crack, approached the house where only the day before he had labored at honest work. As he neared the front porch, he checked the tools he would use this morning—a large knife and a pistol.

Arriving on the porch, he began banging on the door. It took a few minutes for someone to answer, and when someone did come to the door, it was eighty-seven-year-old Mrs. White. She was surprised at who was there.

"Tenny, what in the world . . ."

Before she could say anything else Beard shoved the door open, forcing the frightened woman back into the room, and quickly stepped inside. He slammed the door behind him and, brandishing the knife, said, "I need some money. And I need it now! But first, there's something else I need."

As Donna slept in her bedroom, Tennyson Star Beard, his criminal mind further deranged by the drug that was coursing through his brain, raped the terrified elderly woman.

Donna, wakened by the sounds of the struggle taking place down the hall, jerked up to listen. She could not believe what she was hearing. She sprang from the bed, grabbed a robe, and carefully crept into the hallway. Within seconds her fears were confirmed.

Donna immediately dialed 911. But in her panic, she gave the wrong address.

And then Tennyson Beard, his actions with Mrs. White interrupted by the sound of Donna's voice on the phone, found her.

He now had *two* women to play with.

When the assigned officers responded to the call, they found it to be a false alarm. The lady at the address that had been given out by Communications knew nothing of a call to the police. They weren't surprised. It was probably just another prank call or false alarm. Without a complainant or a good address there was nothing to do but go back in service. They cleared from Klauber Street and resumed patrol.

An hour later, another 911 call came into Communications. This time the address was correct. One of the women had managed to make another emergency 911 call to the police department—and this time gave the correct address. When the officers arrived and began approaching the house, they heard what sounded like screaming and yelling emanating from inside. As one officer reported this new development over the radio and called for backup, his partner ran for the front door and began hammering on it with his fist.

No response. Beard, seeing the officers approach, took the two abused and terrified women into the bathroom, ordered them to stand in the bathtub, and as they obeyed, barricaded the door with a chair. Now he had time to think. Time to plan. Time to bargain with the law.

He analyzed his surroundings. The bathroom was tiny, but it would do. The door was stout, and the only exterior window—an aluminum type with frosted glass that slid sideways—was small. The door appeared to be adequately secured, now that the chair had been angled and jammed up under the doorknob. For the moment he was safe—and in control. The cops couldn't force their way in. And they probably wouldn't even try. After all, he had two hostages.

And a knife and a gun.

6

Officer Ken Hubbs, San Diego Police Department
September 25, 1987

I heard the call come out. My first reaction was that it was just another typical 911 panic call. Someone calls in on the emergency number, gives an address, then simply hangs up. Sometimes the calls are good and sometimes they're not. You never know until you get there.

This one was good. I heard the assigned officers notify Communications that they had arrived on the scene, then within minutes broadcast a hostage situation. And I was close.

I was working patrol in the Southeast Division, and Klauber Street was within my area. I was also one of the on-call SWAT snipers and had my equipment in the trunk of my car. I notified Communications that I would be en route to the location of the hostage situation and accelerated toward Klauber Street.

As luck would have it, I was the first SWAT officer on the scene. It only took a minute to determine that this was indeed an armed and barricaded hostage situation. Quite a commotion was coming from inside the house, and we could hear the panic-ridden voices of the two hostages. I immediately put out a code 11 which would bring the rest of the on-duty SWAT officers to the scene, plus at least five

SWAT officers assigned to the PRT—the Primary Response Team—whose duty was to secure the perimeter. Twelve additional officers and two sergeants of the SRT, the Special Response Team hostage rescue specialists, would also automatically respond. I then transmitted the location for a staging area and advised that I would do the initial scouting for the perimeter positions and sniper locations.

Within minutes Mike Hendrickson, one of our SWAT sergeants, arrived and assumed the job of mission leader. By the time I returned from my scouting mission with a diagram that depicted where the suspect was and locations for both sniper teams and PRT perimeter officers, Hendrickson had established a command post.

"Ken, this guy is really irrational," explained Hendrickson. "The two patrol officers who took the call have been trying to negotiate with the guy and make him give up, but he won't cooperate at all. He's been making all kinds of demands—money, car, guarantees that we'll let him go . . . standard stuff—and he's stated that if he doesn't get what he wants, he's going to kill the hostages."

By now, most of the SWAT contingent was arriving. "How do you want to work it?" I asked.

"We'll probably have to use a sniper-initiated assault. Did you find a place where you can get a shot?"

"The bathroom he's in only has one window, and it's made of that frosted glass that you really can't see much more than a silhouette through. It's on the west side of the house between the houses, so there isn't much room to play with. But I'll see what I can do," I explained, pointing to the diagram to emphasize the layout.

"Okay. Get over there and let me know when you're set up."

I grabbed one of our SWAT officers, Mark Sullivan, who had just arrived and was suiting up, as my spotter. Mark was also a sniper team member and could relieve me on the scope if I became too fatigued. I explained our mission, and that we may have a sniper-initiated assault. And if it came down to that, he or I would be the sniper that fired the shot.

As this was happening, the SRT people had divided up into two teams: a react team, which is an emergency entry team positioned close to the house to react to something spontaneously; and a hostage rescue team that would remain at the command post to formulate an entry plan and prepare for the assault.

The plan was basic: when the shot was fired, the hostage rescue team would move through the back door adjacent to the kitchen, go through the house, make their way to the bathroom, then make entry into the bathroom itself. It seemed simple enough, but anyone who has been on SWAT operations realizes that there are always unknowns that you cannot plan for. The guys on the entry teams had to be flexible—and have a lot of guts.

And a great deal of the success of this mission depended on me. If I missed, or if I couldn't get a shot, then we would have to deal with a drastic change of plans at the last minute. Especially if he began harming the hostages. If this happened, the whole show would be up to the rescue team.

As Mark and I cut between houses a few doors down, I evaluated the neighborhood. It was built back in the prewar years when property was much cheaper than today. All of the homes had extremely large yards of at least a half acre, and these expanses were covered with bushes and other vegetation, and were generously dotted with mature trees. The houses themselves were typical one-story stucco homes with shallow-peaked roofs.

The first place I checked out was the house next door to the suspect. From there, I thought I could get a straight shot through a window across to his location in the bathroom. By this time he had slid the window partially open, removed the screen, and was loudly making demands and threats to officers positioned behind some bushes about forty feet away.

I tried the window directly adjacent to his, which would have been perfect had it not been for one big tree and a bunch of bushes that obstructed my view. I couldn't see him, but I could hear him. And what I heard I didn't like. By the sound of his voice and his attitude, time appeared to be critical. Beard's temper and patience seemed to be wearing thin and he was making more threats than demands, screaming that he would kill the women. I had to find a place, and I had to do it as quickly as possible.

Mark and I searched for a satisfactory position for the next thirty minutes while the officers negotiating with Beard stalled him as long as they could. I climbed to the roof of the first house, I tried a patio, I even climbed a tree. There simply was no place that was ideal that gave me a direct unobstructed view of the bathroom window.

Finally, after walking all the way down the back side of the neighbor's house along a fence line, I ended up in the corner of the lot. There was a six-foot-high chain link fence on one side, a four-foot-high chain link on the other, and from just that spot it seemed I could see the window, just barely, without something being in the way. I pulled my Steyr SSG .308 to my shoulder and eased my eye behind the scope, a 4X12 Bushnell.

I could see the suspect clearly, just underneath the large full branches of a tree, but the foliage was distracting. I checked my scope. It was set on nine-power. I dropped it back to five and rechecked my view. Much better. I could see the window and the silhouette of the suspect's head clearly. The angle of trajectory was about a forty-five-degree angle to the window, and I was looking slightly uphill to an elevation about ten feet higher than my own. It was far from being the most ideal position for a precision shot—but it was the best we could do given the circumstances. I picked up my hand-held radio and keyed the transmit button: "Sniper one to PRT leader."

Sniper one . . . go ahead, came the immediate response.

"We're in position west of the suspect's house, just south

56

of the house to his left. I have a clear, unobstructed view of the suspect's head." This last sentence alerted the PRT leader and the command post that I was ready to shoot. Instead of saying, "I'm all set. I can blow the guy's head off," we just state that we have a "clear, unobstructed view" of the target. Everyone knows what that means.

The word came back. *10-4*. Now they knew.

I tried to adjust my position, but nothing seemed to work. I couldn't get into the prone position because of the obstacles that then presented themselves, and even the sitting position wouldn't work. I was left with the standing, or "off-hand" position. That is one of the most unstable positions a shooter can use, even when you try to use the sling to brace against by wrapping it around your left arm. And the longer you try to hold the standing position, the more shaky you get. Holding the rifle's weight up and concentrating through the scope for long periods eventually makes your arms feel like they are going to fall off. The rifle just seems to get heavier and heavier. The 10.4 pounds of a Steyr SSG PII begins to feel like a hundred-pound weight. I tried to brace myself against the six-foot fence, but it was too wobbly. And the four-foot fence was too low. I just had to make the best of what I had.

And I gutted it out for the next two hours. All of this time Mark continued to hunt for a better spot, but unless he found one, I would have to accept the present conditions and work with them.

I was used to waiting.[1] All of us SWAT team members were. Ours was a waiting game. It went with the territory. Most of the time you never knew when you would get called, so you had little time to prepare for a lengthy siege. But some of the time, when a scheduled event was known of long

---

[1]The "flashback" incidents described here actually happened after the Beard affair. They are told at this point to give the reader another view of police sniper operations.

beforehand, we backed our schedule up and prepared accordingly. As we did on the day Vice President Dan Quayle came to town.

The visit was to include a stop at a small store that dealt with wheelchair parts and prefabricated wheelchairs, followed by a brief visit with the news media and crowd on the sidewalk outside the main entrance to the building. As was standard procedure for these VIP visits of high government officials, the police department was responsible for a sizable portion of the security. The Secret Service handles the security around the president, the vice-president, and their respective families, but just about everything else is covered by the local law enforcement agencies. This was the case when the SWAT team drew their assignments for this particular mission.

We knew it would be a long day, and we had to take our positions well in advance of the arrival of the dignitaries, so we spent the early morning hours tanking up on coffee and having a sumptuous breakfast at a local restaurant. When it came time to head out to the store, where we would be stationed on the roof, we were already prepared for several hours of isolation without resupply.

After arrival, we gained access to the roof and climbed up to take our positions. We had already done all of the scouting and surveillance well in advance, and had completed all of our planning and selected our countersniper and CAT team[2] positions two weeks earlier. Now it was only a matter of getting into position and remaining vigilant while the vice-president did his thing.

Three hours remained before he would arrive. We spent this time surveying the area and generally getting comfortable with the activities below and around us. The time span would also be used to scan the people in the vicinity to get a feel of who belonged or didn't belong. If we saw anyone

---

[2]Counterassault Team.

suspicious, all we had to do was radio it in and they would be checked out.

As it grew closer to Quayle's arrival time, activity picked up. Helicopters were circling in the air overhead, more spectators were arriving, the news media was setting up cameras all over the place, and our guys were scattered around throughout the area in strategic spots. It was a typical VIP security operation.

Finally the limousine carrying the vice-president arrived and pulled to the curb in front of our building. The vice-president and his entourage stepped out and, amid smiles and waving hands, entered the building. After a brief tour, they came back out to the sidewalk directly below us. Quayle began playing the crowd, again smiling and waving for the cameras.

It was a hot, bright, clear day. We had been on the roof for hours, and now we had to stay there and guard the vice-president until he finished talking and departed the area. Only then could we leave the roof.

But one countersniper had a problem. The massive amount of coffee, milk, water, and juice he had drunk at breakfast had run its course and he was beginning to hurt. He had to relieve himself, and with every minute that ticked by, the situation grew worse. Finally he could take it no more.

As Quayle stood below addressing the crowd, our countersniper stepped to an open drainpipe on the rooftop drainage system. A couple of seconds later we heard a sigh of relief as he began to urinate into the opening of the drain.

But what he failed to realize was where it went from there. Until one of us, who is studiously watching the vice-president of the United States—all cameras and eyes locked on him as he delivered his speech—noted something else. There, on the sidewalk just a little uphill from the vice-president's feet, was a trickle of liquid running from the bottom end of a drainpipe that quickly turned into a stream as the volume from the roof increased. And it began to flow down the sidewalk, right by the vice-president's feet, then on down the pavement in front of his entourage.

This was not a simple two-minute leak. This was more of an all-night beer drinking binge hoser. It just kept running, and running. For several minutes. A veritable river of urine flowed by the vice-president's feet.

We'll never know if Quayle ever noticed it. If he did he never batted an eye. But just about everyone else did. With a sidewalk temperature of about eighty-five degrees, it quickly became pretty obvious what it was.

The supervisors didn't see much humor in it, but we countersnipers thought it was rather entertaining.

Even though we spend most of our time on assignments just waiting and watching and never getting to participate, sometimes the job of sniper or countersniper has its lighter moments that makes it all worthwhile. Because of our job, we are normally in a good position of high ground to see all of the surrounding area and everything that's going on. This has its advantages.

In one particular incident, while we waited at our posts on top of a roof at Lindbergh Field for *Air Force One* to arrive with President Reagan, we witnessed a sight that we—and the motorcycle division—would never forget.

On the ramp below, sixty police motorcycles stood lined up in military fashion side-by-side. In front of each motor-cycle stood its rider at the position of "parade rest." The cycles stood freshly cleaned and highly polished; the riders stood smartly behind sunglasses, their eyes locked straight ahead. Their uniforms, resplendent in the sunshine, were sharply creased and their boots spit-shined to a high gloss. They were indeed an impressive sight.

Air Force One landed in good order, taxied across the field, then made a wide turn to come up to its spot in front of the crowd of greeters and dignitaries. The mayor, the chief of police, and every other big guy in town was standing on the hot tarmac to greet President Reagan. I could see every detail of what was going on from my post on top of the PSA[3] building. And I could see what happened next.

The huge Boeing jet with the words "United States of America" emblazoned on the fuselage began to jockey for position in front of the crowd. As it did so, the pilot gunned the engines to provide steerage for the nosewheel as it made its final turn prior to braking to a stop. However, the hot exhausts from the four engines happened to blast across the formation of motorcycle officers—and their bikes.

The first motorcycle in line, struck by the gust of jet blast, blew over into the second. The second, now knocked off balance, did the same into the third. As I watched, a domino effect began to occur. Every motorcycle in the lineup, one-by-one, fell over into the next, knocking it to the ground with a loud crash.

Not one motor officer turned around. They *knew* what was happening. And it continued to happen until sixty motorcycles were flat on the asphalt.

I couldn't see the faces of the riders from my rooftop, but I think I saw a few spines stiffen. And maybe a few butts pucker.

But this day was not one that was humorous. It was deadly serious, and I had to be ready. Especially since the plan of attack depended on me.

I estimated the range. About fifty yards. Close enough to hear the suspect's voice, which came in handy when I picked up snatches of intelligence that I could pass on. At one time I heard him mention something about officers being inside the house with him. I radioed the PRT team leader, "Sniper one to team leader . . . the suspect is making reference to officers being inside the house right now."

Now the CP would know—*if* they had officers already inside—that the suspect also knew. They could relay the information or change plans accordingly. If there were

---

[3]Pacific Southwest Airlines.

officers already inside, then I felt I should again report my status to Sergeant Hendrickson. "Sniper one to command post, once again I have a clear and unobstructed view of the suspect's head."

10-4.

Then I heard Beard say something else. I keyed the radio. "Sniper one to team leader, the suspect has made reference to possession of a forty-five automatic."

10-4. PRT one to Entry one, are you 10-4? Hendrickson wanted to make sure the entry team had copied my transmission. They had. By now, Captain Dave Johnson, the field commander, had joined Hendrickson at the command post. Mike explained to him that the situation was rapidly deteriorating, and that he had a sniper on site that could take Beard out at any time. But Captain Johnson was apprehensive about doing anything. Anything at all. Mike tried to get permission to move on with the mission—to give me the green light—but Johnson held back.

As I was watching Beard, I could see the form of his head come into view, hold still for a moment, then disappear. This happened several times and each time I reported it.

"Sniper one to team leader, the suspect is out of view."

10-4.

Then, almost before I could unkey the radio, "Sniper one to team leader, he's back at the window again."

10-4.

This time Beard froze in position in an ideal spot for a shot. I rapidly keyed the radio. "Sniper one to PRT leader, the suspect came to the edge. I can see him now with a clear and unobstructed view."

10-4. Can you see a weapon?

I studied the form carefully. There wasn't much to see except an outline. "Negative. All I can see is his head." Almost immediately he moved again. "Sniper one to PRT leader, suspect is now out of view."

It was beginning to be a frustrating game of cat and

mouse. I felt like I was in one of those amusement park shooting galleries where the little animal targets rock in and out of view and you have to estimate when they will appear again.

Then there was a new voice on the radio. *411 John, something's up here.*

411 John was one of the officers in the bushes that had been keeping the suspect busy by talking to him when he came to the window. *411 John . . . he's got a female standing around behind him. I don't know what he's getting ready to do. I can't see his hands.*

"Sniper one, ten-four," I acknowledged and drew my scope to my eye.

He's put the two in the bathtub. He says he's going to kill them in a few seconds!

By this time the entry team was standing by for the signal—my shot—to rush the bathroom. But I couldn't shoot until the command post gave me the green light, and Hendrickson couldn't give the green light until Captain Johnson made the decision to take the man out. And Johnson wouldn't give the word. Like the motorcycles behind *Air Force One,* it was a whole row of dominoes that needed a push before they could fall.

Beard's next action forced Johnson's hand. He screamed that in sixty seconds he would begin killing the hostages. Then he began counting down.

Both women were crying and begging for mercy. We could hear their voices clearly as Beard ticked off the numbers. The scene inside the bathroom was one of horror. Though we couldn't tell from where we stood at the time, we later found that Beard had forced both women down into the bathtub and was standing over them with a large knife in one hand, and in the other, a .45 automatic pistol. Both victims were terrified at the look on Beard's face. It was obvious that he would carry out his threat and within seconds they would die.

PRT to Sniper one, Entry one, stand by. Hendrickson put us on alert for action, then turned to argue with Captain Johnson. The clock kept ticking.

Entry team . . . we're at the back door now. The entry team, by announcing their location, signaled that they were ready.

CP . . . he's just counted down to forty-five seconds. 411 John could clearly hear Beard as he marked each second remaining in the lives of the victims.

My target kept moving. Each time I tried to lock him into the center of the crosshairs, he moved away out of view. I clenched my jaw and waited. I felt that his form would probably return to the window. It had better. At least once before he could carry out his promise.

. . . Just counted through thirty seconds. The women are calling for help inside . . .

My heart began to pound. I could feel the blood in my temples and the bitter ironlike taste of frustration in my mouth. I needed the green light. I *needed* the light!

PRT one to Sniper one, have you got a shot?

I grabbed the radio. "Sniper one, affirmative!" I gripped the Steyr and once again tried to lock onto the target with the reticles. Maybe Hendrickson was ready to give me the green light. If he did, I'd take the shot immediately— provided the target didn't move again. Or I didn't. My standing position was still unstable, and as I held the rifle the crosshairs drifted on and off target. I was getting tired.

PRT one to Sniper one, stand by. PRT one to Entry one, stand by for initiation!

Initiation! That wasn't the word I wanted to hear. As soon as he said that I knew that he was thinking of a technique we had practiced called "coordinated fire." Coordinated fire is used only when you have two or more snipers who are supposed to shoot at exactly the same time, such as to take out two or more threats at once. But I also knew what to expect. I knew what the commands would be. And the words I was about to hear would be tantamount to a green light command.

Then, somehow, the words that came over the radio took away my unsteadiness and fatigue. The crosshairs locked onto the target's head as if the rifle were held in a vise.

PRT one to Sniper one . . .

I held my breath and tightened my finger on the trigger.

. . . ready, ready . . . FIRE! Entry, GO!

But Mike, from his position, couldn't see the suspect. He'd given the commands from information he'd received through the negotiators. I only actually saw the suspect on the few occasions when he stuck his head through the window to say something to the officers outside. The rest of the time, on intermittent occasions, I could only see his silhouette through the opaque glass. And even that was hard to see, because he had slid one window to the left until both windows were one behind the other. What I was seeing was a rough form behind *two* pieces of frosted glass. And I'd have to shoot through both windows at once. Provided he held still long enough to take the shot.

His face briefly appeared at the window to announce the end of time. Then he pulled back to do what he promised.

The women were screaming as he turned and hovered over them with the knife. I could see the silhouette of his head move slowly across the opaque glass, slowing briefly as he adjusted his body.

I squeezed the trigger.

The Steyr recoiled, taking my eye from the window. I never saw Beard go down, but I felt confident that he had been hit. Fatally.

My partner, Mark Sullivan, jumped in surprise. He was about fifteen yards away looking for a better spot when the shot was fired. He looked at me, not sure who had fired the round, and asked, "Did you shoot that guy?"

"Yeah. I shot him."

The entry team busted through the back door and raced

for the bathroom as soon as they heard the shot. They staged quickly outside the bathroom door, taking strategic positions on each side, and tried to force it open. It wouldn't budge. They tried again. Still no use.

The two women were inside, screaming in hysteria at what had just happened. But the entry team guys couldn't get the door open to get to them. For Beard's body, shot through the face, had crumpled in front of the chair that he had propped up against the door under the doorknob.

Finally one of the hostages, gaining reason long enough to see what the problem was, reached out of the bathtub and pulled the chair to the side away from the door. The door burst open almost immediately.

I could hear the commotion inside, and for a moment was not sure what was happening. The entry team should have gotten into the bathroom much quicker. But in all, it was only seconds. And finally the issue was resolved.

As the entry team moved the hostages out of the bathroom I marked my spot. The detectives would want to do the crime scene bit with the diagrams, and as soon as they arrived, I knew the entire SWAT team would be taken back to Southeastern Division for debriefing.

I ran what had happened through my mind over and over. Each time the final thought was the same: We damned near had waited too long. I, literally, could not have fired a split second later. This was about as close as I ever want to come.

7

Standoff in Newport Beach

The job of the police sniper sometimes ranges far beyond that of invoking "Rule .308." In fact, in the majority of cases, police snipers find themselves waiting for hours on end without ever being called upon to perform their functions. A SWAT mission is considered most successful when no one gets hurt. The hostages, if there are any, are rescued; the suspect surrenders; property is protected, and finally, the officers involved all go home intact. In most cases this is the end result of negotiations conducted by the specially trained hostage negotiation team. Even when no hostages are involved, the negotiators handle the task with patience and skill until the situation is defused. These incidents range from gangs of trapped "armed and barricaded" criminals to single suicidal maniacs, holed up with hostages, bent on taking as many people as possible with them.

When negotiations seem to be working, the term "time is on our side" holds true. But when unreasonable demands are made, communications break down and the situation begins to deteriorate, the next level of reaction may be to try and force the suspect or suspects from their haven by making it untenable. This might be accomplished by simply firing tear gas into the building, filling it with an irritating

CS gas agent that causes the eyes, throat, and lungs of everyone inside to burn so badly that they are forced to give up.

But this is not always a viable alternative for the police. If their opponents have planned their actions in advance and procured gas masks, or for some reason are not affected by the chemical agent—such as people who are high on certain drugs—then other measures must be taken.

Sometimes the simple act of cutting off utilities to the structure is sufficient. With no lights, electricity, water or gas, the antagonists lose control of their environment. Especially if their telephone is rendered incapable of calling anywhere except the command post—and the hostage negotiators inside. This instills a feeling of isolation and gives the police negotiating team tools to bargain with. In the winter, cold becomes an ally of the police. In the summer, it is heat that quickly builds inside the building, turning it into an oven. Taking away the gunman's comfort is one chink in his psychology into which a wedge can be driven. Taking away his communications is another. No calls to radio or TV stations, no calls to friends or relatives. No contact with the outside. It all works to the advantage of the police.

And, as these necessities and simple creature comforts are eliminated, the passage of time compounds the situation. There is no drinking water, the toilets won't flush, the radio and television won't work—a feeling of complete isolation and loss of contact with the outside world begins to grow with every passing minute.

Still, there are those that continue to resist beyond this point. Cases have transpired where groups of people (such as the Branch Davidians in Waco, Texas, in 1993) have fanatically prepared themselves in advance for almost every contingency. They have stockpiled food and water, flashlights and batteries, portable radios and all manner of military and survival equipment. But this is the exception and not the rule. Most SWAT involvements are the result of spontaneous reactions on the part of a perpetrator who has done little, if any, advance planning.

The next phase of action for SWAT, when all of the above steps have failed or when time *does* become critical—such as a countdown for execution of hostages—falls to the entry team. Commonly referred to as the "door kickers," these heavily armed and highly trained commandos are the officers called upon to assault the gunman's stronghold, force entry, rush inside, and "clear" the building. The word *clear* has a much more sinister, and twofold meaning: capture or kill the bad guys and rescue the hostages without harming them. This is indeed a difficult and dangerous task. For no one knows exactly what they will encounter once inside the structure. Many questions race through the minds of the entry team members as they prepare for the rush: What is the layout of the interior? What obstacles, furniture, and other items will be inside that an assailant might use for cover? What are the lighting conditions? Will it be dark? If there is ambient light, will it be coming through from the outside in a manner that will silhouette them to the opponent? Has the suspect had time or the capability to rig booby traps? A hundred questions, most without answers. It is indeed a time of stress and gut-wrenching anticipation for those about to breach the unknown.

At this point, when the entry team is poised to go, the confrontation is nearing its end. Within minutes, even seconds, the point of no return will have been crossed. And once crossed, it's "go for broke."

The key word throughout all of these phases and elements is *flexibility*. The entire SWAT team must be able to act and react in accordance to an ever-changing situation. The entry team may be on the verge of battering down a door or stealthily crawling through a window, only to be withdrawn at the last second because once again the suspect, after lengthy silence or sudden violent threats, decides to resume negotiations. Or new intelligence has surfaced that indicates that an entry would be disastrous to the hostage or officers.

Whatever the reason, the operation goes back to square one. But not for the police sniper. For the marksman and his observer, it's all the same. Throughout the entire ordeal they have remained in the same mode of operation. They have maintained their position, monitoring events as they unfold on the radio, noting everything that takes place, weathering the elements, exhibiting the greatest of patience as the minutes and hours tick by. And as all of this transpires they realize that it is probably just one more call-out that will end without their direct participation. They will pack up their rifles and go home once again without ever being part of the mainstream of events.

Or maybe not. It only takes one short call from the command post and the sniper becomes the last—and only—alternative. A few spoken words that squawk from the radio: ". . . Sniper, if you get the shot, take him out," or ". . . You've got the *green light!*" sends him into a mental whirlwind of thoughts and feelings. Boredom and complacency are instantly replaced by excitement. The rifleman's chest tightens, his pulse races, his thinking speeds up, senses become super acute, adrenaline blasts away fatigue. He's on the edge. It is for this that he lives. Now it's all up to him.

And then, just when it looks like all of the training, all of the days on the range, will come into play, permission to fire is withdrawn. It's a letdown. And often it's a relief. He knew he could do it, he was ready to do it, but he didn't have to. It's a roller coaster conflict of emotions that not everyone can deal with. But the police sniper must. It goes with the job. It's called "being flexible."

Flexibility can manifest itself in many ways to the marksman. His orders may range from eliminating a violent subject to shooting out a strategically placed streetlight, or anything in between that would facilitate the total mission. Not every shot fired by a police marksman is destined to kill. Such was the case for Officer Mike LaVigne of the

Newport Beach Police Department on Saturday evening, June 10, 1989.

It was a cool, clear night for the beach towns along the coast of Southern California. Even though it was June, summer had yet to arrive, which was not unusual for this time of year. A weather element known as the "Marine Layer" often lingers into July, holding the last vestiges of winter until the Japanese current changes and swings north along the coast, bringing the warmer Mexican water and weather with it. Until then, time spent on the beaches would be limited to only a few hours during the warmest part of the afternoon—provided the morning haze burns off soon enough and the upper layer of gray coastal clouds blows out to sea. It is not the best time for a visitor to judge "that warm California sun."

But it is an anticipatory time of year. The kids are out of school, winter is almost over, and everyone is impatiently waiting for the chance to don a new swimming suit, try a new surfboard, get a tan, or simply kick back and hang out. It's approaching the time of year Californians love.

It is also the time of year when more people are on the streets, stay out later, and make themselves more vulnerable prey to criminals and crazies.

Fifty-three-year-old Frank Musser Johnston was one of the latter. Originally from the East Coast, Musser had migrated to California. His expectations, evidently, went unfulfilled, and his mental attitude deteriorated to a state of depression. For at approximately 8:30 P.M. he wheeled his blue 1979 Oldsmobile Cutlass two-door into the parking lot of the Westcliff Shopping Center in Newport Beach, pulled into a parking space near the front of the northern row of storefront shops, and parked. He opened the door, stepped out, and announced to any passerby within speaking distance that he had a bomb in the car. And he was going to blow the car, the shopping center, and himself, to pieces. He made no particular demands, and was careful to whom he spoke.[1] He only approached women, men smaller than himself, and children. It was as if he didn't want some big guy to say, "Okay, I'll just grab you to keep you from going back to the car, then I'll just call the police." But at the same time, it was obvious that Johnston wanted to draw attention to himself from anyone who did not pose a direct threat at the moment.

And attention he drew.

The Newport Beach Police dispatcher received the call at 9:01 P.M. and immediately dispatched officers to ascertain the situation. Upon arrival, the first officer on the scene could see Johnston pacing the sidewalk, attempting to talk to people as they passed, then going back to his car. He sat down inside the car, closed the door, and began to call out to people from the relative safety of the automobile.

As other officers responded to the area they stopped short of actually coming into view of Johnston. Instead, they contacted store owners over the telephone advising them to close their stores and evacuate the area. As would-be shoppers neared Westcliff Center in vehicles and on foot, they were turned away by the cordon of officers that had established a loose perimeter around the center.

The center itself was not hard to contain. Occupying the northeast corner of the intersection of Westcliff Drive and Irvine Boulevard, the L-shaped structure that contained two banks, a supermarket, and several small stores was naturally cordoned off on two sides by the structure itself. All of the storefronts faced the parking lot, effectively boxing it in on the north and east. Johnston's Cutlass was in plain view among the first row of cars, nosed in against the curb of the sidewalk near the apex of the two rows of shops.

Pole-mounted streetlights illuminated the shopping center and parking lot, but inside the car little could be seen.

---

[1]It was not until after the incident that the police discovered that Johnston was despondent because his live-in girlfriend had just broken up with him and had thrown him out of the residence.

The officers knew that he was still inside, but could not see exactly what he was doing. Did he have a bomb? If he did, would he detonate it? No one had a clue.

But they did know one thing: They could not let him leave. Even if it meant killing him. But other things could be tried first. Other things *had* to be tried first.

8

Officer Mike LaVigne, Newport Beach Police Department
June 10, 1989

Like most police departments, SWAT in Newport Beach is a part-time job. All of the members of the team function in other assignments on a day-to-day basis as patrol officers, detectives, administrators, and other full-time assignments. Of the 155 sworn officers on the Newport Beach Police Department, only sixteen hold an additional duty assignment with the SWAT team. Though we get together once each month for a training period, we seldom see each other the rest of the time unless there is a SWAT call-out. My full-time assignment is as a helicopter pilot for the Air Support Unit, call sign OCEAN—an acronym for Over City Enforcement At Newport.

It was just after 2100 hours when I and my partner, Officer Myles Elsing, monitored the call at Westcliff Shopping Center. I was flying left seat, the pilot's position in the McDonnell-Douglas 500E helicopter, and Myles sat to my right in the observer position. We had only been airborne for a short time when the call came out, breaking the boredom of the early evening hours of a typical Saturday night that begins slow, but heats up as the night wears on. It wasn't the type of call that we would normally "roll" on with a helicopter, so we continued our aerial patrol over the lights of the city in search of other criminal activity.

That changed within minutes with a single call from dispatch: *OCEAN . . . report to the station. See the watch commander.*

Such a call could mean anything. It could be a special assignment that required the services of the helicopter, or it could be an emergency message for either Myles or myself that the watch commander did not want transmitted over the radio. Maybe a family member had had an accident, maybe there was a complaint we had to answer for. There was no way to tell until we arrived. A hundred thoughts race through your mind when you are summoned by the watch commander. I pulled pitch and nosed the machine over to gain airspeed as we offered suggestions to each other over the intercom regarding the purpose of our summons.

We settled to a hover over the helipad and I lowered the collective, settling the machine to the ground. Two minutes later, after the cool-down period prescribed in the checklist, I shut down. The engine was still creaking and groaning as the metal contracted in the cool evening air when Myles and I entered the station.

"LaVigne," said the watch commander, Sergeant Ken Cowell, "we've got a situation over at the Westcliff Shopping Center. Some nut says he's got a bomb and he's going to set it off. We've got the area isolated and evacuated, but right now it's pretty much a standoff. Get your SWAT gear and rifle and grab a car. Get over there as soon as possible and find yourself a spot on some high ground. Whatever happens, we don't want this guy to leave. I don't want some crazy with a bomb driving around town."

"Is this a full SWAT call-out?" I asked.

"Not at this time. For now it's just the patrol officers and you. I don't think this necessitates a full SWAT activation. I

Craig Roberts

just want the people that are already there backed up by a sniper."

"I'll need an observer. How about Myles?" I asked. Elsing was already here with me, and taking him instead of waiting for my SWAT observer would save time.

"Fine. Just get over there and come up on the radio. The supervisor on the scene can brief you when you get there."

Myles and I hurried to the SWAT van and grabbed my black nylon drag bag with all my SWAT equipment and extra ammo inside. I unlocked the arms locker and retrieved my Remington 700 BDL sniper rifle. Chambered in .308 Winchester and mounted with a Leupold Vari-X II 3X9 variable scope, this specialized heavy weapon is basically an offshoot of the big game sporter found in most gun shops. This version, however, is built with one purpose in mind. Accuracy. Accuracy needed by both military and police snipers who must depend upon one shot. The *first* shot. Because of this it is fitted with a heavy barrel and an accurized action. The trigger pull is set at four pounds and all moving parts are milled with close tolerance specifications to provide the smoothest, yet tightest, action achievable on an off-the-shelf sniper rifle. The same basic rifle was used by Marine snipers in Vietnam after the Marine Corps began replacing their pre-1964 Winchester .30-06 bolt-action rifles in 1967. It is a battle-proven rifle of excellent design.

Myles and I drew an unmarked police car and drove to Westcliff and Irvine as fast as traffic would permit. After parking the car, we received a quick orientation from the supervisor on the scene. The suspect was still seated in his car at the sidewalk curb line by the east-west row of shops on the northern border of the complex. Most of the parking lot was empty, but near his car each space was taken by abandoned vehicles that had been left in place during the evacuation. These cars provided him with cover on each side, and the shops offered even more protection to his front. The only point of advantage I could see would be

76

from a position overlooking his car where I could get a downward angle into a window. If I could climb to the roof of the eastern row of shops, perhaps I could crawl to a point where I could shoot down over the top of the parked car to his east. It was the only location from which I might be able to get a clear shot. But even that would be less than ideal because I would only be able to angle a shot in from the passenger side. He would be seated across the car on the driver's side, and unless he leaned over toward the right, I might only be able to see part of his body—if I could see anything at all inside the dark car. But it was the only possibility and we had to go for it.

The fire department had already arrived, summoned early in the incident when the possibility of fire presented itself in the aftermath of a bomb explosion. By using one of their ladders, Myles and I climbed up the back of the center and inched our way to a rooftop hide on the sloped edge of the roof of a savings and loan situated at the corner of the two rows of shops. It was as close as we could get and was slightly higher than the surrounding structures. The savings and loan was the keystone of the center, with the surrounding shops extending away to the west and south. Being one of the largest businesses in the center, it extended out into the parking lot on the southwest corner until it formed a square building four times larger than the shops in the wings. The roof sloped up on all four sides to a flat apex on top. It was on the south slope that Myles and I settled in.

I inched my way on my belly to the comb,[1] raised my head slightly, and peered over. Below and to my front, not more than forty yards away, I spotted the Cutlass.

"I see it. It's still there," I advised Myles. He joined me

---

[1] The peak or top edge of the roof that the sides slope away from. In this case, it is the line formed where the west and south roof sections meet at an angle that runs from the gutter line to the ridge line.

and brought a special twenty power spotting scope mounted on a plastic shoulder stock up to his eye.

"Yeah. No movement as far as I can see. I'll report in." Myles eased back away from the edge and radioed the command post.

I began to evaluate my position. Visually, as far as covering the car, it was as good as we could expect. But other than that, it was less than desirable. We were lying on an angle of about thirty degrees, an angle that canted to the left and forced me to lie at an uneven plane in reference to the target. It would be very uncomfortable to maintain this position for long. It wasn't like lying on a flat roof, or a sloped roof that you lie uphill on to look over the top of the comb. Instead, it was about as unstable a position as a sniper could encounter. And to make matters worse, I was a left-handed shooter! To bring my rifle to bear I had to figure out how to prop myself and the weapon up in a manner that, if I had to take a shot, would not knock me sideways down the roof.

I scooted my body around until I found the best angle possible. It wasn't much of an improvement, but it would have to do. Myles sat slightly behind me, watching with the spotting scope and handling the radio.

Myles was a helicopter pilot. He was not a trained observer in the police sniper sense, and never even considered the possibility that he would be drafted into the role in a come-as-you-are assignment. When he started the shift he would never have believed that he would end it, still dressed in his tan flight suit, on the dark rooftop of a shopping center overlooking some nut with a bomb parked only forty yards away. It wasn't exactly the type of job helicopter crews become part of. Though flying police helicopters is a dangerous business, airspeed and altitude are two natural defenses that come into play against armed criminals encountered during police work. These are two advantages we have over our brother officers on the ground. A helicopter moving at sixty miles per hour or more, circling in the air several hundred feet over the ground, is an extremely hard target to hit. Speed and distance are the only two advantages we have, but they are very *effective* advantages. Now here we were, probably well inside the burst radius of high explosives, and our "altitude" was, to say the least, insufficient.

As a rifleman, I had another problem. Just to the right of my line of fire, on the edge of the roof to my front, was a cube-shaped clock tower. It extended above the gutter line by about eight feet—just enough to present an obstacle and limit my fan of fire to the right.

I analyzed my predicament. I was a left-handed shooter, trying to remain stationary on a platform that sloped away steeply to the left, armed with a right-handed rifle—which would force me to raise my right elbow, while using my left elbow for support, to work the bolt. I had to shoot at a downward angle, around a clock tower, under artificial lighting conditions, over the roof of one car, into the darkened interior of the Cutlass at a target that was on the opposite side of the vehicle. I didn't feel good about this.

I reviewed my orders. They were fairly basic. I was to do whatever was necessary to keep the vehicle from leaving the parking lot. But what would that take? I wasn't sure. And I wasn't sure exactly how I would accomplish this. I began to feel that I was in the proverbial "trick box." A box from which the best-laid plans backfire at the worst possible moment. Only time would tell.

As we watched the Cutlass, several attempts were made by the other officers to communicate with the suspect. Using a PA system, supervisors attempted to talk him out of the car, tried to reason with him, find out what the problem was, anything that would establish a dialogue that might defuse the situation. None of this seemed to have a great deal of impact on him. He did, however, write a few notes and hold them up to the open window. Officers tried to read the notes with binoculars—no one wanted to approach the car for obvious reasons—but this proved almost impossible. I could see him make some sort of hand signals through my scope, confirmed by Myles through his spotting scope, but they were meaningless.

I adjusted my scope for the short range, cutting it down to three power, to get the widest field of view. It seemed to help, but not enough to make out detail. As I concentrated on the car, trying to pick up whatever I could, we received a radio call. Myles answered.

"Mike, they want us to try and shoot out a tire. Can you get a shot?"

I shifted the rifle. I could see the right rear tire of the Cutlass, but the others were blocked by the car he was parked next to. "Yeah, I can. But it'll make a hell of a lot of noise. It might scare him, and if it does, he might blow us all up. Tell the command post that."

Myles quickly relayed the information and the CP agreed. Instead of the Remington, they decided to send up a silenced H&K MP-5 submachine gun mounted with a 3X9 Leupold scope. Within minutes it arrived, brought up the back of the building in the same manner as we had used to access the roof.

I selected "semiauto" to fire a single round instead of a burst, brought the stubby black weapon to my eye and sighted in. The tire was easily visible in the magnified view of the scope. I held my breath and squeezed the trigger. The weapon coughed one time, sending the suppressed 9mm round into the tire. It did the trick.

I laid the MP-5 to one side and picked up the Remington. If I had to shoot through the body of the car, the metal wouldn't deflect the high-velocity Federal 168 grain Sierra boat tail hollow point.

It was now about 2230—10:30 P.M. It seemed like we had been on the roof much longer, but that was probably due to the discomfort we were experiencing. I settled down and shifted my body slightly, trying to gain a modicum of comfort. No luck. I just had to gut it out.

Then I heard it. The cranking sound of a starter. I took my eye off the scope just long enough to see that the suspect had started the Cutlass and was beginning to back out of the parking space. Either he didn't know the tire was flat, or he didn't care. Myles and I had both witnessed people driving on flat tires, relying on just the rim to make headway. He wouldn't be able to go very fast, but he wouldn't be immobile either. He had to be stopped. There was nothing that would keep him in the parking lot if he headed for the street.

The radio chatter picked up. Short transmissions from various officers strategically placed around the location crackled with warnings. *He's backing out! I can see the suspect vehicle trying to leave!*

And it was up to *us* to stop him.

I got back behind the scope. I leveled it on the car and concentrated the crosshairs on the body as it backed out. I felt that maybe I could disable the car further if I could just get a shot or two into some critical component—if there was time. Just give me a shot at something vulnerable. . . .

The car continued to back up. I shifted the rifle. As the Cutlass cleared the parking space the front end came into view. I watched intently as the right side fender filled my scope. I placed the crosshairs just above the front wheel well and took up the slack on the trigger.

The Remington had no sooner recoiled than I worked the bolt to chamber a new round. I fired again. The second round struck right next to the first.

But still the car continued to back up. I frantically worked the bolt again. Obviously neither of the shots hit anything critical. I just had to keep trying.

Now I wasn't sure exactly what I should aim at. I just decided to crank another round into the engine compartment and hope for the best. I squeezed the trigger again.

This time something happened. The car lurched to a stop, the engine running roughly for a few seconds, then dying. The suspect tried to restart the engine but it wouldn't catch.

Myles and I held our breath. If this guy was going to get mad and detonate the bomb, this would really give him an excuse. But nothing happened. He just sat there. I'm sure he was confused, trying to reason what had happened, and I prayed he would rethink his situation. Maybe give up.

As I waited to see what would happen next I remembered how many shots I had fired. I only had two remaining rounds in the rifle: one in the chamber and one in the magazine. Without taking my eye from the scope I called out to Myles to bring me some ammo.

Myles, not being a trained SWAT observer, thought we were out of ammunition. He grabbed the radio, keyed the mike, and announced in an excited voice, "We need ammo! We need someone to bring us some more ammo *right now!*"

I couldn't help but chuckle. It sounded like we were pinned down and were being overrun. "Myles, I've got plenty of ammo in the rifle pack. Just get a box and hand me a few rounds."

"Oh. Right," mumbled Myles as he grabbed the rifle pack and unzipped the ammo compartment.

As he did this I couldn't help but think what an outstanding job he had done so far. Even though he was an untrained sniper observer, he had performed flawlessly. His handling of the radio, the spotting scope, and observation functions were every bit as good as any SWAT observer could have done. I felt completely comfortable with him.

Then the night came alive with the sound of a PA system. A police car had been pulled up to within seventy-five yards of the Cutlass and a negotiator began to speak over the public address system. He tried to reason, to cajole, to coax the man out. But the suspect would have none of it. He remained fixed behind the wheel as if all of this were only a temporary setback.

Then the decision was made. Tear gas would be used to

run him out of the car. Officers armed with a twelve-gauge shotgun loaded with Ferret CS gas projectiles approached the right side of the Cutlass, stopping about thirty feet short to use another parked vehicle as cover. From there, they could see the right side windows of the car. It would be a straight shot.

The gunner leveled the shotgun on the car and pulled the trigger. The report reverberated through the still night air as the small tear gas projectile zipped toward the car. The Ferret is a small-finned projectile similar in shape to a tiny aerial bomb. Inside, it carries a breakable bladder containing three centimeters of CS-type chemical gas. It will penetrate a hollow-core door and still carry its charge through, and into, the room beyond.

The Ferret broke the glass and burst into the car, vaporizing into a cloud of gas. We waited for a few seconds, but the suspect didn't come out. The officers fired another, and another. Each hit its mark, but the man remained inside the vehicle, apparently not fazed. Finally, the gunners shifted to the back post supporting the roof of the vehicle. They hit it square, sending white clouds of gas drifting around and through the car. But those, like their predecessors, were not effective. The man inside simply grabbed handfuls of tissues from a box and covered his face. I couldn't believe it. Twenty-four Ferrets were fired, and all he needed was tissue paper to filter the gas and wipe his eyes! This was one tough dude.

It was time to call up some heavier artillery. The twelve-gauge shotgun was replaced with a 37mm gas grenade launcher. This single barrel weapon resembles a stubby shotgun with a bore similar to that of a one and a half-inch water pipe. It breaks open just like a single-shot shotgun, then is breach-loaded with one large bullet-shaped tear gas round about eight inches long. The breach is then closed and a large hammer cocked prior to being fired. It contains a great deal more chemical agent than the tiny Ferret rounds.

The gunner, Officer Mike Pule, took aim at the rear

window support post and let loose his round. But the shot missed its mark. Instead of bursting inside, the shot carried right through the car, out the shattered back window, and then out on the parking lot beyond, where it skittered around spewing gas.

Pule decided to change the angle. He had to get a shot into the car in a direction that would keep it from passing through the windows. To do this, he relocated to the ridge line of the roof over the shops in front of the car. This would put the next shot at a downward angle, forcing the round to impact into the seats and lodge tight.

He aimed carefully at the unoccupied passenger side and fired. The projectile broke through the windshield, leaving a hole surrounded by shattered glass, and slammed into the empty seat. Gas began once again to fill the vehicle. Still, the suspect refused to budge.

At this point it was decided that tear gas wouldn't work. Negotiations were resumed.

Finally, at 1:00 the next morning, we began to receive an indication that the man was ready to surrender. Myles and I hoped so. I wasn't sure how much longer we could maintain our awkward body positions. My muscles and elbows were all throbbing in protest at having to fight the sloped roof for so long.

The main concern at this point was twofold. First, that he leave the explosive device in the vehicle, and second, that he be prevented from returning to the car after he exited it. I wasn't sure how they were going to do that, but it would prove interesting.

He was told to slide over to the passenger side of the car, open the door, and leave the vehicle. He hesitated at first, but then slowly began to comply. He eased over to the right side, then opened the door. He paused for only a second, then stepped out of the car. As Myles and I watched, he was ordered to remove his shirt. The officers that stood poised to rush the car wanted to make sure he didn't have the bomb or a weapon on his person. He complied, then shuffled toward the rear of the car and stopped by the flattened back tire.

Then I saw how he was going to be restrained from reentering the car. One of Costa Mesa Police Department's K-9 German shepherds, trained to hold someone at bay as long as they make no threatening moves, appeared and took a position within attack distance of the subject.[2]

The man would have been just fine if he had not moved. I couldn't see exactly what he did, but whatever it was, it triggered the dog. He hit the man in the leg, knocking him to the ground, and began shaking his ankle violently. The suspect yelled more in fear than pain, but the diversion kept him occupied long enough to permit other officers to take the car. The Orange County Bomb Squad, which had been standing by nearby for some time, moved in to deal with the explosive device.

Myles and I crawled down from our perch. When we got to the car we found out that the "bomb" was nothing more than a paper bag containing some personal effects. But there was no way of knowing this in advance, and every bomb threat is, and has to be, handled as if it were the real thing.

I examined the car and the point of impact of my three rounds. Three holes sat neatly grouped together halfway between the top of the right wheel well and the hood line. Another was just a few inches to the right on an equal plane. We opened the hood to see what this bullet, the final shot fired that stopped the car, had struck.

Inside, we could see where the first two shots struck noncritical components such as the alternator and air conditioner. But the third shot, the one that put the engine out of commission, amazed us. It was one of those one-in-a-million shots that has to be credited more with luck than skill. For as unlikely as it was, the bullet had cut *three* spark

---

[2]Costa Mesa borders Newport Beach on the northwest. They had volunteered assistance with a K-9 unit.

plug wires in a row! The Cutlass's V-6 engine lost half of its cylinders to one single bullet. It was a lucky shot, but it was enough.[3]

The mission was a success. We *had* kept the suspect from leaving Westcliff Shopping Center. And it had not been necessary to take him out. It would have been unfortunate if we had had to neutralize a man over a brown paper bag.

But if the order had come, that's exactly what would have happened. You don't have time to think about it. You just do it. It's the job.

---

[3]A traffic officer, upon examining the bullet holes in the fender, stated, "It looks like our snipers need more training. They missed the tire all three times."

9

Trouble in the High Country

Not every SWAT incident occurs in big cities. Occasionally, situations develop in rural areas far from the freeways and lights of the metropolises that stretch the capabilities of small law enforcement agencies to the breaking point. It is then that the tiny contingents of sheriff's deputies or community police officers who police the "outback" find themselves faced with odds that are not in their favor. To deal with these scenarios, most agencies band together and come to one another's aid. As in the days of old, when posses were formed to counter gangs of outlaws, deputy sheriffs, state police, highway patrol troopers, even fish and game rangers respond to calls for assistance from brother officers. But even then, altercations occur that require more than the presence of a number of men with badges armed with pistols and shotguns.

One such incident took place in the small resort town of South Lake Tahoe, California.

Lake Tahoe is a large mountain lake that rests in the high mountain country of the Sierra Nevada range on the California-Nevada border. Surrounding the cold crystalline waters of the lake are rugged mountains covered with stately ponderosa pine trees. The entire vicinity has long been popular with tourists. Vacationers come from all fifty states, Canada, Mexico, and Europe to enjoy the pure, clear, clean mountain atmosphere. In the spring, summer, and fall, hunters, boaters, and fishermen inundate the local communities in fantastic numbers. In the winter, they are replaced by skiers who race down the packed slopes of some of the finest ski areas in the world. And to add further attraction to the locale, a short drive away is the Nevada border. Here, numerous casinos pull in thousands of people who enjoy the bright nightlife of the shows, restaurants, and gaming tables. It is because of these attractions that the surrounding towns have blossomed in the past fifty years from small vacation cabin communities to major resorts.

The town of South Lake Tahoe lies at the southern tip of the lake. Known by the locals simply as "Tahoe," it is a nerve center for the visitors that flock to the forested vacation land of the Sierras during the tourist seasons. And for those who like the wild nightlife, the gambling community of Stateline, Nevada, is just across the nearby California-Nevada border, which is little more than a dividing line between the two communities. Historically, Tahoe developed from tiny residential sections that grew around scattered general stores that straddled the main highway. Because of the sporadic expansion of the various clusters of cabins and businesses, modern million-dollar homes can be found next to tiny cabins built before World War II. It is an unregimented community where property lines are almost undistinguishable, and few fences mark boundaries. Tahoe is best described as a hodgepodge community of the new and the old, the rich and the not-so-rich.

The population of permanent residents numbers approximately thirty thousand; however, in the tourist seasons this number swells to over one hundred sixty thousand. And as in any resort community, the crime rate is directly proportional to the number of transients. Those that come into town from the big cities bring big city crime. Armed robberies, burglaries, auto thefts, and drugs increase, sometimes to the point of being more than a small police department can handle.

The biggest influx of tourists occurs between Memorial Day and Labor Day. In those months the motels, cabins, and campgrounds are full of people in a party mood. It is a festive time of year, and with the passing of the winter snows, it is a period when people can move about unhindered to enjoy the sights, meet new friends, and generally have a good time. It is also a time of year when criminals take advantage of opportunity.

In the mid-1970s, when the following story transpired, the South Lake Tahoe Police Department could field only fifty-one officers, ten of whom comprised a young, sparsely equipped part-time SWAT team.

When thirty-one-year-old police detective Paul Habelt first heard the call come over his police radio, it was nothing to get excited about. Just a simple "disturbance" call involving an argument over a poker game. Routine. Two patrol officers acknowledged the call, and since he was close, he decided to drop by and see if he could be of help.

A few minutes later the dispatcher upgraded the call.

Units responding to the Kelmont Arms Apartments on Ski Run Boulevard, be advised that the complainant said the subjects inside have guns.

But Habelt didn't hear this transmission. By the time it came out he had already arrived at the scene and had left his car.

He entered the two-story Kelmont Arms and took the elevator up to the second floor, where the "disturbance" was supposed to be taking place. As he did so, the two patrol officers arrived, entered the building at the opposite end, and began ascending the stairs.

When the doors of the elevator opened, Habelt walked into the hall and immediately saw that the door to the apartment in question, located across and slightly down the hall to his left, stood partially ajar. He drew his Smith & Wesson Model 19 .357 magnum as a precautionary measure, walked down the hallway, and pushed the door open.

At that moment a hand appeared from around the edge of the wall of the apartment's interior entryway to the living room. In it was a .45 caliber Colt automatic pistol. Before Habelt could react, the confined entryway reverberated with a deafening muzzle blast. This shot was followed by three more in rapid succession.

One bullet struck the detective in his right shoulder, spinning him sideways. The next hit him in the biceps of his left arm.

Habelt, now coming to full realization of what was happening, desperately tried to return fire. He managed to get off two rounds before his right forearm was shattered by a bullet, forcing his hand to release his gun, which fell to the floor.

The helpless detective now took the fourth round fired by his unseen assailant. It entered his jaw at one side of his chin, traveled along his jawbone, deflected down his neck, then traversed across his back to lodge in his shoulder. Bleeding heavily, he fell to the floor just inside the door.

The gunman, a bushy-haired twenty-four-year-old drug dealer from Los Angeles named John Locklear, stepped over Habelt and peeked around the doorway to examine the hall. At the end of the hallway he spotted the two patrol officers who had charged up the stairs at the sound of gunfire. Without hesitation, he stepped out into the hall and discharged a round in their direction. The two officers, caught in the open, desperately kicked the door of another apartment open and dove inside. Then, before they could gather their wits and return fire, Locklear ducked back into his apartment and slammed the door shut.

He then stepped over Habelt and looked down. Habelt was lying on his back, bleeding and helpless. The detective's eyes followed Locklear—and the pistol that was slowly raised until it pointed directly at his face.

Habelt knew it was the end. There was nothing he could do but await his fate. He steeled himself, then turned his head away and closed his eyes to await the shot.

Locklear pulled the trigger. The big Colt recoiled in an ear-shattering blast, ejecting the spent cartridge onto the floor next to Habelt. Locklear then turned away and walked back into the living room, out of sight of the downed police officer.

But Habelt wasn't dead. Locklear had managed to miss him from a distance of *two feet!* The only explanation offered later was that Locklear was so high on drugs that his aim was skewed. And he didn't even realize that he had missed.

Habelt, fighting back the effects of shock, lay still for a moment to compose himself. Then, drawing from an inner reserve given those caught in the most extreme conditions of stress, rallied his strength and began inching his way toward his gun.

As he drew close he extended his arm. But his hand, because of the traumatic nerve damage inflicted by the bullets, would not close on the grip. His only hope now was in escape. He had to get out of the apartment before the gunman could return to discover his error and finish the job. Habelt, moving as quietly as possible, dragged himself toward the door.

Succeeding in reaching it undetected, he reached up and tried to turn the knob. But the blood that now covered his hand and arm caused his hand to slip on the metallic surface. He tried again, and again. The effort was useless.

He sank to the floor and forced himself to breathe in measured gasps. As he sat there, fighting back the darkness that preludes unconsciousness, he noticed that the door was not completely closed. When Locklear had slammed it, he did it with such force that it had bounced back open far enough to expose an inch of light from the hallway. If he could just get the door open, he might be able to crawl out into the hallway and escape.

The wounded detective was beginning to grow weaker by the second. He knew that if he lost consciousness, he would bleed to death where he lay. He had to force himself to at least try and get out of the apartment. It was his only chance.

Mustering up every bit of strength available, Habelt grasped the edge of the door. He pulled slowly, praying the door would not make any noise.

The door inched open.

Down the hall, the two patrol officers saw the door open and readied themselves for another onslaught. But what came out of the apartment was not the long-haired gunman who had first accosted them. Instead, it was the bloody form of Paul Habelt.

Leaving their position of cover, they charged down the hall, grabbed the detective's clothes and, as fast as the weight of Habelt's now limp form permitted, dragged him back to the stairwell—and safety.

Within minutes their call for help and the words "shots fired, officer down" brought every available man on duty rushing to the scene. Officers from the California Highway Patrol and the El Dorado Sheriff's office, receiving word of what had happened in South Lake Tahoe, dropped whatever they were doing and accelerated toward the city to lend assistance to the small department.

As the units arrived they began setting up a perimeter around the apartment building. But this was not an easy task. The apartment faced Ski Run Boulevard, an extremely wide main street that provided no concealment to officers who had to cover the front of the structure—and the sliding glass patio doors on the balcony of Locklear's apartment. From the apartment, Locklear held the high ground and could command all approaches from the front. Only by crouching behind their cars could officers maintain any semblance of tactical positioning.

As outside units arrived, the highway patrol set up blocking points on Ski Run Boulevard to isolate the scene from civilian traffic, and El Dorado deputies reinforced the

Tahoe officers on the perimeter itself. Then, with the perimeter strengthened, Tahoe officers closed in to contain the scene as tightly as possible.

One officer made his way to a telephone pole located in front of, and just north of the balcony. From there, he could watch the glass doors of the apartment, and if a shoot-out transpired, return fire with a twelve-gauge Remington 870 shotgun.

Inside the apartment, Locklear took stock of his situation. He and his younger brother, Wayne, and a third cohort named Barry Chretian were not happy about the way the situation was developing. No matter which window they looked out, all they could see were police cars and cops. It was obvious that they were surrounded, and the only hope they had would be in the three hostages they held.

During the night, the Locklear brothers and Chretian had perpetrated a scam that they had anticipated would bring in some money. The plan was to host a poker party and invite some of the local drug dealers to come over, gamble, get high, and buy some dope. But after they arrived, the threesome planned to rob them of their buy money. The con went sour sometime during the early morning hours and one of the dealers, taking advantage of the commotion caused when guns were produced, managed to escape and called the police. Now four of his counterparts, terrified at what John Locklear had done to the cop at the front door, cowered in the apartment at gunpoint.

Sometime during the night Locklear had ripped the telephone from the wall to isolate his victims. Now he had no way of negotiating with the police. The hostages were worthless unless the cops could be told that they were there.

Locklear ordered Chretian to bind the hostages with cords. Chretian, now having second thoughts after witnessing the violent actions of Locklear, tied the four people loosely. He hoped that if Locklear lost complete control of his actions at least a few of the hostages could get free and defend themselves or escape. Such an action might be his only bargaining chip for mercy later should he live long enough to go to trial.

As the hostages were being bound, Locklear began thinking of how he might communicate with the police. The only possibility that came to mind would be to use a hostage as a shield and to negotiate from the balcony. This course of action determined, he selected George Stedler, a drug dealer who, unknown to the police at the time, was himself a wanted felon from San Francisco.

Locklear opened the sliding patio doors and forced Stedler out onto the balcony. As Stedler stepped out, Locklear shoved his arm out of the opening in the door and followed him with his pistol. The officer behind the telephone pole, seeing the pistol in Locklear's hand, brought his shotgun to bear and shouted, "Drop!" to Stedler to clear him from the line of fire. But Stedler, instead of dropping out of the way, attempted to escape by diving toward an adjoining balcony. At that moment Locklear shifted his aim and opened fire on the officer.

The officer, now trying to use the narrow telephone pole as cover, returned fire. A single errant pellet from one blast of the twelve-gauge hit Stedler just as he cleared the rail to the adjacent balcony, clipping his descending aorta. As he fell to the balcony, Locklear withdrew into the apartment and disappeared from view.

Stedler, bleeding internally, died within seconds. His lifeless body now rested in plain view on the balcony overlooking Ski Run Boulevard.

To the gathering crowd of curious tourists and onlookers, many of whom were inebriated from all-night binges at the local twenty-four-hour clubs, the excitement became quite an attraction. Several individuals, feeling their quota of alcohol, offered advice and commentary. One middle-aged man declared, "What they need to clean that nest out are some old combat vets like us. Give me a BAR[1] and we'll

---

[1]Browning Automatic Rifle.

blast the place apart!" Another, taking a different approach, claimed he knew Locklear and that all the cops had to do was let him go up to the apartment and hold a casual conversation with him, after which he was sure to surrender.

The standoff at the Kelmont Arms was rapidly becoming a zoo.

Besides having to deal with the gathering crowds, the officers manning the perimeter in front of the Kelmont Arms now faced the prospect that standard tactics and issue weapons might not provide the best solution to the problem.

What they needed was SWAT.

10

Patrolman Lance Young, South Lake Tahoe Police Department
September 3, 1975

I hung the phone up in a state of shock. My mind was trying desperately to sort out the words just spoken by the dispatcher. Paul Habelt had been shot. I just couldn't make that register. I had wanted to ask a hundred questions, to find out what had happened, how bad he was, when did it happen . . . but there wasn't time. I had to get moving. The SWAT team was being activated, and I had been caught on my day off, baby-sitting my two small children. I had to notify my wife at work that I had been called in, then drop the kids off at the day-care center we used when we both worked before I could even head for the rally point at the station.

I called my wife and quickly explained that we had a major incident in progress. I told her that we had an officer down and SWAT was being activated. I tried to sound calm, but it was hard. I knew that she could sense by the tone of my voice that this was a serious, and obviously dangerous, situation. I explained that I would have to get going and not to worry, and that I would drop the kids off and that she would have to pick them up after work.

I piled the kids into the car and headed for the preschool. As I drove I thought about Paul. We had occasionally worked patrol together during the five years I had been with the Tahoe police and I knew him to be a fine, dedicated officer. Like most of us, Paul was a "lateral" transfer to South Lake Tahoe from another department. Previous to being hired at Tahoe, he had worked on the Oakland Police Department where he had experienced his share of hot calls. It was ironic that he had survived the streets in the Bay area only to get shot in Tahoe. I couldn't help but wonder why he was involved in what normally would have been a straight patrol call since he was a detective, but then I knew that if anyone needed help and he was near, he'd volunteer to assist.

Tahoe is a small department, and as such, everybody knows everyone else. It is a very close-knit community where each officer knows everything about the others. It's not like a major department where officers only know those that work out of their station, or maybe just their shift. In Tahoe everyone is on a first name basis and there are very few, if any, secrets. For this reason Paul's shooting hit us all close to home.

I dropped the kids off and drove to the station. It was here that we were supposed to meet, draw out gear, and receive a preliminary briefing before going out as a unit to Ski Run Boulevard. It was just after noon when I arrived.

The briefing was short and to the point. We were filled in on what had happened and how the scene had been secured. That was about it. After that we were told to get over to the on-scene command post and report in for assignments. I grabbed my SWAT equipment and rifle from the station, retrieved my Second Chance bulletproof ballistics vest from my locker, pulled on my blue jumpsuit, and headed for Ski Run Boulevard.

Our SWAT team was young at the time. We had been in existence less than a year, and the training we had came from some of us taking vacation to go to schools provided by larger departments, then returning home to train our guys. Another officer, Roger Taylor, and I had been lobbying with the administration for quite some time to establish a SWAT team. Roger had come from the Santa Barbara Sheriff's office, and I was from Monterey Park, down in the Los Angeles area. We had watched LAPD form its team, along with some of the other large departments, and were convinced that there was a definite need for a specialized team in our area to handle just such an incident.

The brass had finally condescended and allowed us to form a team of ten officers. But the logistical support was weak. It was like "Well, maybe we can give these guys a little something and they'll get off our backs." But all they gave us were the blue jumpsuits which they provided to all patrolmen anyway. We just removed the big "Police" patches from the backs and said, "Okay, this is our uniform."

All of the nonexpendable equipment was provided by the officers of the team. We bought our own rapelling ropes and caribiners, our individual load-bearing equipment, and even our own weapons. As for tear gas, we drew outdated gas grenades that were procured when the department was formed in 1965. When I originally inventoried the stock I had the feeling that it had come from some Third World nation that was trying to dispose of it. I had serious doubts whether it would even work or not. Every date stamp on the munitions had expired long ago.

We even provided our own gas masks. These ranged from fairly modern military M-17s to old M-9s with the screw-on side cannister. We could only hope that the charcoal filters would still work.

Training consisted of what we could do in-house. But we did the best we could with what we had. The only redeeming factor was in the choice of sergeants picked to head the team. Dean Paulson, a former canine officer, happened to be very tactically oriented and very enthusiastic about SWAT. Under his leadership, we managed to get together on a fairly consistent basis to hold training sessions. If it were not for our own initiative at the time, Tahoe would not have had a SWAT team on this day. And this was to be our first full-blown major action.

Arriving at the command post, I was met by my spotter, Ron Lichti. He, like Habelt, was a working detective. He had driven straight to the scene when he heard the call-up and had not had time to get his SWAT gear. Because of this he was dressed in a sport coat and tie. Nowadays, SWAT personnel in most departments normally carry their gear with them at all times to be ready at a moment's notice to respond in short order fully equipped. But in those early days of SWAT we had a lot to learn. Needless to say we made a strange looking pair—and Ron's attire would later prove to be extremely disadvantageous to a sniper team's role.

Dean Paulson was already at the command post when Ron and I reported in.

"I want you guys to try and pick a spot where you can cover the apartment and get some observation of the place," said Dean. "What we need now is some intelligence. We need to know what's going on in the apartment. Use your binoculars and scope and see what you find out. Then let us know on the radio what you can see. All we know is that there's some crazies inside armed with at least two guns who've already shot one officer, and fired upon several others. According to the guy who escaped earlier, who is the one that gave us the original call, there were three suspects and four other hostages still inside. But one of the remaining hostages has already been taken out. We're not sure exactly what happened, but it appears that one of the suspects shoved the hostage outside to use as a shield. Then there was an exchange of gunfire and the hostage took a hit in the crossfire. Right now his body is up on the balcony next to the suspect's place."

"What about negotiations?" I asked.

"We're working on that, but we can't get through by

telephone. Meanwhile, we need any information you can provide. And if you can, try to find a position where you can get a shot at the bad guy in case we get the go-ahead."

Ron and I shouldered our gear and moved out. The first thing we had to do was take a look at how the motel was set up and how the surrounding area was laid out. Ski Run Boulevard is a major access street that branches off of Highway 50 and runs through the center of town, then up into the mountains until it reaches Heavenly Valley ski resort. It's a very wide street that's lined with small stores, cabins, and motels. The Kelmont Arms is on the west side, and directly across the boulevard to the east are a number of small cabins, many of which are seasonal residences that are closed much of the year. Ron and I worked our way to the opposite side of Ski Run Boulevard, then behind the cabins and through the trees to stay out of sight of the kill zone until we came to the area directly across the street from the Kelmont Arms.

We then looked around for a place to set up that would give us direct visual contact with the front of the apartment building. We wanted high ground to put us level, or maybe above, the suspect's apartment. That would be the only way we might be able to see what was happening inside. We considered climbing a tree, but quickly discarded that idea. The only trees around were ponderosa pines with branches too narrow to support our weight, and the thick clusters of needles were too dense to see through. Our only hope would be the rooftop of a building.

Almost directly across from the suspect's apartment was an unoccupied cabin. The roof, pitched steeply to shed the heavy winter snows, appeared to be high enough to serve our purposes. From the peak we might be able to see the balcony, windows, and the sliding glass doors. But first we had to get up there.

We looked around for something to stand on. The only thing we could find that appeared substantial enough to hold our weight was a discarded washing machine that was resting next to the cabin's back wall. Ron, being the observer, climbed up first onto the edge of the asphalt-shingled roof and as I covered him, cautiously inched his way up the steep incline to the peak.

By now curious people were beginning to come out of the woodwork. Because of the amount of winter snowfall there are virtually no fences in Tahoe. Therefore, there is little in the way of obstacles to impede foot traffic. Everyone in the vicinity who wanted to see what all the commotion was about began showing up in droves, many walking up behind us. It was becoming a major job just to try to keep them back. People were walking up saying, "Hey, what's going on?" I tried to tell them to go back home, to stay out of the way, to clear the area, but they'd only reply, "Hey, man, we've got to see what all of the cops are doing," and "I know my rights. You can't make me leave." It became impossible to deal with the number of rubberneckers that were flooding into the area. I gave up trying.

Ron checked out what he could see of the scene from the top of the roof and called down. "This looks like a pretty good vantage point. We're directly across from the apartment. Come on up."

I slung my Remington Model 700 BDL on my shoulder, and wearing my backpack, crawled up to join him. Reaching the peak, I proned out on what was about a forty-five-degree angle and looked over the top. I was astounded at what lay before us. Dozens of police cars from various agencies, both marked and unmarked, were scattered up and down Ski Run Boulevard. Both uniformed and plainclothes officers crouched low behind the vehicles, guns drawn, watching the apartment. Onlookers milled around in large groups, many of which stood on line with the police cars, all of which were in the kill zone. It was like the circus had come to town and everyone came to see the sideshow.

Across the boulevard I could see the apartment building.

A large white sign on one end proclaimed KELMONT ARMS MOTEL APTS, and below that a smaller sign said VACANCY. To the right of the building two officers hunkered behind a concrete block wall. One was barely discernable in the shadows of a ponderosa, but I recognized the other as Frank Gonzalez, a friend of mine who had followed me to Tahoe from the Monterey Park Police Department. Frank, I could see, wore a shoulder holster and held a pump shotgun. At the other end of the building, over the office, was the suspect's apartment. Just to the right of that, on the balcony of the next apartment, was the body of the dead hostage.

I analyzed our position. Behind us were several large ponderosas that would help in hiding our silhouette from the front, and to one side was a chimney that might further break up our outline. Still, I felt somewhat exposed because of having to look over the top of the roof. We would just have to try and stay as low as we could.

Our view of the apartment was good and the structure of the cabin provided fairly good cover against handgun fire for the majority of our bodies. But if the bad guys produced a rifle, we'd have to abandon the cabin in a hurry. The main disadvantage was the incline of the roof itself. It was so steep that it was extremely hard to cling to. It would prove very tiring to maintain this position for any length of time. I hoped that we would not have to be there too long.

I drew my scope to my eye and examined the suspect's apartment. There was a metal rail that ran around the balcony. Behind the rail was a sliding glass door that was partially open. To the left of the door was a row of small aluminum frame windows. It was now about 1:00 P.M., and with the light conditions outside at that time of day and no interior illumination, it was impossible to see anything inside. And even if the light had been favorable, most of the windows had curtains that had been drawn closed. The intelligence we would be able to provide to the command post would be limited.

"I estimate the range at about one hundred yards, maybe

a little more," I said to Ron. "And I can't see into the apartment at all."

Ron, scanning with his binoculars, agreed. "We'll just have to wait and see what happens. At least we have a clear shot from here if someone comes out onto the balcony or tries to shoot out of a window."

Ron pulled the radio out of his back pants pocket and reported in. "Command post, this is Lichti. We're in position on the roof of a cabin directly across Ski Run Boulevard from the front of the suspect's apartment. We can't see inside, but we've got an unobstructed clear view of the front of the apartment." Before he could finish his report someone in the apartment broke out a small window. "Stand by . . . there's some activity. Someone's breaking out a window." He released the mike button and we watched for a moment. A face appeared in the opening.

The words of a terrified man echoed across the wide highway. "He's going to kill us if you guys don't back off! He's going to kill us! Do you hear me? If you guys don't get away from here, he's going to kill us all!"

Now we had some intelligence. "Command post, it appears that a hostage is shouting out of the window. He's making some demands."

Command post . . . what kind of demands?

"Something about if we don't back off, he's going to kill them all."

10-4. Keep us advised.

From a position near the apartment, one of our captains, Don Johnson, saw the first opportunity to initiate dialogue with the captors. Using a bullhorn, he replied, "Tell them we can't back off, and we can't let anyone go. I want to talk to whoever is in charge up there."[1]

"He won't talk to you," shouted the hostage. "Not

---

[1]The dialogue between Captain Johnson and the hostage used in this chapter is taken from research of articles written by on-scene reporters and from the recollections of Lance Young.

103

face-to-face. He just says that you have to back off and let them go. If you don't they'll kill us all!"

Because of the distance, Ron and I couldn't pick up on all of the words. But we could hear enough to know that the suspects were going to be hard to negotiate with. And to make matters worse, Johnson was not a trained negotiator. For that matter, neither was anyone else on the Tahoe department at that time.

Inside the apartment, Locklear had taken the bound hostage he had selected as his mouthpiece, shoved him belly first over a kitchen sink, and jammed his face through the opening of the broken window. Unwilling to present his own head to possible police fire, he forced his victim to serve as the go-between. The longer the hostage was there, the more frightened he became and the louder he screamed the demands.

"He wants a shotgun and a car! Get him what he wants or he'll kill us!"

"We can't give him a car. And we're not going to give anyone any guns," returned Johnson. "If he harms anyone else, we'll have to do something. I don't think he wants to get himself killed!"

"He doesn't care about his life! How many people do you cops want dead?"

"We don't want anyone dead. Just tell him to throw out his guns and come out. We don't want to hurt anyone," said Johnson.

"Get that car and shotgun for them. Do you hear me?" yelled the hostage. Then, as if he knew someone outside, "Al? Do you hear me? He's going to shoot me and blow up the building. What's wrong with the cops? Al, do you hear me?"

Johnson tried again. "Throw your guns out the window!"

"They aren't going to!" These last words sounded like the hostage was near hysteria. "He says that in eight minutes he's going to kill me, so do what he says. He says he was in Vietnam."

"We aren't going to start any shooting," Johnson shot back. "We aren't the VC."[2]

The man was beginning to panic. "Do as they say. They want guns, cars, and ammunition. They're going to kill us all. Are you going to stand around and watch us all get killed? They mean it. Don't you believe me?"

Johnson played for time, cajoling the hostage-takers as well as he could. "Talk to them and tell them to get their guns out the window and nobody will be hurt. The officer who was shot is all right and we don't want anyone else hurt."

"They want guns and they want a car. Do you hear me? They aren't going to just give up."

"No guns and no car," replied Johnson.

"Then you're going to have a bunch of dead people up here! They're not going to throw their guns out . . . and he has a gun at my back and a knife at my heart!"

Johnson remained inflexible. "No guns. No car."

By now the command post had decided that something had to be done to facilitate negotiations. The bullhorn and the screaming hostage only provided amusement to the crowd of gawkers, many of whom were now joining in with innovative suggestions on how to handle the situation. The command post called us to inform us of their next plan.

Command post to all units, the telephone company is hooking up a phone in the apartment next door to the suspect's apartment. As soon as they're done, an officer will come out to pass the phone across to the suspects. Hold your fire.

A few minutes later an officer came out of the neighboring apartment carrying a telephone and a long coil of cord. Ron and I watched as he inched his way along the balcony until he could throw the phone across to Locklear's balcony. This done, he quickly retreated from view back into the apartment.

---

[2]Viet Cong.

So far, Ron and I had no idea who was who inside the apartment. The only person we had seen up to this point was the hostage that had been shoved up to the window. We needed to figure out who the hostages were and who the suspects were. The only way we could do this was to write down everything we saw: physical and clothing descriptions, who was bound and who was not, anything that would give us a clue as to who the bad guys were—and how many suspects were involved. All we knew at this time was that there were "multiple suspects." If we got the green light we had to know exactly who were targets and who were not.

As we watched, a man appeared on the balcony. His hands were tied behind his back and his feet had been bound together. A length of cord ran from his ankles back into the doorway of the apartment. Locklear, using the cord as a leash, was not taking any chances with this hostage trying to escape.

The captive, showing all appearances of being under extreme duress, hopped out to the edge of the balcony, bent over, and using his teeth, retrieved the phone. He then turned and hopped back inside. Within a minute or two the command post established communications with Locklear.

By this time, Ron and I were becoming very uncomfortable. The asphalt shingles of the roof were starting to get very hot. The clear atmosphere of Tahoe's 6,200 foot elevation contained almost none of the pollution or dust particles found in the air at lesser elevations. Because of this, there was little to block the ultraviolet rays of the sun. An eighty-degree day feels much hotter in the mountains than in the lowlands, and anyone who has spent time on the ski slopes knows how easy it is to burn in the high country. My dark blue jumpsuit was becoming unbearable, and Ron's civilian clothes offered him almost no protection against the sun's rays—or the heat of the roof. As the telephone negotiations between the apartment and the command post wore on, Ron and I suffered.

Finally, after frying on the roof for what seemed like an hour, an angel of mercy appeared.

"Hey, is there anything I can do for you guys?"

I looked around. Behind us on the ground stood a fireman. "Yeah, you sure can. We need something that we can use as a barrier to insulate us from these shingles. They're hotter than hell."

"I'll see what I can do." He analyzed our predicament for a moment, then disappeared. A few minutes later he returned with a ladder and a couple of blankets. The ends at the top of the ladder were curved into two hooks that could be used to grasp a wall or other obstacle.

"It looks like if you just used the blankets, you'd slide right off of that roof. Hook this ladder over the peak and you can use it for support." He passed up the ladder and the blankets. I brought the ladder up to my right side, hooked it over the peak as instructed, then braced my right foot on one of the rungs. Ron took the opposite side, using his left foot on the ladder. With this, we were able to lie on the blankets and have a secure position. I now felt much more stable in case I had to make a shot.

I threw my backpack on the ladder and began going through it. Inside I found my beanbag support that I had made by sewing up a sleeve from a shirt and filling it with little polypropylene plastic pellets that had spilled from a beanbag chair we had at home. Unlike a bag filled with sand, the pellets were extremely light, which made the support easy to carry around in my pack. I set it up on the peak of the roof, made an indentation in it with my hand, and rested my rifle in the notch. In this situation, the bag worked well. Bipods would have been useless on the roof, as the pitch was much too steep for them to rest on the opposite side.

The rifle itself was a .223 caliber Remington Model 700 BDL bolt-action sniper rifle with a Redfield 3x9 scope. Though most departments nowadays use at least a .308 Winchester round, in 1975 the .223 was a popular choice for urban police sniping because of the fear of collateral damage caused by a heavier round penetrating through and beyond the target. The arguments for the .223, which is the same round as the military's 5.56mm M-16 cartridge, consisted of "What happens if a heavy bullet goes through the opposite wall and enters the house next door and kills an innocent bystander?" To a certain degree, the argument was valid. However, the disadvantages of a .223 far outweigh the safety factor. Virtually any obstacle, including a window, can deflect the lightweight, high-velocity bullet. This is not a good property for a bullet used by a police marksman who often faces opponents who are behind cover. But in 1975 SWAT teams were still in the learning stages.

I rechecked my body position and again began observing the apartment through my scope. I now noted that I could see a little bit through the window that framed the hostage's face. Even though Locklear now had a telephone, he kept the hostage jammed up to the window. Probably for shock effect, or to make a point that he was still in control. I could see movement in the background, but it was still too dark inside to make out any details. My concentration was interrupted by a voice to my rear.

"Hey, can you use a phone up there?"

I looked around. Down below was a telephone lineman. Without hesitation I replied, "Absolutely."

The lineman tapped into the cabin's telephone line, checked the phone for a dial tone, then passed it up. If more guys like the fireman and the telephone man showed up, we'd soon have all the comforts of home. I dialed the command post and reported in. We now had direct communication that couldn't be intercepted by people with police radio monitors, and an additional benefit in that our conversations could be longer and provide much more information without tying up the police channel. It was with the phone that we discovered that another hostage had escaped through the apartment building. The suspects now held only three hostages. We were also told that another hostage had escaped, but this one turned out to be one of the original bad guys, a fellow named Barry Chretian. Chretian had quickly rolled over, turned informant, and given up the fact that only two hostage-takers remained: James Locklear, and his younger brother, Wayne. Now we had descriptions of everybody and finally knew who all the players were. Ron and I now felt much more confident in taking a shot should we get the green light. There was only one hostage left that we had not seen, but it would be obvious if he appeared because he would probably be bound like the others.

Chretian also stated that the only weapons the Locklears had were pistols. Ron and I breathed a sigh of relief at this. Now we didn't have to worry about rifles or shotguns.

As the telephone dialogue between the command post and the suspects progressed, an agreement was finally reached with James Locklear to let his brother, Wayne, go over to the neighboring apartment for face-to-face negotiations. By this time, the officers in the next-door apartment had pulled the dead hostage inside, leaving the balcony clear.

The next telephone contact between myself and the command post informed us that the younger Locklear would be coming out dressed in only his pants, no shirt. We were to visually check him out and make sure he was not carrying any firearms. Two minutes later he came out and crossed over the railing, and was immediately challenged by the officers inside. "Stop right there! Raise your hands. Do a three-hundred-sixty-degree turn."

Ron and I both watched to see if he had any weapons tucked into his belt, but at the same time tried not to split our attention from the main apartment too much. As the suspect crawled over the railing, I shifted my attention back to the windows and door while Ron kept his attention focused on the suspect. Satisfied that he was not armed, Ron advised the command post.

Waiting inside the neighboring apartment were Captain Johnson and a deputy district attorney. For the next thirty minutes the DA, the captain, and Wayne Locklear argued over the details of a deal that James Locklear had proposed. As this went on, the hostage with his face still stuck in the window began to shout out more demands. "Let them go so we can go! Can you hear me? Just let them both go!"

Four hours had passed since our SWAT team call-up. It was now 4:00 P.M., and for the first time James Locklear made a mistake. He walked up behind the hostage in the window and looked out. It was my first look at his face. My adrenaline began to pump as I gripped my rifle and put the crosshairs right on his head. His description and hair style matched what the command post had given us. I knew we had our man.

It was perfect. His brother, unarmed, was in the next apartment. Locklear himself was now centered in my scope. All I had to do was squeeze the trigger and the situation would be over. Ron called the command post.

"This is Lichti. We've got the suspect in our sights. He's standing in the window, the window is open, and we have a clear shot. How about a green light?"

Then the answer came back: "Negative."

We couldn't believe it. Here was a guy who had shot one of our buddies, fired at several more, kept the whole police department—not to mention the deputies and highway patrol officers—tied up for most of the day, still held three hostages that he could begin shooting at leisure, and they wouldn't let us take him out. Ron and I were more than a little upset.

"I wonder what's going on?" asked Ron.

"I don't know. We could have ended it right then. But I'll tell you one thing, I'm sure going to find out when this is all over."

As we gritted our teeth and did our best to restrain our anger, the younger Locklear exited the neighboring apartment, crawled over the railing, and returned to his brother's location. A discussion followed, after which he came back out to return to where Captain Johnson and the assistant DA waited. Over the next hour, we watched him repeat this activity several times. Three times during that period we had perfect lineups on Locklear while his brother was absent. Each time our request to take a shot was denied.[3]

The negotiations were now becoming quite lengthy. As time wore on, the twilight of the evening hours brought long shadows from the ponderosas, signaling the approach of darkness. In the mountains, night comes quickly as the sun sets beyond the ridge lines. As it began to grow dark, lights blinked on in the apartment. We then could see movement inside. Someone was walking around, silhouetting himself as he passed the windows. It could only be Locklear. But there was nothing we could do but watch and report.

Then came more demands. James Locklear had not backed off from his original diatribe one bit. "If I don't get my guns, if I don't get my car, if I don't get my airplane, I'm going to start killing the hostages!" Then he set deadlines.

The deadlines came and went, but Johnson and the chief were inflexible. No guns, cars, or airplanes. Period.

As the sun set beyond the mountaintops it began to get cold. Ron was becoming quite uncomfortable in his civilian clothes, and my jumpsuit provided hardly any more protection against the biting breeze. And we were getting tired. Fatigue was taking its toll on our bodies after hours of fighting the incline of the roof and trying to stay alert in the heat, and now the cold. Our muscles were starting to cramp because of the constant battle of having to cling to the ladder with one foot while the other foot dug into the asphalt shingles.

---

[3]Lichti and Young discussed where a shot could be made without having to worry about the penetration factor of the .223. All but one window were closed, and the glass doors were only open enough to let someone slide out sideways. They discussed bringing a shotgun up to the roof and having Ron fire it through the glass door, followed by Young's shot with the rifle. But the range was too great for accuracy. The "hostage window" and the narrow opening of the door were the only choice.

By midnight we were physically whipped. Our mental facilities were beginning to drift and we could tell that our discipline was starting to fade. We weren't paying attention the way we had when we had first arrived. But still we had to maintain our post. The only good point during this time was when someone brought Ron's jumpsuit to the cabin and passed it up. He managed to struggle into it and gain a bit of comfort. I, meanwhile, dug a sweatshirt out of my pack and put it on under my jumpsuit.

At 2:30 A.M. we finally had a break in the negotiations. John Locklear agreed to let the hostages go if we would give him a written guarantee that his brother would not be prosecuted. For some reason the deputy DA agreed to the terms. Then Locklear told them to write it up and call his attorney in Los Angeles for his approval. If his attorney agreed, then he'd give up. Additionally, the captain promised that if he let everybody go, we wouldn't do anything until daylight.

He'd given the suspect the timetable. Locklear could do anything he wanted until then, including get some sleep. It was a bad tactical decision, but there was nothing anyone on the SWAT team could do about it. Not even Paulson, who was by now extremely frustrated with the meddling of the brass on what should have been exclusively our operation.

The DA wrote up the guarantee and called Locklear's lawyer in L.A. In short order it came back approved.

Now that we were out of the picture until dawn, Ron and I were allowed to come down and go to an empty apartment nearby and get some rest. It was a welcome respite. But before we started for the apartment, we went over to the command post to talk to Sergeant Paulson.

"What's the deal?" I asked. "We had the opportunity and could have ended the situation right there. We had that guy dead in our sights and couldn't get the green light." He could tell I was really disgusted at the turn of events. After all, what had we been training all this time for?

"The chief didn't want to take a shot because the newspapers would crucify us for shooting the guy in the middle of negotiations."

I almost choked. I had to regain my composure before I could ask, "Well, that's kind of a calculated risk, isn't it?" What would have happened if one of the hostages had been killed at one of the deadlines? Then what? And now, what if he doesn't come out in the morning? Someone is going to have to go in after him. Do we really want more officers to put themselves in jeopardy? If that happens, some of our guys are going to have to make an entry and he's going to have a chance to shoot another officer."

Paulson just looked at me. I could tell he had already thought of all these things, probably several times. I was preaching to the choir. Finally he said, "There's just not much we can do about it now. Go and try to get some sleep."

While Ron and I were getting some downtime, Locklear began taunting the officers on the perimeter. Several times during the night he came up to the sliding glass door, gave the cops outside the finger, then laughed loudly and danced around like "See? I can do anything I want and there's not a damned thing you can do about it. I'm still in control." It was extremely frustrating for the perimeter guys to watch this and not be able to do anything about it. But other than these displays of cockiness on Locklear's part, the remainder of the night passed without incident.

At first light Ron and I were back on the roof. For the next two hours we watched the apartment and waited. Nothing happened. Then at 8:00 A.M. we got a call. It was Paulson. "Lance, come down and come on over to the CP. I need to talk to you."

"I wonder what this is about," I said to Ron. He simply shrugged his shoulders and continued to watch the apartment. I slid down the roof, hopped onto the washing machine, then worked my way behind the houses toward the CP until I could cross the kill zone at the narrowest point. I tried to run across the kill zone, but my muscles were so sore and cramped up from the long hours on the roof I could barely hobble across the street.

When I finally reached the command post I almost lost control at what I saw. Everyone there was drinking hot coffee, eating snacks, and generally having a pretty easy time of it. None of the guys on the perimeter had coffee, or food, or an opportunity to get out of the cold like these people. It made me sick.

I walked up to Paulson. "What do you want? What is it you can't tell me over the phone?"

Paulson grabbed my arm and took me aside, out of earshot of the brass. "He's refusing to come out. He's not going to come out at all. We're going to gas the place, and if that doesn't work, we're going to have to make entry."

"I knew it! Damn! I just knew it!" I spat. Then I thought about the gas. With the outdated stuff we had I had my doubts that any of it would even go off. Then I thought about why Paulson had called me over to the CP. "Who's going to make entry?"

"I would like you to. Would you?" He didn't order me, he just asked. I was one of the few who had been to the schools and was a logical choice for the entry team. Paulson also knew me. I was young and gung ho, and he knew that even though I was a sniper, I would also, if need be, serve as a door kicker. But first I had to know something.

"Let me ask you one question," I replied. "Are you asking me to make entry, or is the chief asking? Because if it's the chief—the same guy who declined the opportunity to take this guy out from long distance without any threat to anybody else, then, no. I'm not going. If you're asking me, I'll do it."

"I'm asking you to do it."

There was nothing left to say except, "Okay. I'll do it."

We formed the entry team with three guys. I would lead, backed up by an officer named Rob Ingloia who was armed with an AR-15. Bringing up the rear would be another officer with a twelve-gauge shotgun. Together, we practiced the entry in an apartment that was similar in layout to the one we would be going into, paying particular attention to any nook or cranny where Locklear might hide. It was then that I could see what had happened to Habelt. When you entered the apartment, there was a wall on the right that screened off the living room area so that you couldn't see into the apartment. You had to go into the hallway and then immediately come around the corner of the wall to engage anyone in the living areas. We practiced going in high and low, trying to figure out how we could gain a tactical advantage in the safest manner. As soon as we felt comfortable with a technique we told Paulson we were ready to go.

While we waited for the brass to give us a signal, we had time to sit and think about it. The omnipresent thought in my mind was that this guy had already shot a cop, and I felt that he was going to shoot it out with us when we went in. The scene that was painted in my brain just wouldn't go away. It kept playing over and over. I had an extremely strong urge right at that moment to just stop everything and take a few minutes to call my wife and just say, "Hi. I'm thinking about you."

I walked over to a phone and dialed my number. There was no answer. She had left to take the kids to preschool. I hung up with the feeling that I just might not see her again. I thought about the standard joke that we always used when I came home from a dangerous assignment, where she'd say, "Well, are you okay?" and I'd say, "Of course. I wasn't in any danger. I always stay back at the command post and run the coffee and donuts for the commanders." I never really let her know what was going on. But knowing me, she knew better.

I pushed the thought out of my mind and went back to where the entry team waited. It was time to do business. Paulson was waiting.

"This guy is not going to get an opportunity to engage us," I said matter-of-factly. It wasn't a question, it was a statement of fact. "We go in, he's the only one who's there, if he tries anything at all, we're dumping him. We just are not going to give him the opportunity to engage us first."

"I understand," said Paulson. "Be careful."

We pulled our gas masks on, double-checked our weapons, entered the building, and moved into our final position in the hallway outside Locklear's door. As we lined up I stared at the white-painted door and tried to imagine what awaited us inside. Was Locklear there, pistol ready, just waiting for us to come in? Or would he burst out of the door before we were ready and shoot it out with us at close quarters? If he did that, there was no place for us to go for cover in the narrow hallway. He could easily hit one or more of us. It would have been so much safer for us all if the chief had given me the green light the day before when I had Locklear lined up in my crosshairs. But he didn't, and now we had to do it the hard way.

As soon as we lined up we notified our people that we were ready and they could hit the place with gas. As the officers with the grenade launchers took aim I heard someone with the bullhorn give the final ultimatum. "Come out with your hands up or we're going to gas. Come out with your hands up!"

Somewhere inside a muffled voice shouted back, "I'm not coming out. You're just going to have to come in and get me!"

In my mind's eye I could see one of our gas men, Officer Phil Crough, lining up his 37mm tear gas launcher and pulling the trigger. I pictured the outdated round going *bloop* and falling out of the end of the tube to the ground at Phil's feet. I shivered at the thought.

But it worked. I heard the Flite-Right projectile crash through a window, hit something solid inside, and then fall to the floor. Within seconds the hissing cannister filled the apartment with a gray-white cloud of gas. Almost immediately we could hear the sounds of someone coughing and retching inside the room. It was a beautiful sound.

We waited for the gas to do its work, and as we waited I heard a gunshot. I thought, *Damn. This guy has just committed suicide.* This thought was followed by the realization that if I went in there assuming he's no longer a threat, he'll be alive and waiting and the gunshot was just a hoax. I started telling myself, *Stay alert. Stay awake. Be watching for whatever is moving.*

It was time. I kicked the door. It flew open and Rob and I prepared to charge in. Just as I started to move, the radio said that the suspect was coming out onto the balcony. I turned to Rob. "We can't assume that he's the only guy," I yelled through the gas mask, my voice deadened by the hot, sweaty rubber. "We've got to take the apartment room-by-room."

The next radio transmission announced that the suspect was now out on the balcony and that he was at that moment being taken into custody. As soon as the transmission ended, Rob and I charged into the apartment. The first thing I saw was the blood on the doorjamb, the wall, and the floor. My mind flashed to Habelt. *This is the spot where Paul was shot.*

Room by room we searched the apartment, then exited out onto the balcony. I couldn't believe what I saw. Instead of SWAT officers, Locklear was in the custody of *the chief and the captain!* Somehow they had managed to get into the picture and put the grabs on Locklear in front of all the news cameras. I was disgusted.

After securing the scene for our B.I. man, we returned to the station for debriefing.[4]

I was exhausted. So was everyone else. It had been a long, hard night and now the adrenaline had finally subsided. I was ready to collapse. I asked Paulson, "Where are we going to have our debriefing?"

---

[4] "B.I." is one of the standard terms in California for Bureau of Identification. In Tahoe's case, the B.I. consisted of one man who handled the crime scene analysis.

Dean was silent for a moment, as if something were bothering him. Finally he spoke. "The chief said everything went so fantastic that we're not going to have a debriefing. Everyone can go home."

I couldn't believe it. The debriefing session was a necessary part of our operation. It was the best time to talk about what we had done right and what we had done wrong. We needed it in order to try and make sure we didn't repeat any mistakes. And there had been several. We wanted input from both the SWAT team guys and the guys on the perimeter. But this time we wouldn't get either. I felt that I knew the reason. The chief and the captain had jumped the balcony, pushed their way past two SWAT team guys to make the arrest, and they didn't even have masks on. The glory hounds probably didn't want to hear any gripes about their little publicity stunt.

I went home to stew.

The next day I picked up a copy of the *Los Angeles Times*, the out-of-town newspaper that I had delivered in Tahoe to keep up with events from the geographical area where I grew up. On one of the pages a composite police sketch of a fuzzy-haired, hippy-looking white male stood out under the headline *Rites for Ex-Officer Today*. I read on.

> Services are scheduled today for William George
> Roberts, 51, a retired Los Angeles policeman shot
> to death Friday in the parking lot of a West
> Hollywood supermarket.

The article went on to describe the service, who would be in attendance, and Roberts's police service record. It also stated that he left behind a wife, a son, two daughters, a sister, and his mother. The bottom line simply said: "The killer remains at large."

I studied the picture. "Damn. I've seen him before." Then it hit me. "Damn! It looks like *Locklear!*"

It didn't take much investigation to make Locklear on the

murder. When he was searched in the El Dorado County Jail, retired officer William G. Roberts's Bank of America credit card was found in Locklear's wallet. And to add insult to injury, the .45 automatic he had used to shoot Habelt was the gun that he had taken from Roberts's body.

I left Tahoe a short time later. There were several reasons for my disenchantment. But one of the main reasons was the way the administration handled the Locklear incident.

I went back to the Coast in search of a more professional department—an organization that would know how to handle a situation and how to back its personnel. I found it in a large agency north of Los Angeles and spent ten great years involved with a SWAT team which grew and progressed each year.

I now work as a sergeant in the Major Crimes Unit, and have been involved in some very interesting cases. Police work is in my blood, and there are few days that go by when I don't feel that I've somehow made a contribution to society. But occasionally, when I think back to that hectic day south of Lake Tahoe, I still have a sense of frustration and disgruntlement. I can't help but think that I had a cop killer right in my crosshairs—and because of a fear of the media, a small town chief refused to give me the green light.

11

Insanity on Locust Street

There are a lot of things that a police officer can take. By the very nature of the job, officers consistently experience things far beyond those witnessed by the average person. Grisly auto accidents, bloody murders, suicides of the most creative and horrible means, the aftermath of airline and train accidents, every possible shocking scene one could imagine hardens the police officer. He or she, after a few years of dealing with such sights becomes hardened. They have to. A mental wall must be built that protects one's sanity. Only those who develop a strong psychological self-defense system survive in the world of law enforcement. Those that don't, or can't, quit.

But for those that stay and make a career on the streets, who become mentally tempered, there is still one thing—one type of call—that reaches deep inside and rips their heart out. It's the call, or the scene, where children are involved. Every cop has a soft spot toward kids. Especially the younger age groups. If a child is the victim, threatened or harmed in the slightest manner by some adult, the police will react swiftly and with any force necessary to assure the safety of the child. In the words of one officer, "You can do about anything you want and I won't get shook up or overreact or get mad. You can rob a bank, burgle a house, steal a car, beat someone up in a bar fight, even commit

120

murder, and I won't get excited. I can deal with that. But don't mess with kids. You mess with kids, I really, really get pissed. If anything is going to bother me, it's that. You want to shoot it out with *me,* that's fine. You want to fight with someone? Fight with me. Whatever you want to do, I can handle it. Just leave the kids out of it."

But it all goes with the job. No matter how much an officer hates to hear a call go out where children are victims, the calls still come. And someone has to go.

On Friday night, September 8, 1989, a hot, dry night by Milwaukee, Wisconsin, standards, thirty-one-year-old Roderick Kenneth Harris went in search of his girlfriend, Ernestine Williams. Even though she had filed a restraining order against him because of his past acts of violence toward her and her two children—of whom he was the father—Harris was determined to find her and force her to take him back.

At approximately 9:30 P.M. he arrived at 614 East Locust Street, a single-story older residence in the east side of Milwaukee not far from Lake Michigan. This was the house of Williams's baby-sitter where his daughters, aged five and eight, were being cared for. Ernestine would return to pick up the children within minutes and he would be ready to confront her.

Over the objections of the baby-sitter, Harris forced his way inside. Fifteen minutes later Williams arrived. But as she started to go inside, she saw Harris. Instead of confronting the six-foot, two-hundred-pound man, she fled and called the police. As she was doing this, the baby-sitter managed to get the eight-year-old out of the house to safety. But she couldn't do anything to help five-year-old Melissa Williams. For Harris, now agitated that his plan had not worked and that he would soon have to face the police for violating the restraining order—a sure trip to jail—held her hostage.

Squad 51, a two-man patrol unit, was dispatched to the

scene. They arrived at 10:10 to find Harris standing just inside the open front door of the residence, holding the child around the upper body with one arm, while in his other hand he waved a large butcher knife dangerously close to her throat. And just to make sure the officers understood how serious he was, he cut the child a few times. But the wounds were superficial, just enough to draw blood. Just enough to make a point.

"I'll kill her, man. I'll kill her and myself," he screamed. "Just back off. I'll kill her, and I'll kill you, too. I spent five years in Vietnam[1] and I ain't afraid of nothing. Besides that, I ain't got nothing to lose. I've got lung cancer and only have two weeks to live. I ain't going back to jail."

The officers attempted to negotiate: "Hey, man. Just be cool. Put the knife down and no one gets hurt. No one wants to harm you. Just let her go and we'll talk about it."

"Not until I get Ernestine back. Send her in here," he demanded. But that couldn't be done. The police cannot put someone who is not in jeopardy into such a situation. And there was no guarantee that even if they did, Harris would let Melissa go.

Squad 157—Detective Lieutenant Michael Krzewinski —was summoned to take over negotiations. And at the same time it was determined that the standoff, which had become a full-blown hostage situation involving an obvious mental case, might also require the services of the Tactical Enforcement Unit—Milwaukee's version of SWAT.

At 10:25 P.M. the call went out.

---

[1]This was a bogus statement. The normal tour in Vietnam was one year for the army and thirteen months for the Marines. Few people did more than two tours at the most.

12

Officers John Gutmann and Ron Lindsey, Milwaukee Police Department

September 8, 1989

When the call goes out for SWAT, things happen fast. One minute, you're working some routine call, or taking a report, or maybe just clearing roll call, or even asleep at home when an alert sends you into high gear. You drop everything you're doing and race to the scene, seldom knowing at that time just exactly what you're getting into. Such was the case when the alert went out for the Tactical Enforcement Unit—Milwaukee's version of SWAT—to respond to a hostage situation in the lower east side of the city.

My partner, Ron Lindsey, and myself were working the evening shift out of Metro Division when we got the call. It had been a pretty routine night so far, considering that it was a Friday, and we were in the process of booking a prisoner at the station when we were notified of the alert. We dropped everything and ran to our car.

As we raced through the night, dodging traffic and taking shortcuts toward the rally point—an intersection near the scene where the command post was being established—I thought of the call-outs Ron and I had been on before. Most of them, at least for us marksmen, were like the old military saying, "Hurry up and wait." You rush to the call, scramble to get into position, then wait. And wait. Usually you end up being the eyes and ears of the CP. The marksman watches the scene through the scope, relaying what he sees to the observer. The observer does the same with his binoculars. Both observations are relayed to the CP. It's an important job, but other than having a ringside seat, you seldom get much more involved. But when you do, when the order is given to take someone out, you have to be ready. And you have to have a good team that can react instantly. Because that's usually all the time you have—an instant. You have to really be tuned into each other. You almost have to be able to know what your partner is thinking, or what he is going to say before he says it. You have to really click. You know that you've really got it together when, if he's the observer, and he says, "Shoot!" you've already started squeezing the trigger. Ron and I are like that.

We're also what one might call a "salt-and-pepper" team. Ron's black and I'm white. This gives us an advantage on the streets. No matter where we work, people can identify with us. But when they try to use race against us by trying to identify with one of us and not the other, they lose. If someone comes up to Ron and says, "Hey, brother . . ." he promptly sets them straight. "You aren't *my* brother. We don't have the same mother and father. *This* is *my* brother," he says, pointing at me. It really disarms them. Ron and I, "brothers of the badge," work well together.

Ron is also a trained marksman. It was just the luck of the draw that I would be the triggerman this night.

Within fifteen minutes we arrived at the intersection of Locust and North Booth, the location where the command post was in progress of being organized. Unit 792, Sergeant Michael Kuspa, met us there.

"Let's get over to the scene and get you two set up. There's a house across from the bad guy that looks directly into the front of his place. Let's check it out," advised Kuspa. Ron and I grabbed our gear and followed.

We entered through the back door of the house directly across from 614 East Locust, the house where Harris held the little girl at knife point. We quickly located the most advantageous position for a marksman: the living room that overlooked the street and the front of the single-story frame house where everything was happening. Ron opened the window and laid a sandbag on the sill to serve as a rest as I pulled a large easy chair up to the window and readied the rifle. As I scoped the house, Ron pulled up another chair and began scanning with the binoculars.

What we saw was terrifying. Directly to our front, approximately thirty-five yards away and almost directly in the line of fire, stood Lieutenant Michael Krzewinski, one of our field supervisors, negotiating with this large black male in the doorway of the house. Krzewinski stood at the base of the steps to the front of the house, and Sergeant James Oliva, one of our Tactical Enforcement Unit sergeants, stood just to his left. The man, Harris, held his daughter, Melissa, in front of his body as a shield. In his left hand he held the knife. And we could both make out cut marks on the child. They appeared to be slashes, but obviously weren't too deep due to the relatively minor amount of blood.

I had a straight shot into the front of the house through the open door. The only problem was Krzewinski. If I received permission to fire, and Krzewinski moved only slightly to the right at that moment, I would hit him. Even if he didn't, there was little margin for error on my part.

Ron and I discussed how we might get Krzewinski to move if we received the order to shoot. We agreed that the CP had to get the word to him, or Oliva, to shift left quickly if and when the time came. Ron relayed this information to Unit 5, Sergeant Oliva, and the command post.

I checked the time. It was 10:56 P.M. The rest of the

Tactical Enforcement officers would have by now contained the perimeter. But they wouldn't be too close. Streetlights illuminated the neighborhood and any sign of more police might rattle Harris into doing more harm to the girl. We didn't want to do anything to escalate the situation, but at the same time the unit needed to find a way to move as many officers as necessary to positions as close as possible in case a takedown team or entry team was needed. And by the way Harris was acting, we didn't have much time to mess around with. The CP was frantically working on a solution.

For a few minutes everything happening across the street appeared to remain unchanged, then we witnessed something incredible. Lieutenant Krzewinski tried to talk Harris into a hostage exchange. Him for the little girl! Harris wasn't interested. He evidently distrusted the lieutenant. Then we couldn't believe what we saw next. Krzewinski, in a desperate attempt to sway Harris and allay any suspicions of trickery, took his pistol out, opened the cylinder, and dropped the bullets on the ground! Still Harris was not interested—at least in using a cop as hostage. Instead, he said that he would let the girl go if he could have Ernestine instead. This was out of the question. There is no way one civilian hostage can be exchanged for another. And as for Krzewinski's offer, it was rapidly nixed by our own CP. Sergeant Oliva quickly came on the radio.

Unit five to Squad 157 . . . no, you don't do that![1]

Harris, denied his counteroffer, decided to improve his position. He backed away from the doorway and disappeared into the house.

"Damn!" I spat. "I've lost him."

"Hold on, John. I think he's just moved farther back into the house," Ron said as he focused tightly on the binoculars.

Then the streetlights went out. The CP had evidently got the power cut so that our guys could get closer undetected.

---

[1] Radio call signs: Unit 5 was the entry team commander, Squad 157 was Lieutenant Krzewinski.

Things were beginning to really happen fast—faster than we had ever seen before.

Harris, still throttling Melissa, and once again in clear view straight through the house to my direct front, was now facing Krzewinski—and me—with his back propped against a doorjamb near the far end of the central hallway. As I focused on him through the scope, he screamed, "I'm going to draw blood!" At this, he drew the knife down to the terrified child's throat and began to make slashing motions. Tiny Melissa, her face contorted in terror, sobbed, "Don't kill me, Daddy."

I gulped and grasped the Remington tightly. As I caressed the trigger nervously, a million thoughts burst into my mind. You go to a hundred of these things every year and it gets almost routine. You always picture the guy who comes out shooting with a gun and there's not much to think about. You just ace him. But this was different. Things were escalating too quickly. No room to think, plan, or reason. It was coming down faster than we had ever seen. I'm thinking, *Oh, shit. This thing is really escalating. I might have to shoot—it looks like I'm going to have to shoot here. If I don't, he's going to kill the child.* Then I think, *Am I really seeing this? Is this a dream—or a nightmare? I can't really be seeing this.*

My heart was racing. I knew it was going to come down to us—to me—to end this. I *knew* it was going to happen. It was going to happen within seconds. I could feel the trigger. My finger had already begun to put pressure on it. All I needed was the word. But what if no one gave us the go-ahead? What if they forgot about us? Should I take the shot anyway? I'm not going to let him kill the child. I'm *not* going to let that happen.

I thought about my own kids. I have three daughters, one of whom was born prematurely and has cerebral palsy. My wife had to quit her job to take care of her full time. We had sacrificed for our kids and would continue to do so. Kids are worth it. They're all we really care about in this world. After all, when we are all gone, they are the ones that have to carry on. I knew Ron was thinking the same things. I could just tell, I guess because we could almost read each other's mind. Ron has four daughters, and one of them was born prematurely and has a learning disability. So here we had two fathers of daughters facing another father of daughters. And we were probably going to have to kill him. It was a heart-wrenching scene that was quickly becoming numbed with anger. Anger that we were put in this position, and anger for what this idiot was doing to that baby.

As these thoughts sorted themselves out Harris was yelling at Krzewinski and Oliva and the girl's mother, Ernestine, who now stood nearby, "If I can't have Ernestine, I'll kill the girl. You want to see blood? I'll show you blood. I'm going to start sliding down this door, and when I get to the bottom, the kid will be dead!"

Krzewinski began saying anything he could think off. "We all have problems, we can work them out. Don't you want to see that little girl grow up?"

"I don't care! I don't care!" screamed Harris.

Melissa was struggling, crying, trying to get away. Harris, growing more hysterical by the second, still clutched her tightly to his legs. "I drew blood and now you want to see some more."

"Please don't," cried Melissa. "Please *don't* . . ."

Harris raised the knife in the air and began to slide down the doorjamb.

"Tell Oliva to get Krzewinski out of the way," I instructed Ron. I didn't have to. He'd already transmitted the instructions.

It was like a machine where all the parts begin to move at once: I centered the Leupold's crosshairs on Harris's head, just above his right eye; Harris raised the butcher knife into the air, shifted it to a stabbing position and began to slide down the door; Krzewinski leaned to the left; I took up the slack on the trigger . . . my mind raced. . . .

We've got a job to do. . . .

I've got a job to do. . . .

"He's going to stab her," exclaimed Ron. Then the knife began to come down. *"He's stabbing her! Shoot!"*

Just as Ron said that, Oliva's voice came over the radio. *Unit three! If you have a shot, take it!*

But before the last words were spoken the 150 grain Remington softnose was on its way. It was almost like three guys pulled the trigger at once.

Krzewinski later said, "I heard a shot over my shoulder. Then I could see the man's head explode. I could see the splash of blood, and suddenly the child standing up. I thought the child was hit. She was stunned. She kept looking at me. I yelled, 'Run, honey! *Run!*' "

I watched the little girl hesitate, then run directly toward us—and the front door—directly into the lieutenant's arms. She never looked back. I was glad she didn't. I didn't want her to have to live any more of that nightmare, to remember forever what her father looked like with half of his head gone.

I relaxed, then took a breath. It was the first I remembered taking in a long time. As I did, Ron grabbed the radio. "How's the child? How's the child?"

She's fine.

I never knew exactly how I would react after a shooting. This one was my first. I was extremely happy about saving the little girl's life, and I knew I was justified in terminating the situation. But I began to think about other things once she was safe. The first thing I thought about was the press. How were they going to react to this? Milwaukee is a city of about three-quarters of a million people of all classes. Kind of a potpourri of rich and poor of all races. The department has a strength of around 1,800 personnel in all, and there's always something in one or more of our newspapers about the police every day. And the press here is hardly ever sympathetic to the police side of a story. Sensationalism and hatchet jobs of the cops must sell the most papers. When you read about something in the paper, it doesn't matter if the guy you take down is a shit head. It doesn't matter if he's a scum bag who's been involved in robberies or homicides and dope. Instead, when it comes out in the news, all of the guy's relatives come out of the woodwork and talk to the reporters and all of a sudden the guy is the "father of the year." I was afraid of this happening here.

As it turned out I was surprised. Every article that came out praised what we did. They all basically stated that we had no choice, that we tried everything we could, and finally the guy made us take him out. In one article, the reporter wrote:

> When they took the life of Roderick K. Harris Friday night, police officers also were taking the only option left open to them. Had they not done so, a five-year-old girl might have died instead. . . . The courage, experience, and skill of several officers that night ensured that Harris was the only victim of his threats and instability.

He went on to say:

> Harris was an unstable, dangerous man with a weapon, threatening to kill a five-year-old girl. His actions forced police into a situation in which they had to shoot.[2]

There were other articles that came out in the next few days, and all of them either treated us fairly and factually or they praised us. I couldn't believe it. These reporters were actually treating us like we were human.

The next thing I thought about were the after-action things like the police investigation, the coroner's inquest, and the district attorney's opinion. You always have to go

---

[2]Editorial, *Milwaukee Sentinal,* September 9, 1989.

through these things, and it's like you are the suspect of a crime. They take your rifle away for analysis, keep you at the station for hours answering questions, give you three days off to stabilize while they investigate it, and make you see a shrink. But as it turned out, the shooting was so straight-up that the district attorney, Robert Donahoo, came out to the scene, videotaped interviews with witnesses, reviewed the case and said that the shooting was completely justified and no inquest was granted. It was the only case any of us could remember where they didn't hold an inquest.

Still, even though all of these things were positive, I couldn't help but have some bad feelings that lingered on. I still feel sorry for the little girl, Melissa, having to go through all of that. It hurts to think what kind of memories she will grow up with. I think about it when I go to sleep at night, and I think about it when I get up. But if I had to do it all over again, I'd do it. And I wouldn't hesitate. Anytime there's a child in the equation, you don't think about yourself or your feelings, or what you might think or feel later. You just think, *Someone's trying to hurt a kid, and I won't allow that to happen.* I think—I *know*—every officer feels this way.

The bottom line, when it's all said and done, is that we had a job to do. And we did it.

Officer Ron Lindsey, watching the action unfold through his binoculars, gives the perspective of the sniper observer.

All of us that go out in the unit are trained to be riflemen. So at the drop of the hat, any of us could be the guy sitting behind the scope. On this day, it happened to be John who drew the job.

As luck would have it, I was the spotter for this call. I'm sitting in a kitchen chair next to John, who had pulled up a big easy chair behind the window to put him on a level plane with the windowsill. He had the rifle resting on a sandbag that I had brought and was scoping the house across the street where the suspect was. I sat just to one side with the binoculars and radio.

As I watched, I could see this guy standing just inside the front door of the house. In front of him, at the base of the steps, was the lieutenant. This put the lieutenant between us and the assailant—right in the line of fire. The man, who gripped his struggling daughter tightly around her upper body and throat, was very, very agitated. I could see that the little girl had already been wounded, but most of the injuries appeared superficial. But I could also see a very large butcher knife in the man's left hand, which he held in front of her in a manner that indicated that he could easily slash her throat.

I couldn't help but think that usually you go to these things and you figure, *Well, we probably won't have to shoot the guy. They'll talk him out.* But this guy, from his actions and statements, was more crazed up than most of those we had encountered in the past. I was catching snatches of what he was saying, and could hear him yelling, "I'm going to kill this kid and there's nothing you can do about it. I don't have anything to lose. I've got a brain tumor. I've got lung cancer." He was saying that he had all these terminal illnesses, which to me made him sound like he was trying to force the issue—to commit "suicide-by-cop." It's happened before in various incidents around the country. Some crazy decides to end it all but wants to go out in a big confrontation with the police. He wants the cops to shoot him. He may have planned it that way from the beginning, or maybe if there's media coverage, he decides during the incident that he wants everyone to see his last moments on earth.

In this particular situation, the first and foremost thing that we were concerned with was the safety of the child. And as I'm watching this guy jerk this baby around, threatening her with this huge knife, I want to do something. Anything. I want to make him stop. It's very difficult to handle something like this when a child is involved. A cop, especially one hardened by years of police work, can mentally handle just about anything that he comes across and remain cool and collected. But don't mess with kids. You mess with kids and no cop is going to stand by and let that happen. Most of us have our own kids—I have four, John has three—and we've got a special fondness for them. Kids are innocent bystanders and victims that are absolutely helpless against adult aggression. To stand by and watch all of this happening right in front of me was tough.

But my job was to continue to watch and report everything I could see to the CP. It was really frustrating. You want to react, to intervene, but can't. As marksmen, we had to just stand by and let the other officers handle the close-up work.

As I'm watching through the binoculars, I see the lieutenant, who is doing face-to-face negotiations with the guy, start creeping up to him very slowly. He's beginning to close the distance as he talks. It appears that he is trying to reason with the guy, coax him to let the girl go. He's saying things like, "It's not worth it. It can all be worked out. How about just dropping the knife and we'll get this all straightened out."

As he's trying to get the suspect calmed down, he's inching closer. Finally he stops in front of the steps at the bottom of the front porch. Then, as John and I watch, the lieutenant did something I couldn't believe. He took his gun out, opened the cylinder, and dumped the bullets out. He then offered to trade places with the little girl. This was creative on his part, but tactically it's a definite no-no. You *never* give up your gun, and you *never* exchange places with a hostage. But as luck would have it, and much to our relief, the suspect refused the offer.

The proximity of the lieutenant must have bothered the man because he quickly stepped out of sight. This was frightening. What was he going to do? If he wanted to hurt the girl now there was nothing that we could do to stop it from our position. You can't hit what you can't see.

Then he reappeared. He had retreated farther back into

the house, stepped into a bedroom on the right side of the hall, taking the child with him, then came back to a position where he could see the lieutenant. The lieutenant had not moved. He still remained by the steps of the front porch—and was still in our line of fire.

John was concentrating on a sight picture over the lieutenant's shoulder and I was watching everything I could see through my binoculars. Though I could "visual" the guy plainly inside the lighted house without them, I could get a better look at his face and judge his emotions through the glasses. Up to this point there was little else we could do. Though he was making threatening motions, he was still holding dialogue with the lieutenant. I felt that this would be one more time when a suspect was talked into surrendering.

Then the dialogue broke down. With a single statement he started the clock ticking. "When I slide down on the door frame, I'm going to stab her." As he said this, he began moving the knife across the child's body in a cutting or slashing motion.

The lieutenant tried desperately to get him to stop. He called out things like: "Hey, calm down. Don't do anything stupid." But the man had already made up his mind. As we watched in horror, he began sliding down the doorjamb. And he began to raise the knife into the air.

"John, he's getting ready to—it looks like he's going to stab the child," I blurted. Just then he changed his hold on the knife into a stabbing grip with the point downward. All it would take was a single movement and the child would die. I could just see that long blade going clean through her tiny body. My mind was racing, searching for a solution, desperately seeking any possible thing that could be done to stop him. There was only one.

"John, I think you're going to have to take him. He's going to stab the child, John. *Take him!*"

At that precise second, Sergeant Oliva's voice comes over the radio. "Unit three, if you have a shot, take it!" But the command was not necessary. Before either of us had finished our sentence John had fired.

I could see the impact through the binoculars as if it were right in front of me in the same room. The bullet struck the man on the right side of his forehead just above the right eyebrow. I could see his scalp, brain matter, and other tissue hit a refrigerator in the kitchen behind him. The knife was frozen in midair as he began to slump to the ground. I knew, by the damage that I'd just witnessed, that he was already dead. The shock of the bullet's impact alone, square into the "no-reflex zone," saw to that.

Immediately the lieutenant, who had leaned to one side when Oliva told us to shoot, called out to the little girl: "Run, honey. *Run!*" And she did. She ran directly into his arms without even looking back. Two thoughts hit me then. First, the little girl would not have to grow up with the memory of her father, missing most of his head, crumpled on the floor. Second, that what we had just done really worked. All of the training, all of the practice, paid off. They teach you that a shot through the "no-reflex zone" will knock out the central nervous system instantly. An attacker, hit there, can't even pull a trigger. And it worked. Like someone had flicked a switch off. The guy just stopped. Everything shut down. He went limp and was no longer a threat.

"John, take a deep breath," I said as I turned my back to the scene. I took one myself. I pulled some chewing gum from my pocket and put a piece in my mouth. I offered a piece to John. We sat there for a moment in silence, then I asked, "You okay?"

"Yeah." That's all he said. We just sat there, waiting for the investigators to arrive to reconstruct the events and examine the scene, and just—as they say on the street—chilled-out.

As we waited I mulled over what had just transpired. To me, it was a perfect shooting. We didn't have a choice. The guy didn't leave us one. It was him or the child. That's no choice in anybody's book. But *he* had a choice. He could have just given up—let her go—and that would have been the end of it. He made his choice and forced us into ours. I asked John, "Why didn't the guy give up? Why threaten the kid if he's got a problem?" John didn't have the answers. Neither did I.

When I went to see the psychiatrist later on, my biggest concern was for John, being he pulled the trigger. I kept asking, "How's John? Is he okay? I'm more worried about John." I had been in Vietnam as an air policeman in the air force and had shot three guys over there. This was different, but because of my background it had less impact than if I'd never been in this type of situation before. But there were sleepless nights. Probably because of the little girl being in the middle of all of this. She was terrified and I could see the fear in her face. She was crying and screaming as she was being jerked around and threatened. I hated that. I kept seeing it over and over in my mind. But the realization of what could have happened if we hadn't been there made the whole thing much easier to deal with. And the bottom line is that we did what we had to do. The guy forced our hand.

To take someone's life is nothing to be proud of, but it had to be done. Whatever the man's problems were, they were not serious enough to cause that child the stress that he did and to create all that turmoil.

The really odd thing about this incident is how fast things happened. We were used to waiting for hours upon hours as situations develop and are finally resolved. This one lasted a matter of minutes. John and I were at the station booking prisoners when the deal went down. We took off and flew out to the scene and within twenty minutes it was all over. It was one of the quickest confrontations I've seen in the nine years I've been on the unit. When I've been the rifleman, I've sat in the window for four and five hours looking at a guy, scoping him, targeting him, and nothing happened. Then the negotiators talk him out, or he goes to sleep, or they take him out with gas, or Unit 5[3] goes in and pulls him down.

It could have been me behind the trigger. You've just got to try to prepare yourself for it. But I don't think anybody can ever say, "I'll do this," or "I'll do that." I tell a lot of younger guys when they talk about it, "You don't know what you're going to do. There are no textbook solutions. When you realize that you're just about to take out somebody's father, or brother, or son, you just don't know how you are going to react or what you are going to do." It's easy to be a Monday morning quarterback. But it's different when you are on the scene, behind the rifle.

It's a hell of a lot different.

---

[3]Entry team.

13
The Man Who Held Himself Hostage

Cops see a lot of strange things. Perhaps more than anyone else in the world. If it were possible for the average person to sit around with a bunch of off-duty police officers and have a few beers, one would hear the saddest, the funniest, and the strangest stories ever told. Law enforcement personnel, by the very nature of the work, find themselves eyewitnesses to events that the majority of the human race only reads about later. And even then, the whole story is seldom told.

Police officers, deputy sheriffs, state troopers, and federal agents are a closed-mouth lot. Part of this is a basic distrust of the media, part a sense of "not taking the job home," and to a greater extent, knowing that only another officer will understand or appreciate a story related from a cop's perspective. Things are said between officers that the general public will never be privy to. But if one *could* get on the inside for just a little while, and could understand the unique—sometimes morbid—sense of humor, the hardened thought processes, and the job-related prejudices of the average lawman, it would surely be an enlightening experience. But that seldom happens. Few outsiders are taken into confidence by the men and women who wear the badge. Besides, even if they heard many of the stories that are related between those of the fraternity that speak its own language, they'd never believe them.

One such story, told only between cops because most "civilians" would never believe it—or see the humor in it—would serve as a prime example.

The officer involved in this story was a product of the 1950s when police departments hired patrol officers who, because of size, were physically able to take care of themselves in any type of physical confrontation. Education and intellect were not top priorities. A successful applicant did not have to have a college degree, be able to quote case law or utilize college psychology when dealing with people. He only had to be big. The bigger the better. In this case, our officer closely resembled a gorilla. He spent more time in the gym than in intellectual activities. And it showed. At six-four and 250 pounds of solid muscle, he was indeed an intimidating figure—a virtual Neanderthal with a neck almost as broad as his shoulders that tapered up to the top of his head like a pyramid. In the words of an officer who worked with him, "You couldn't ask for better backup if you got into a fight, but you sure didn't want him to do your thinking for you. He wasn't stupid, but he was, for lack of a better description, a bit slow in the brain-box department."

This particular officer, whom we shall call "Sledge" for his hammerlike fists, answered a routine (read boring) call to a residential neighborhood in an average American city. The call came out:

Baker fourteen, see the lady, 2312 East Rosedale.

He wrote down the address, then picked up the microphone and acknowledged receipt of the call. "Uh, Baker Fourteen, ten-four."

He knew that the calls that had little, if any, information broadcast often proved to be the most dangerous. And he knew that sometimes you have to milk the dispatcher to get more information that may provide a clue on how to approach the call. One didn't want to drive up in front of a complainant's house, step casually from the car and approach the front door if the "information" you were about to receive concerned a rabid dog on her porch, or a mental case with a hatchet hiding in her bushes.

"Baker fourteen, what's the nature?"

Baker fourteen, it's some type of pet disturbance. That's all we have.

"Pet disturbance?"

10-4. A distraught female called in and said she could hear her cat in her basement making strange sounds. She's afraid to go down there and see what the problem is.

"Baker fourteen, ten-four." He hung the mike on the dash, wrote down the time, and slipped the patrol car into gear. "Sounds like a call for the friggin' dog pound," he mumbled as he pulled away from the curb.

When he arrived at the house in question, a frantic elderly lady stood on the front porch wringing her hands. "Officer, over here! Please, you've got to do something."

He unfolded his bulk out of the car, screwed his hat onto his head, and began to walk across her front yard. "What's the problem, ma'am?"

"My cat's in the basement making horrible noises. I think she's caught in something, or she's in some kind of pain. It almost sounds like a fight, but I don't have any other animals. I'm afraid to go down there. Maybe she's sick. Oh Lord, I hope it's not rabies. . . ."

"Rabies?" The word stopped him dead in his tracks. He turned around and trudged back to his car.

"Where are you going?" asked the lady, now worried that the police might abandon her.

"Be right back, ma'am. Just gotta get something else."

He opened the trunk of the car and pulled out a Winchester twelve-gauge pump shotgun, slammed the trunk lid, worked the slide to chamber a round, and returned to the porch.

The woman's eyes were wide with fright. "What are you going to do with that?"

"Just in case, ma'am. Better be safe than sorry. If the cat's got rabies, I ain't gonna let it bite me. And there ain't anything you can do for 'em except put them out of their misery. But don't worry, I ain't seen any rabies around here in years."

"But do you need such a *big* gun?"

"If I gotta shoot, I don't want to miss. Them pesky animals can be on you in a flash. No sense in taking chances. But like I say, it's probably nothin'."

"Well, please be careful. The steps to the basement are next to the kitchen."

Sledge found the steps and started his descent. He could hear the screeching of the cat, interspersed with a strange hissing and growling sound that was unfamiliar. It indeed sounded like a fight. But the lady said that she had no other pets. "Friggin' cat's gone nuts," he mumbled. "That's all I need. A mental friggin' kitty that thinks it's a friggin' tiger."

He reached the bottom of the steps and peered around the basement. The room was lit by a single sixty-watt light bulb that left the far end of the basement almost completely dark. It was from this part that the sounds emanated.

Sledge cautiously shifted his bulk farther into the room, straining his eyes into the darkened corner. He brought the shotgun to his shoulder, pointed it in the direction of the commotion, and slowly advanced.

All of a sudden the cat appeared. It erupted from the dark corner as if it had been launched by a catapult. Sledge, startled at first, quickly regained his composure and stood his ground. The cat, ignoring the huge policeman, turned back to face the darkness. Its back was arched and its fur stood up in the classic feline fighting position. Fangs bared, it hissed into the dark.

Sledge examined the animal, looking for any evidence of rabies. But all he could see was a cat that looked like it had just come out second best in an alley fight. Then beyond, in the dark, he could see two glowing eyes that began to move toward the cat. As he watched, he leveled the shotgun.

Then it all made sense. A full-grown male raccoon,

crouched low, snarling a guttural challenge, sprang into the light to face the cat for another round.

Sledge slipped the safety catch off and fingered the trigger. "I'll end *this* shit right here." He tracked the raccoon as it circled the cat, finally drawing a bead as the animal paused momentarily to snort in defiance at its opponent.

He pulled the trigger.

Ka-BOOM!

The little old lady, who stood at the top of the stairs safely out of sight, jumped at the clap of thunder that echoed from her basement. "Oh, my God, what happened?"

Sledge, ejecting the spent shell from the smoking Winchester, turned and yelled up the steps. "It's okay, ma'am. It was just an ol' 'coon. I blasted him."

"Oh my. Well, what about my kitty?"

Sledge shrugged his shoulders. "If you say so."

Ka-BOOM!

Unless you're a cop, you would find this story hard to believe. And you might not see the humor in it. But that's to be expected. As they say, you'd just have to have been there.

And that's the problem with sharing experiences and stories with the uninitiated. That's why police officers have a hard time relating to the general public in an off-duty environment.

It is unlikely that this story would happen today. The profile of the modern law enforcement officer is much more sophisticated. The men and women faced with the perils of the streets in this modern age of technology are selected more for brains than brawn. They are more intellectual and better educated. They handle things differently than their predecessors. They are, in the words of today's police administrators, "more professional."

Many older officers will argue with this presumption. They will tell of times "back in the old days," when cops were cops. They will say there were two forms of justice: that of the courtroom and that of the street. If the lawyers got the villain off, he still had to worry about running into you on the street. They will say that all of that college classroom education goes out the window when the fists fly or the first shots are fired.

And some of the younger officers will agree. But it's after a few years on the streets dealing with the dregs of society, and the same amount of time in the courtrooms dealing with unethical lawyers and a judicial system that seldom works, that these attitudes develop. It doesn't take long for a young, intelligent man or woman who dons the shining armor of a rookie cop in a crusade against evil to realize that once they pin on the badge, they move into a different world—a world that exists outside that of "normal" society.

In this world strange things happen. Incredible things that if addressed by national television would provide material for an entire staff of writers. Things that newspaper reporters cannot do justice to, even if they had sufficient information, in an entire half-page article. But a cop, who is not a trained journalist—and is not attempting to stir public emotions—can get it all down in a few paragraphs on a police report. All the facts, all the necessary items needed in court, enough for the detectives to follow up on, everything the system calls for. There is no "color" in the written report, no emotions, no feelings, no gut-wrenching, gripping account of what happened a few short minutes ago, but there's enough. Enough to provide a synopsis of crimes most horrible, discernable only to the eyes of experience. The eyes of another cop.

Still, the stories are there. They happen, somewhere, every day. And when a police officer says, "It's the weirdest thing I ever saw," it must indeed be in the nature of the most bizarre, the most freakish, of happenings.

One such incident occurred on a cold, wintry night in November 1988. The place was Milwaukee, Wisconsin.

Henry Smith, a black man in his early fifties, had a problem. He had just shot his ex-wife through the face with a .22 caliber revolver, fled the scene, and had gone home to figure out what to do next.

Police and an ambulance arrived at the location of the shooting and the officers quickly determined the identity of the perpetrator. The victim, though wounded in the cheek and jaw area, was conscious and provided her assailant's name, address, and physical description.

It was a routine call. A simple matter of classification on a report form heading that said it all in one word: *shooting*. They had a victim, a suspect, and an address. All they had to do was go there, and if the shooter was home, arrest him.

But Henry Smith wasn't going to make it quite that easy. When the officers arrived, they found Smith barricaded in his second-story apartment holding a cocked revolver to the chest of a hostage.

And the hostage was himself.

14

Officer Robert Connolly, Milwaukee Police Department
November 8, 1988

We were close. Real close. The range from my position to the suspect was only about thirty feet. At this distance, the 4X Leupold was a bit of overkill. I and my observer, Officer Wayne Kozich, were on a second-story balcony overlooking a small courtyard, and almost directly across from us were windows to the suspect's apartment. We could see him inside, pacing back and forth, crossing in front of the lighted windows of the apartment holding a cocked pistol to his chest and talking on a telephone. From the radio traffic on my portable, I knew that he was talking to the negotiators. They were trying to talk him into giving up, but so far had been unsuccessful.

To my right, inside an apartment, was the other Tactical Enforcement Unit sniper team. The rifleman was my friend John Gutmann. His spotter was Officer Bill Wiley. They occupied a good position that permitted them to sit back in the shadows looking through an open window that allowed them to see pretty much what I could. But they had a bit more area inside that extended to the left than I had, and I had more to the right. By crossing the angle, our two teams could create a fan-shaped wedge that gave us better coverage than one team would normally have.

The problem for Wayne and me was that it was cold. Real cold. It was in the lower thirties, and even though there was no wind, the chill was biting. I worried about the numbing effects, but there was little we could do but gut it out.

To compound the situation, I could not find a comfortable position to get into. The only rest I could find for my rifle was the steel railing around the balcony, and the height of the railing precluded me from sitting down. I had to crouch awkwardly to bring the weapon to bear, and due to the discomfort, had to keep changing my posture. It was a miserable situation.

To take my mind off my predicament I focused my attention on the suspect. I could tell he was very agitated. Whenever he passed the windows, dragging the phone cord behind him, I could see by the expression on his face that he appeared nervous and apprehensive. I could also tell that he wasn't concerned with presenting himself as a target because he gave us plenty of opportunities to shoot if we wanted to. It was obvious to us all that he was suicidal. Or if he wanted to appear that way, he was doing a fine job of it.

In my mind, I couldn't see what we, as marksmen, could do about all of this. The guy was not presenting a danger to anyone but himself. About the only thing I thought we might be able to do is take him out if he started shooting out of the windows, or if the entry team had to force entry and he turned on them. But even then, we could only cover them if he was still somewhere in front of one of the windows and didn't take cover behind something. I picked up the radio and called John.

"Unit two to Unit three, do you have a visual on the suspect?"

Affirmative. But only when he crosses a window.

"Same here," I replied. "I guess as close as we are we could probably shoot the gun out of his hand just before the entry team has to go in, but I can't think of any other thing we can do."

Bill and I thought maybe hitting him in the shoulder might do the trick. But I imagine since he doesn't have a hostage or anything that we'll just end up waiting him out.

"I hope we don't have to wait too long. It's getting kind of chilly out here."

I hear that, partner. Are you guys doing okay?

"We'd be glad to change places with you in that nice warm apartment," I offered.

No thanks. We like it right where we're at.

I laid the radio down and continued to watch. And watch. Minutes turned into hours and still the man refused to give it up. But I could see he was getting tired. At one time he decided to sit down at the kitchen table to use the phone. As I watched, I noted the details of the room. To the left was a refrigerator, to the right the rest of the kitchen, and behind him an opening that appeared to lead to the rest of the apartment.

Finally, at about 2:30 A.M., he did something to break the pattern we had been watching for over four hours. He laid what appeared to be pill bottles on the table and began opening them.

Command post to all units . . . the suspect is going to give up. As soon as he takes some medications he'll be coming out. Hold your positions.

"Finally," I said to Wayne. "It's about time. It'll be nice to get inside and warm up."

Wayne didn't reply. Instead, after watching the apartment for a few seconds, he asked, "Why is he still holding that gun to his chest if he's going to give up?"

I turned my attention back to the windows. As I did, Wayne continued evenly, "He's moving again."

I focused my eye through the scope and saw the man pick up a big brown winter coat and begin putting it on. It was all over. Almost.

For some reason, he had kept the gun in his hand. And

when he turned back toward the window, his elbow hit the refrigerator.

There was a muffled *bang,* and his facial expression turned into a wide-eyed "Oh shit! What did I do?" look. It was as if he couldn't believe what had just happened. As I watched in bewilderment he crumpled to the floor. He had shot himself right through the heart.

I grabbed the radio. "Unit two to Unit three, did you see that?"

Affirmative. At least I think we did.

Then the command post came on. *Sniper teams . . . did you take a shot?*

"Team two, negative," I replied.

Team three, that's a negative. The guy looks like he shot himself. But it looked like an accident.

There was a pause in the radio traffic. It was like no one could believe that one minute the guy was coherent and was ready to give up, then the next had blown himself away. Right away the command post came on again. *Unit five, take it down.*

Unit 5, the entry team, hit the apartment like gangbusters and within seconds we could see them searching and securing the scene. A few minutes later the paramedics arrived but it was too late. He was dead.

Later, John and I compared notes. He and Bill had witnessed everything Wayne and I had. "I can't help but think that maybe we could have done something," said John. "Maybe disable the guy so he couldn't have killed himself. But then I think that if I'd taken out a shoulder or arm, we'd have people asking, 'Why did you shoot the guy? He's a cripple for life and it's your fault.' Still, I think that being a cripple is better than being dead. But what if I took the shot and missed? And the guy gets startled and pulls the trigger. Whose fault is it then?"

I agreed and added, "The problem as I see it is here we have a guy who is threatening no one but himself. What are we supposed to do? If we try anything we might just aggravate the situation. When you think about it, we really had no choice but watch the whole thing happen just the way it did. What I hate is the fact that after all that time, the guy was finally going to give up, and through a freak accident, does what everyone was trying to prevent. I just can't believe the irony involved in this."

"Yeah," said John. "When that gun went off it really surprised me."

"Not as much as it surprised him."

• • •

I guess one could say that this mission had been a success in the way it was conducted. Everything had been done according to the book and it had worked. Except for one thing. The gunman ended up killing the hostage.

15

Drugs, Guns, and Money

Kalamazoo, Michigan, is not a city that springs to mind when one thinks of crime. With a population of just over seventy thousand, Kalamazoo might even be considered a small town by midwestern standards, and as such, would have small town problems. But that's not so. Because of its geographic location—almost exactly halfway between Chicago and Detroit—the crime rate is much inflated. Each of these centers for crime in the Great Lakes region is no more than 140 miles away. Any drug dealer, burglar, or robber that conducts business or has connections in both cities must pass through the heart of Kalamazoo on Interstate 94. Another major metropolitan area, Grand Rapids, lies just 50 miles north on Highway 131. All of this makes Kalamazoo a popular getaway spot—for criminals.

It wasn't always this way. Prior to 1983, Kalamazoo was a relatively quiet town. But in that year drugs entered the scene in major proportions. Since then the crime rate has increased steadily until, per capita, it now exceeds many of the larger cities. In one six-month period alone in 1991–92, Kalamazoo had fourteen homicides. In comparison, Tulsa, Oklahoma, with a population almost six times that of Kalamazoo, had only four homicides during the same period.

And Kalamazoo doesn't have a police department.

Unlike most municipalities, there is no division in emergency services. In the majority of American cities there is a distinct division of responsibilities between the members of the police department, the fire department, and emergency medical services.[1] In Kalamazoo, the officers of the Department of Public Safety do it all. Each man and woman of the department's 260 sworn personnel is trained in law enforcement, fire fighting, and emergency medical treatment. As one Kalamazoo detective put it, "You have to be able to drive the fire trucks, run the hoses, work the pumps, patch up wounded people, investigate traffic accidents, work burglaries and homicides, and do just about everything else in between. We all wear the same badge and do the same work." Kalamazoo is not the only city with such an organization—many small communities are forced to have a similar structure because of budget and manpower constraints—but it is the largest such department in the nation.

In the late 1980s, the pressure from the increased criminal activity began straining the system. The rise in drug-related violence, homicides, robberies, and other high-risk encounters where the suspects had more potent firepower than the police created a demand for something that the Department of Public Safety did not have: SWAT.

By 1989 the Special Weapons and Tactics Team had grown to eighteen members representing various divisions in the department: one lieutenant, eight sergeants, one detective, one deputy fire marshal, one crime prevention officer, and six public safety officers. And in that year the

---

[1] Emergency medical services normally consists of an ambulance service. The quality of the service varies around the country. Some services must employ trained paramedics, while others simply have ambulance drivers and attendants trained in basic first aid. In some cities the fire department provides the paramedic services on a first-response basis prior to arrival of an ambulance.

team was called out no less than seven times—three of which were for barricaded gunmen.

Sunday, June 11, 1989, broke clear and hot in Kalamazoo. People had been looking forward to the day because it was the date of the annual Kalamazoo Air Show, one of the major highlights of the summer season. A county-fair atmosphere filled people with excitement and anticipation. In the air over the fairgrounds, various historical aircraft, stunt planes, and other flying machines would perform.

Many of the officers of the DPS would be there to handle security, public relations displays, and offer medical aid to anyone in need. Even the SWAT team made its appearance to exhibit items of equipment, weapons, and their new SWAT van. It would be a fine day, and being Sunday, probably a slow day in the criminal world. The chances of anything major happening that would demand the services of SWAT were slim. But the men dressed in the dark blue uniforms of the team who stood in the hot sun, patiently repeating answers to questions asked by fascinated visitors, did not know what was happening just across town.

It was a nice day for a drive, and Walter Casey had decided to take advantage of it. At fifty years old, there were few other diversions that an older man could take advantage of in this neighborhood.

As he pulled up to the intersection of Clay and Burdick streets, he was flagged down by a young man standing on the curb. "Hey, man. How about a ride? I just need to get up the street to my lady's house."

Casey looked the boy over. He didn't appear dangerous, and he was going that way anyway. "Sure, get in."

As they drove, Casey asked, "What's your name?"

"Curt."

"Curt what?"

"Just Curt." It was obvious to Casey that the young man

didn't want to get too friendly. A few blocks farther, "Curt" motioned to the curb. "Stop here. I gotta talk to someone."

Casey pulled over in front of 1618 North Rose and stopped. Within seconds, a lady came out of 1626, the house next door.

"Hey, Christine," jived Curt. "What's happenin'?"

Christine McCone, the new arrival, replied, "Nothin' shakin', Curt, how you doin'?"

Petty small talk followed for a couple of minutes, during which time Curt got out of the car to talk to McCone on the sidewalk. The chatter stopped when a third party came out of Christine's house—with a pistol. He came down the steps and walked up the sidewalk to Curt.

"Hey, man. What the fuck you think you're doin'?" he demanded, making sure Curt could see the gun.

"I ain't doin' nothin', man. Just talkin' to the lady here."

"Yeah, well, that ain't your lady. So just get the fuck back in the car and leave." With this statement, the gunman raised the pistol, a .32 automatic, and brandished it menacingly.

Casey was getting worried. He didn't like guns, and he didn't like anyone who had them. "Come on, Curt. Get in and I'll get you out of here."

"You heard the man. Get the fuck out of here."

"Yeah, I'm goin'. No need to get all uptight," said Curt, crawling back into the passenger seat. But he obviously wasn't leaving fast enough for his antagonist.

The man with the gun, a drug dealer named Oliver Lavert Hughes, stepped in front of the car, racked the slide back to chamber a round, raised it toward Casey, and pulled the trigger. The bullet struck the hood of the car and ricochetted up into the windshield, shattering it and scaring the hell out of Casey.

Casey stepped on the gas, almost running over Hughes, and fled the scene. Five minutes later he was home. He promptly called the police. Curt, not interested in dealing with the police, disappeared down the street.

Sergeant Tommie Sykes and PSO Frederick Stovall got the call. Sykes related what happened next in his report:

> Casey said that the person that shot at him was still at the location inside of 1626 North Rose Street. He was very impatient when we tried to get more information about the incident, and within minutes he got into his car and told us to follow him so he could show us where the subject was.
>
> We followed him to the house and parked. Stovall and I got out of our cars and approached the residence from the south, but as we came close, a black male wearing clothes that matched the victim's description came out of the back of the house and began running east toward Burdick Street.

Sykes took off in pursuit. He followed Hughes through the neighborhood, trying to close the gap, but the younger man finally outdistanced him and disappeared. Sykes immediately called for assistance and requested a perimeter be set up so that the suspect could be contained and a search initiated.

Hughes, searching desperately for a safe place to hide, found the back door of 112 Martin Street standing open with only the screen door closed. He opened it and walked in. Inside, Madinah Edmondson sat in the living room waiting for her husband to return from work. She heard the door close and thought it was him. It wasn't.

"What you doin' here? Who are you?" she demanded, shocked at the sight of this man who stood sweating profusely and breathing heavily in her living room.

"They're tryin' to kill me. You gotta let me hide here," he gasped, eyes darting around as if searching for something to crawl under.

"Get out of here! You don't belong here . . ." began Madinah. But he cut her off with a wave of his hand. Then, as she stared in disbelief, he reached into his pocket and pulled out a wad of money. Thousands of dollars.

"Here, keep this. Just let me hide someplace and don't tell no one I'm here," offered Hughes.

"I don't want your money," said Madinah, backing away. She now knew that this man must be a drug dealer. Only dealers carried that kind of money. Then she heard something outside on the back porch. It was Robert, her husband. "Robert, there's a strange man in here and I think the police are after him."

Robert burst in through the back door and faced Hughes. "Get the children out of here and call the police!" At this, Hughes retreated toward the back of the house.

Madinah, quickly rounding up her two children, left the house and ran down the street to a neighbor to call the police. When the dispatcher answered, a frantic voice reported: "Send the police to 112 Martin Street. There's a strange man in my house. My husband's there with him now."

The dispatcher, realizing that this was probably the suspect that had just escaped from Sykes and Stovall, notified all field personnel that she now had a possible address for the suspect's location—and he may now have a hostage: Robert Edmondson. Then she reminded them of one more factor.

Attention, all units, suspect is wanted for assault with intent to murder . . . and is to be considered armed and dangerous.

16

Public Safety Officer Al Morris, Kalamazoo Department of Public Safety.[1]

June 11, 1989

It was one hell of a hot June day and I was glad it was almost over. We had been outside all day, and the heat and humidity had taken its toll on us. It was the annual Kalamazoo Air Show, an event that brings the public out for miles around to enjoy the presentation of aerobatics, static displays, and other exhibitions of interest. Those of us on the recently formed Kalamazoo SWAT team that had been "lucky" enough to be selected for the assignment, had taken turns minding our SWAT tactical equipment display that had been set up as part of our public relations effort.

By 4:00 P.M., the festivities neared an end and we began

---

[1] The Kalamazoo Department of Public Safety has not endorsed, approved, verified, or participated in the publication of this chapter. Detective Al Morris has provided this information from his own recollections, experiences, and public records. This disclaimer is provided to satisfy the requirements of the Kalamazoo DPS Policies and Procedures.

breaking down and packing up the display. It had been a long day and all of us were ready to call it quits.

But that day, unknown to us at the time, was far from over. We had no way of knowing what had happened on North Burdick, or what was at that moment transpiring on Martin Street. At 4:20 P.M., we found out. Captain Weston, our commander, came with the bad news.

"We've got a SWAT call-out. Some guy took some shots at someone, then when the officers arrived to investigate, he took off on foot. They chased him to a house on Martin Street and he's supposed to be barricaded inside. They're holding the scene but they want us to take over. You guys take the van and follow me."

Captain Weston, breaking traffic for us with his red lights and siren on, wasted little time getting to the scene. Twenty minutes later, after a wild ride through air show traffic, we arrived at the command post. The briefing lasted five minutes. The whole thing seemed cut-and-dried. The bad guy, a twenty-year-old male named Oliver Lavert Hughes, was holed up in a two-story, wood-frame house at 112 Martin Street. And according to what information was available, he may even have a hostage.

It was enough. We received our position assignments and began drawing our equipment. My partner, Detective Jerome Bryant, and I drew the responsibility for covering the three and four sides of the house. In SWAT operations, the four sides of a building or scene perimeter are identified by a numbering system that is nationally recognized. Each side is numbered in clockwise order. This makes any assignments or plans formulated at the command post understood by all in short order, and later, any activity that is noted and transmitted over the radio comes across both concise and accurate. In this case, the three-side was the backyard, and the four-side was where a hedgerow with trees separated a detached one-car garage from the house to the west.

The neighborhood was in an older section of town and was comprised mainly of two-story, wood-frame houses that were seventy to eighty years old. Mature maple trees, shrubs, outbuildings, and fences limited any fields of fire or clear view to the bare minimum. One look at the area with sniper tactics in mind immediately made us realize that we would be working within the inner perimeter. Any farther away and we wouldn't even be able to see the house with all the obstacles in the way.

Realizing this, I selected a 5.56mm AR-15 with standard iron sights. There was no reason to take a telescopic sight-equipped, long-range rifle when I knew that any shot taken at the suspect would probably be in the twenty- to thirty-yard range. A scope would only prove a hindrance, and since I would be shooting on a level plane toward the house, a larger round, such as a .308 round, might go clear through the structure and hit an innocent bystander. The 5.56mm round, known to sportsmen as .223 caliber, will normally deflect or disintegrate on the first hard object it hits—such as a wall, even if it's made of wood or plaster.

As we drew our equipment, the main thing on my mind was the heat. My secondary job was team paramedic, and I was concerned with dehydration. I wanted everyone to drink as much as they could before deploying and had ordered a cooler of pop and water to be delivered to the command post. It arrived as we were being briefed and I made sure everyone drank all they could hold. We didn't carry canteens, and I knew that once we were scattered on the perimeter there would be little chance to drink anything, especially if any of the team were in isolated or exposed positions. As it turned out, I was right.

Jerome and I made our way through backyards until we came to the back of the house in question. We began visually scanning our area of operations and spotted a hedgerow of shrubbery and bushes that would offer us concealment in a spot that could cover our sector. But a wire mesh fence stood between us and the hedgerow.

"From what I can see, that row of bushes looks like the best place. But first we're going to have to get there," I said to Jerome. "If we try to crawl over this fence, the bad guy will have an open shot at us."

"No problem," said Jerome. "I'll just run back to the command post and get some wire cutters. It'll take a few minutes, but we can cut a hole and crawl through."

"Good. I'll wait here and cover what I can until you get back."

Bryant quickly pulled back and disappeared in the direction of the CP. While I waited, I could hear things beginning to happen on the radio: Officers were busy evacuating the surrounding houses, others were preparing to cut off the gas to the house, the command post was requesting a representative from Consumers Power to be dispatched to shut off the electricity, and the telephone company was contacted to "freeze" the phone line. This latter action would keep Hughes from talking to anyone other than the negotiators.

Everything was falling into place. We had the situation under control and it was now only a matter of time. But time was what I was beginning to worry about. Even though it was now past 5:30 P.M., the heat had not seemed to dissipate at all. I was beginning to get thirsty again and there was nothing I could do about it. If I was suffering, I knew that the temperature would eventually begin to affect all of the officers on the perimeter. Heat casualties became a very real possibility.

Jerome returned with the wire cutters and quickly snipped a hole in the fence. We crawled through and established ourselves by the hedgerow, settling into positions where we could watch the house without being seen. For the next hour-and-a-half we lay there, baking in the heat, watching the house, and listening to the radio. Our thirst was almost unbearable, and now to add to our misery, swarms of mosquitoes joined us for their evening feeding frenzy. I began mentally cursing the weather, the bugs, the suspect for putting us in this situation, and life in general.

And I didn't like where I was at. It just felt wrong. I couldn't cover the house as well as I would have liked, and I didn't like being in a place that offered no protection against incoming bullets. Finally I'd had enough.

"Jerome, this place sucks," I rasped with a parched throat. "I'm going to shift positions. See that garage over there? Cover me. I'm going to get next to it where I can get a better view of the house."

Jerome looked at the garage in the next yard over and signaled that he understood. I gripped the AR-15, crawled to my feet, and moved out in a crouch. Even though this would distance us by about thirty yards, we would still be able to see each other. And that was important. For safety reasons we always worked in teams of two and tried never to get beyond an effective covering distance from our partner.

I reached the wall of the garage, a single-car, weatherworn structure that was beginning to sag and lean. I crouched low, crept along the base until I had a clear view of the house, then dropped to my belly. I was right. It *was* a better location than the hedgerow.

The range was about twenty-five yards. Plenty close enough for the AR-15. I looked back over my shoulder and could see Jerome watching me. I signaled that everything was fine and that I would remain where I was. He nodded and turned his attention back to the house.

My throat was parched, my mouth dry. Visions of an ice-cold beer floated through my mind and I cursed myself once again for not bringing anything to drink. I shook off the thought and tried to focus my attention on the house. I was beginning to wonder if we were on a wild-goose chase. There had been no contact with the suspect since we had arrived, and Jerome and I had even discussed the possibility that he had gotten away in the time between when we received the call-out and when we arrived. But the command post felt he was still there, and ours was not to reason why.

For the next twenty minutes I lay on the ground, trying to ignore my thirst and the mosquitoes that buzzed by my ears looking for—and occasionally finding—a meal. The radio was almost dead, leaving me with no diversions to break the boredom and misery. The only transmission of interest that punctuated the monotony crackled at 7:21 P.M. when a team escorted the representative from the power company to pull the electric meter to cut off power to the house.

As the time dragged by, my shoulders and neck began to ache from keeping my head raised and my elbows were growing sore from propping the rifle up. This was not exactly what I had envisioned when I volunteered for SWAT. I consoled myself with the fact that if anything happened, at least I would be close to the action. I didn't realize how true that last thought would prove to be.

By 7:40 I began to worry about what we would do if nothing had happened before dark. Though the days were long in the summer months, the sun could be expected to drop below the horizon by 9:30. Already long shadows were beginning to stretch across the yard from the buildings and maple trees. If this thing continued on into the night the command post would have to come up with some type of artificial lighting.

I looked at my watch. 7:45 P.M. Still plenty of time.

Then I heard something. It sounded like a little piece of glass falling to the floor inside the garage! Something was in there. I froze and listened, but there were no other sounds. I turned to Jerome and signaled that I had heard something inside the garage and that I was going to check it out.

I rose to my hands and knees, backtracked a few feet, and eased my head up to where I could see into a small, dirty window. Squinting into the darkness I noticed something moving. Something small. Then I breathed a sigh of relief. It was just a cat.

I gave Jerome the okay sign and settled back down. I once again eased my body next to the rotting plywood wall and tried to make myself as comfortable as possible. I thought how strange it would be, after all of this, to find out that the suspect had escaped undetected from the house and had been hiding in the garage—*my* garage—all of this time. But I knew that was impossible.

Then I heard something else. This time it sounded louder, and heavier. I cocked my ear. *What in the hell was that?* I asked myself. Whatever it was, it had brushed against the wall right next to me. And it sounded like something big. Surely the cat couldn't have made that sound.

Again I rose and retraced my steps to the window. I waved at Jerome and, pointing at the garage, signaled with four fingers—the signal that I might have someone inside. He shifted his stance to cover me and his face frowned intently as he watched me rise up to the edge of the window.

I "quick peeked" inside and immediately saw something large and dark move. It was some kind of silhouette in the shadows, but it moved. And it wasn't any cat. I signaled with four fingers again, this time much more dramatically, and reached for my shoulder microphone.

"Morris to command, I've got movement in the garage next to the suspect's house on the 'four' side."

By the time I unkeyed the mike, Bryant had cleared the fence separating the two yards and was approaching the garage. The bad guy had evidently heard me transmit and I could hear him again moving inside. He was slithering toward the door.

I shouldered my rifle, clicked the safety off, and quickly moved to the front edge of the wall where I could cover the driveway. If he bolted from there, he could run down the driveway toward the street, or cut either right or left and attempt to escape through the backyards of the surrounding houses. To cut off his escape I would have to be ready to react as soon as he cleared the entrance.

As I reached the corner of the garage I could see other SWAT guys appear out of nowhere and quickly set up in strategic locations surrounding me. It was perfect timing on their part. For immediately the suspect, wearing exactly what had been earlier described by witnesses, came through the door.

"Police officer!" I yelled. "Get your hands where I can see them!"

He looked at me and hesitated. I could see that he was sizing up the situation, trying to decide if he could run and make it. I screamed the warning again. Still he refused to comply. I could see the look in his face, the look that said, "I don't think you'd shoot. I think I can get away."

"I said, *get your hands in the air where I can see them!*" This time I leveled the AR-15 between his eyes and donned my most intimidating look. It was enough to convince him. He raised his hands.

Then, from out of nowhere, Jerome blasted by and ran right in front of me to grab the guy. I wasn't ready for this. I thought, *What in the hell is he doing in the kill zone? If this guy has a buddy in the garage, he can take Bryant out. Shit, we didn't even know this guy was in the garage in the beginning, and we don't know if there's only one.* I was really pissed.

Hold your positions, the radio squawked. It was Lieutenant Berglin, our supervisor. *Everybody hold your positions!*

I looked around. Officers, seeing Bryant take the guy down, had begun leaving their positions of cover to get in on the action. Berglin's orders put a stop to it.

"Jerome, get the hell out of there and bring him with you!" I yelled, covering him as well as I could with the rifle. "Get him over here to me." But Bryant, having his own plan in mind, cuffed the guy and started dragging him down the driveway toward the street.

I was still worried about the garage. I backed up and again peeked through the window. I couldn't see anything, but still I felt that we had to check it more thoroughly. I grabbed my shoulder mike. *Morris to all units, we've got to clear this garage.*

It was reassuring to know as I was saying this that there were twenty tactically trained officers covering my butt, many of whom would respond without question and would immediately know exactly what to do.

Ten minutes later the garage was declared clear by two officers from the perimeter team. I went in and looked around. The place was full of junk. Old tires, bits of wood, piles of clothing, and other trash littered the place. Then I saw where the suspect had hidden. Against one wall, the same wall I had used for cover, he had lain down and covered himself with old clothes. I stepped over the garbage and examined the spot. It was no more than an inch from where I had been. The only thing separating me from him was a half inch of rotten plywood. All he had to do was shoot through the wall and I would have been dead. And we had lain there together, with only him knowing how close we were, for almost two hours.

It was undoubtedly a record event, distance-wise, in the annals of police SWAT sniper history. I could just see the notation written in a sniper log: "Range to target: half inch." The more I thought about it, the more it bothered me. I like to be in control. I like to know that I'll see the suspect before he sees me—*if* he sees me. But in this situation, the bad guy was in control. He knew exactly where I was, and I had a false sense of security by taking it for granted that the bad guy was barricaded in the house. Hell, they're *always* in a house.

Except when they're in a garage.

When they say, "Long distance is the next best thing to being there," they're wrong. For a sniper, long distance is better than being there. Much better.

17
A Cold Winter's Night

For the average person, thoughts of the winter holiday season bring a kaleidoscope of pleasant visions to mind: Christmas decorations on city streets; strings of colored lights outlining homes; malls bustling with shoppers; Christmas trees resplendent in ornaments and foil, gifts wrapped and waiting below their boughs; parties and good friends smiling, and hand-bells being rung by red-suited Santas.

The holiday season ends with New Year's Day when people stay home to recuperate from the previous night's festivities and settle down to watch parades and football games on television. It is indeed a cheerful time of year.

But for police officers nationwide, it is a tragic time of year as well. Drunk drivers cause accidents, often resulting in fatalities; death messages must still be delivered; family fights develop for various reasons that end with someone— usually the wife—being assaulted, and someone—usually the husband—going to jail. Armed robberies, burglaries, and other crimes of larceny increase. And for people already suffering from depression or loneliness, the season is the low point of the year. Because of this last factor, suicides increase, adding personal tragedy to far too many families.

For law enforcement officers, caught between the holiday festivities of their family lives and the grim realities of their daily jobs, this time of year has two faces. They know it, and they deal with it. It goes with the territory. But sometimes, when the man behind the badge just begins to think that maybe the season will pass with no major incidents to mark the end of the year, and that perhaps, just this once, he too can enjoy the days of "Peace on Earth, Goodwill toward Men," fate intervenes. And it only takes one radio or telephone call to destroy the season.

For Kentucky State Police Trooper Jim White, a sniper on the Post 12 Special Response Team located at Frankfort, Kentucky, that call came four days after Christmas 1985.

In stark contrast to the big city police departments, where officers work relatively small districts or beats of densely populated urban areas, state troopers cover extremely large, sparsely populated sections of their state. And unlike the city officers who have partners, or can summon help from a district only blocks away and expect it to arrive within minutes, troopers normally work alone. This puts the nearest backup officer several miles away. For this reason, troopers and other rural law enforcement officers have grown to depend upon each other. If a call for help goes out, anyone and everyone, whether they be other troopers, deputy sheriffs, town marshals, or police officers, respond. In the law enforcement community, it's one big family.

Such was the case on December 29, 1985, when the Kentucky State Police received a call from a municipal police department in need of assistance.

Newport, Kentucky, is, by most standards, considered a small town. The 1980 census put the population at 21,587. But because of its geographical location—directly across the Ohio River from Cincinnati—the small town has big city problems. Criminals know few boundaries, and the river, with its two major bridges crossing into Kentucky, offers no obstacle to their intentions. Because of this, the crime rate in Newport is far out of proportion to that of its population—and its police department. And occasionally, as is the case with communities with limited manpower and resources, help is needed from outside. Newport Police Chief Rick Huck and his officers had been dealing with a very bad situation for some time. For six hours a suspect had been holding two teenage boys hostage. Huck's men, after receiving the initial call at 3:00 A.M., had responded quickly, effectively contained the assailant, evacuated the surrounding homes, established a command post in a church parsonage near the suspect's apartment, manned a perimeter, and begun negotiations. It was a sterling performance, but it had taken time. Four hours. Huck's men were cold and tired. They had accomplished a great deal but were worn out. By 7:30 A.M. Huck put out a call to Post 6, located 30 miles away in Dry Ridge. Two hours later Terry Evans and the Post 6 SRT team arrived. They were indeed a welcome sight.

"Glad to see you boys. We can sure use the help. My men are beat. I've got to get them some rest. Can you take over the inner perimeter?" asked Chief Huck.

"No problem, Chief. Can you fill me in on what's going on?"

"Sure. Here's the deal. Sometime last night we got a disturbance call at 836 Isabella Street. That's where the suspect was staying or visiting when he went off the deep end. To make a long story short, he took the two boys in there hostage. One, Larkin Wordlow, is sixteen. His brother, Robert, is fourteen.

"The situation deteriorated and we ended up calling out our SWAT team. After we set up the command post we managed to call the assailant and establish communications. But he's kind of incoherent. He says that he's already killed two boys in the past two days, but we haven't been able to establish that for certain yet. He's made various demands, but nothing that we can work with."

Evans made notes. "What's the suspect's background? Anything on him yet?"

"Yeah. Name's Dennis Lucas, white male, age twenty to twenty-one. He's shaved his head and eyebrows, if that tells you anything. His psychological profile, which was done about three years ago, shows that he has an IQ of seventy-six."

Evans shook his head. "Real genius, eh?"

"Yeah. The bad part is that his evaluation says that he has absolutely no regard for human life. And from what we've been able to establish, he's pretty well armed. Nothing heavy, but he's supposed to have some type of homemade machine gun, a .380 pistol, and a .357 magnum pistol. He's shooting from the front door quite often. There's a little window in it that's broken out and he just walks up, sticks his arm out, and fires away at anything that moves. He's already told us several times on the phone when he can see police moving around—and that he's going to kill them."

"What's the house like?" asked Evans.

"It's a two-story building, but the top and bottom apartments are separate. The bottom apartment, the one Lucas is in, has a front and rear door. The front door faces the street and is located on the left, or south, end of the building as you face it from across Isabella Street. There is a large picture window next to the door. The upstairs apartment has stairs that go up the back side to the entrance door. There's no entrance in front for that one. It's a corner house, and across the east-west street on the south side is the Corpus Christi Church."

"How much of the neighborhood have you evacuated?"

Chief Huck outlined an area on the map. "About two blocks all the way around. That should take care of any stray shots from a pistol."

"Okay, Chief. If you'll man the outer perimeter, we'll take over the scene and inner perimeter. I've got two of my hostage negotiators on the way in: Sergeant Joe Whalen and Trooper Mike Evans. We'll put them on the phone when they get here. Meanwhile, we'll relieve your men. Any decision we make from now on out will be a joint decision;

however, the Kentucky State Police must have the final word."

"Sounds good to me."

At 9:30 A.M. Lieutenant Terry Evans called his captain, Dale Fortner, to advise him of the situation. By 12:10 P.M., the lieutenant's scenario worsened when new information arrived. His command post log entry breaks an intensive and dangerous event into basic police language—and adds three more players to the game:

> 1210: [A] Subject ran out from upstairs apart-
> ment and suspect began shooting again. Suspect
> [Lucas][1] saw Tpr. Daley across the street and
> began shooting at him—fifteen–twenty shots.
> The subject was from the upstairs apartment.
> He gave us information that one twenty-five-
> year-old white female and two children, three
> and five years old, were still upstairs.

Evans positioned two sniper teams in strategic locations. One in a church located across the street from the suspect's house to the south, the second in a third-floor window of a single-family house directly across Isabella Street to the east. The remaining members of the Post 6 SRT took up advantageous positions wherever they could be found. And settled in to wait.

But it was an exciting waiting period. Lucas, screaming and yelling epithets from within the apartment, stomped back and forth through the room, firing shots at random, and pausing occasionally to shoot through the little window in the front door. It kept everyone on their toes—and under cover.

By 1:30 P.M., Lieutenant Evans decided to call for additional help. The temperature was below thirty degrees

---

[1]Bracketed statements are author's explanations.

Fahrenheit and there were just so many hours a man could stand remaining immobile in such an environment. A phone call to dispatch Post 5, located eighty miles away at La Grange, to saddle up their SRT team and start toward Newport.[2] They were to bring their marksman and observer.

Troopers Marshall and Downey, the marksman and observer from Post 5, arrived a little before 3:30 P.M. and relieved one of the Post 6 sniper teams. Other troopers from Post 5 began replacing the cold, tired Post 6 men on the inner perimeter, who were taken in turn to a nearby motel for much needed rest and warming. So far, since taking over the perimeter, other than ducking the intermittent bursts of shots fired by Lucas, the standoff was a routine SWAT-type operation. By 3:25 P.M., Captain Fortner had driven to Newport from Dry Ridge and had taken overall command of the operation.

An hour and ten minutes after Fortner's arrival the situation took another twist.

"Captain Fortner, we got a problem here," advised one of the negotiators, cupping his hand over the telephone. "Lucas says that at five o'clock he's going to shoot one of the boys and throw him out the rear window!" The negotiators were finding Lucas almost impossible to reason with. Instead of making demands that could be discussed, Lucas merely exhibited an almost uncontrollable rage.

"Keep talking to him. Try to calm him down. Change his mind," ordered Fortner.

The personnel in the command post waited in an atmosphere electric with dread. By now the small rectory of the Corpus Christi Church was filled with representatives of local, state, and federal law enforcement agencies. Besides Captain Fortner, Chief Huck, Lieutenant Terry Evans, and the three negotiators, Sergeants Lewis Hankins and Joe

---

[2] Lt. Evans had alerted them originally at 10:13 A.M. and put them on standby status. They were ready to move out when he called at 1:30 P.M.

Whalen, and Trooper Mike Evans, there were Colonel Ken Page of the Newport Police Department, Special Agent in Charge (SAC) Joel Carlson of the FBI, FBI Hostage Incident Instructor Agent Bernie Thompson, and U.S. Attorney Lou Defalaise. Everyone waited quietly, feeling helpless and frustrated, as the seconds ticked by.

But five o'clock came and went and Lucas failed to live up to his threat. The command post breathed a sigh of relief.

Fortner read the psychological evaluation on Lucas. Lucas was a violent individual with a hair-trigger temper who suffered from paranoid schizophrenia. He had possible homicidal tendencies, and indeed had made claims of killing two boys the week before. He noted that the report had been written by Lucas's group counselor, a Harrodsburg, Kentucky, resident named Rusty Weitzel, who had worked with Lucas after previous brushes with the law. Harrodsburg was 135 miles away, 35 miles southwest of Lexington. But a state police car could get the man to Newport in an hour-and-a-half at the latest if he could be located. He got on the phone to headquarters. "Have Mr. Weitzel picked up by a Post Seven officer and get him transported here as soon as possible."

Negotiations dragged on throughout the afternoon, wearing Lucas down as the hours went by. By 6:00 P.M. it was dark. The prospect of facing a night that would drop into the teens was not one welcomed by the SRT members. Still, with the lives of the two young hostages at stake in the downstairs apartment, and the woman and two children in the upstairs apartment, there was little choice.

Fortner considered his manning problem and his options. There were an insufficient number of troopers to cover both the sniper posts and the perimeter positions throughout the night without relief. Fresh troops were needed to change out those freezing in a night that sparkled with crystals of frost in the air that began to form a blanket of white on the roofs of the houses. With the temperature dropping to an expected fifteen degrees, they would be hard-pressed to maintain their positions for more than an hour or two at a time. He needed more men.

And to cap that, at the same time there had been a new turn for the worse in developments involving negotiations with Lucas. Fortner's report noted:

> At approximately 2100 hours, negotiations had totally broken down. Lucas was raging, firing shots, and continually threatening to kill Robert and Larkin Woodlow [sic] and throw the bodies out into the yard. Lucas was also calling the radio stations telling them he was enlarging the hole into the second floor and was going to take the lady and her two small children as hostages.

Even Rusty Weitzel, who had been on hand for several hours after his rapid transport to Newport, and had attempted to help with negotiations, had given up on dealing with Lucas. It was now a police matter, pure and simple. Go in and get him, and in the process, rescue the hostages—or take him out with a sniper's bullet before he can harm them.

It would be safer to take him out with a shot. Fortner notes that at 2130, 18½ hours since the original 3:00 A.M. call:

> I called Major Rakestraw[3] and told him of the graveness of the incident and that we were intending to take the life of Lucas by our riflemen if he came out of the house or presented a clear shot while shooting at our personnel. Major Rakestraw agreed this was probably the only thing left to do.

There were no guarantees on how long it would take before Lucas presented himself for a shot by one of the sniper teams. Fortner had to be ready for an even longer

---

[3]Headquarters on-call staff officer.

standoff. This would require more men—especially marksmen. When the time came, the riflemen on duty had to be at their sharpest. Well rested and ready. Not numb from cold and sleepy-eyed from fatigue. With the addition of another team, they could be rotated on an effective basis that would ensure alertness and capability when the moment came to take the shot.

Fortner weighed his options. His next unit of choice for call-up would be Post 12, located at Frankfort, eighty-five miles away.

At 9:40 P.M., a request was made through Major Tom Rakestraw for the Post 12 Special Response Team to rally at Newport as soon as possible. Seven minutes later, Lieutenant Dave Williams of Post 12 called back. He and six men would arrive by midnight.

And he would bring their sniper team, Trooper Jim White and his partner, C. H. "Chuck" Reed.

18

Trooper Jim White, Kentucky State Police
December 29, 1985

The call came in at 9:24 P.M. I had been relaxing at home when the phone rang, disturbing the few remaining hours of my Sunday evening with the family. It was the Post 12 dispatcher.[1]

"Jim, there's a big deal going on up in Newport. Some kind of hostage situation. The Dry Ridge and La Grange posts are already up there. I'm calling to let you know that our SRT team and you and your partner are on standby. If they call us in, be ready to roll pretty fast."

"You called Brumfield yet?" I asked, referring to my partner, Detective Stewart Brumfield.

"He's on vacation down in Ashland. We're trying to get hold of him now, but if you get called in on this one, you're supposed to take Chuck Reed as your observer," said the dispatcher, referring to Trooper Charles H. "Chuck" Reed, the next marksman on the list.

---

[1] Post 12 is the Frankfort post. Each post, besides having a numerical designation, is referred to by the name of the city or town it is in or nearest to. Post 6 is also known as the Dry Ridge post. Post 5 is the La Grange post.

"Okay, keep me advised."

I hung up and went back into the living room. I had no sooner settled down to finish my TV show when the phone rang again. "It's a go. Be in Newport by twenty-four hundred hours."

By the time I arrived in Newport a system had been established to handle incoming units. We were to meet at the Newport Police Department, link up with a Kentucky State Police sergeant who would guide us to the command post, then receive a briefing there before being posted. This would keep any of our units that were unfamiliar with the area from wandering around lost, or worse, unwittingly ending up in the danger area around the suspect's house.

I pulled into the Newport PD parking lot at 11:25 P.M., thirty-five minutes to spare before the arrival deadline. Within minutes the entire Frankfort post Special Response Team had arrived, and, led by the sergeant, moved out to the scene.

The briefing at the command post brought us up-to-date.

I made notes on the descriptions of the two hostages and the suspect. It wouldn't be hard to tell them apart, especially since this Lucas had shaved his head and eyebrows. If I received permission to shoot, it would be hard to mistake the target.

The briefing was thorough but quick. By 12:25 Chuck and I were being led to our position, the third floor of a house directly across the street east from Lucas.

It was cold. The temperature had already dropped to twenty degrees and was still falling. I could see why the boys that had been here all day and into the night were ready for some help. At least inside the house, Chuck and I would have it a bit better than the troopers outside on the perimeter. Or so we thought.

We came to the house and entered through the back door where Lucas couldn't see us. It was dark inside. All of the lights had been turned off to eliminate the chance of being backlit or illuminated, and we had to lug our gear up three flights of stairs using only the bouncing beams of our flashlights.

We killed our lights on the third floor and cautiously entered the room that overlooked the front of the suspect's house. Inside, the Dry Ridge sniper team sat patiently behind a table that had been shoved up against a window that faced the street. On top of the table, resting on bipods, was the marksman's issue Steyr SSG Model 69 with its Leupold scope.

"You boys about ready for a break?" I asked, noting the gaping hole in the lower portion of the window that had been broken out to accommodate muzzle blast. Cold air came in, lowering the temperature of the room quite noticeably.

"You bet," said the rifleman. "Glad to see y'all could make it. Hope you brought your long johns. Get's a bit chilly up here."

"We can handle it. How's the view?" I asked.

"Not bad, not great. It's a down-angle shot and the only thing you've got is a small window in the front door that he occasionally takes potshots out of. There's a big picture window, but they don't want us shooting through it. It's supposed to be some kind of tempered glass or something and no one is sure what it will do if hit by a rifle bullet."

I knew that bullets do strange things when they hit various objects. Different thicknesses and consistencies of barriers, such as plastic, metal, wood, and glass, behave differently. Often unexpectedly. And we couldn't take any chances on a real-life situation with our shot not breaking clean, or just as bad, exploding razor-sharp shards of glass into the room in an uncontrolled pattern.

The Dry Ridge boys picked up their gear and turned the position over to us. I extended my Harris bipods and set my Steyr on the table. The chair that the previous shooter vacated was stacked with clothes to elevate him high enough to put him on line with the target house, which appeared to be about thirty feet lower in elevation than the windowsill. I sat down and tried it for size. A few adjustments and it fit fine. I could sit on the pile of clothes, pull the rifle to my cheek, take up a sight picture, and see the front of the house just fine.

As Chuck set up to my left, I gave the target house a going-over. The house was bathed in light from portable floodlights previously set up by the Newport police. It was a two-story frame structure with the front door of the lower apartment on the left side as I faced it. In the center of the wall was the large picture window, and to the right, somewhere in the north wall, was a brick chimney that protruded slightly above the roof that now sparkled with white frost. There was hardly any front yard to speak of. The front porch basically dropped off to the sidewalk.

The neighborhood was an older one. Two-lane asphalt streets separated blocks of one-, two-, and even a few three-story houses and apartments. For some reason, the houses on my side of the street looked quite a bit better than the ones on the other side. I didn't try to understand the significance of this beyond the possibility of the street being some kind of dividing line between classes or status. Or for this night, maybe between the good and the bad. Or life and death.

As I scanned the target, moving the rifle slowly from left to right, my bipod legs grabbed at the table making the weapon vibrate slightly as it moved. I picked up a rag and put it under one leg to reduce the friction. I tried moving the rifle again. No vibration. It slid smoothly from side to side, one leg serving as a pivot point. I jacked a 168 grain boat-tailed hollow point into the chamber, feeling the bolt slide smoothly and locking home with a distinctive click. I then checked the magnification setting on my 3.5X10 Leupold. It still registered my normal setting of ten power.

Satisfied that everything was ready, I eased the rifle's butt to the table and settled in for the long haul.

One of the worst jobs in police work is the stakeout. They seem to last forever. Hours and hours of boredom watching absolutely nothing until someone moves or something happens. Much of SWAT work is the same. If the suspect stays hidden inside a building, refusing to come out or do something to break the boredom, you just have to steel yourself to remain vigilant and ready to move or react in an instant. Because that's when it happens. As soon as you relax, get complacent, your suspect makes his move. For the SWAT sniper team, posted in some building, or on some rooftop, or lying prone on the hard ground for hours and hours on end with your neck and shoulder muscles aching from keeping your head up all that time, and your elbows sore from holding binoculars or the rifle in position, there is no room for complacency. Or boredom. Or inattention. Your focus *has* to be on the objective.[2]

And this takes patience. That's the key word to all SWAT operations. The hostage negotiators have to have that quality, as do the command post personnel, the paramedics, the entry team guys, and everyone else involved in an ongoing operation that lasts sometimes for days. It's the name of the game. Outwait, negotiate, and wear down the opposition. To those of us in Special Operations, we've heard it a hundred times from our instructors and supervisors: "We've got all the time in the world."

But for the law enforcement marksman and his observer, it takes more. We don't get to kill time by rehearsing an entry in preparation for an assault or rescue like the "door kickers." We don't get to hear everything that is going on like the folks in the command post. We just have to wait, our

---

[2]Lieutenant Evans notes in his report: "12/30/85: 0030 hours. Post 6 SRT left the scene to return at 0700 hours." They had been on the scene approximately seventeen hours.

attention focused like a magnet on what is happening in our area of responsibility until the situation is terminated one way or the other. And normally, it's terminated by the negotiators, or maybe the entry team. It's only when all else fails, when nothing short of taking the bad boy out, that we are called on to do our part. We don't necessarily like that part of it, but like the man says, "It's a dirty job, but someone has to do it."

The temperature by now had dropped a few more degrees. It was cold. Bitter cold. And getting colder. The broken window let the winter in, making the area around the opening a pocket of frigid air. But at least we were better off than the guys out on the perimeter. Though there wasn't much wind, the walls around us kept what little windchill factor there was outside.

I looked across the street and estimated the range to the front door. That would be just about the only area of engagement we would have. The other sniper team, located in the Corpus Christi Church south of the house, could cover the backyard and back door, and the tiny south lawn, but all Chuck and I had was the front door. Lucas would have to come out of it, or at least stand behind it long enough for a shot—if we were authorized to shoot at all.

"Looks like about sixty to seventy yards," I said to Chuck.

"You talkin' about to the front door?"

"Yeah."

"I agree. Better split the difference and make it about sixty-five," said Chuck. "How about the downward angle?"

"Shouldn't be too much of a problem. I'll just have to remember to aim a little low." We both knew that a downward shot, shooting from a high position to a low position, was affected slightly by gravity. Some instructors tell you that the bullet tends to rise, others say that it just doesn't drop as much as a flat trajectory shot—such as on the rifle range that parallels the ground. So to compensate for this factor, you have to aim a little low. At the ranges police snipers shoot, this is only a matter of a couple of inches at most. But it makes a difference. When you realize that the "no-reflex zone" in the head is only a narrow band about two inches wide—running around the head about eye level—a half inch can make the difference between a solid hit that severs the brain stem, keeping the suspect from even pulling a trigger, or giving him the chance to jerk off a round. If he has a cocked pistol or sawed-off shotgun against the temple of a hostage, or a knife to their jugular, your shot can inadvertently cause him to kill the hostage. It's happened.

But sometimes, maybe far too often, you don't get the ideal shot. You've just got to go with what you can. If you can get a clear shot and there's no hostage or innocent bystander standing close to where your bullet will go, you just do the best you can.

Chuck was also a sniper. He'd had the training and could have just as easily been behind the rifle as me, but he hadn't shot this rifle before and it was zeroed for me. So I was going to have to be the shooter. It was a simple luck of the draw.

We weren't alone in the room. Two other men, Trooper Danny Reed and Sergeant Robert Milligan, were also there watching the house from our vantage point. But the main purpose of this particular position was as a sniper post.

As we waited, taking turns watching the house, occasional radio messages squawked from the portable radio keeping us informed on what was happening. Most of it was routine chatter: people needing relief, errands to be run, questions asked or orders given by the command post, just normal stuff. But the radio was also our source of news. If negotiations broke down, or if Lucas wanted something new, or his attitude had obviously changed, or he made new threats, we knew about it.

But to gain some of this information, the negotiators at the command post had to keep Lucas on the phone. If he hung up and didn't yell anything from the broken door window for perimeter troopers to hear, then we had no idea what was going on inside the house. All we had to go on were these two means of communication. The phone and the window.

That changed briefly when arrangements were made with the telephone company to use a little-known means of eavesdropping technology. The technicians have the capability of making some changes in the system that disables the switch-hook. Hanging up the telephone no longer cuts it off. You can still hear what is going on in the room even though the suspect thinks that you are disconnected. But the quality is poor. The farther away the suspect is from the phone, the weaker the transmission. Just like leaving a receiver on a table and walking away. You can hear doors opening and closing, a bit of conversation, stuff like that. But little else.

It was better than nothing, but it wasn't totally satisfactory. If there were no noises at all, we became a bit nervous. What was he up to? This guy was a loud, obnoxious, egotistical sort who stayed calm very little. We had to have a better way to monitor him.

The FBI solved the problem for us. In the early morning hours of December 30, they provided the command post with a high-intensity microphone and transmitter that, if placed inside the suspect's house, could pick up a cat walking across the floor. But how would we get it inside? If we had a way to do that, we could have already taken Lucas out as well. Still, there had to be a way to sneak a small object such as a microphone into a position that would at least monitor the interior.

Then someone came up with an idea. Trooper Stewart Brumfield, my regular partner and himself a Post 12 sniper,[3]

---

[3]Brumfield was called in from vacation for the incident. He did not have his sniper rifle with him at the time and therefore doubled as part of the entry team.

and one of our Frankfort post members, Trooper Gregg Muravchick, would get up on the roof of the adjoining house, cross to the roof of Lucas's house, then try to drop the microphone down the chimney with a cable. If they could do this undetected, the command post could monitor not only what was going on, but by the sounds of the movements, just about where Lucas was at.

I looked at the roof. It sparkled white with frost. One slip and Lucas would probably know someone was up there. There was no telling what would happen then. But it had to be tried.

Brumfield's team managed to locate a ladder and gain the roof of the house next door. Carefully, moving slowly, they eased across the roof, taking the ladder with them, and approached the edge of the roof nearest the suspect's house. By using the ladder as a bridge between the two buildings, they crept across until they were solidly positioned on his roof. They froze and waited for a reaction. There was none.

Brumfield crept to the chimney and began lowering the microphone. Within seconds he had extended it almost forty feet. It was enough. They beat a cautious, silent, retreat.

For the next seven hours the command post listened. Lucas moved about, loudly swearing to himself and making various threats, moving furniture and, more sinister, making scraping noises like he was still trying to carve a larger opening at the ventilation hole that led to the apartment above. If he succeeded in this, he would then add three additional hostages to his stable. And we were helpless to do anything about it. If our entry team tried to get in, he could kill one or both of the boys. If they tried to cross the street or backyard to get to the stairs that led to the upstairs apartment, they had to cross a kill zone. And so far, the lady and two girls upstairs had not been in extreme danger. This appeared to be about to change.

The street brightened with light a little after 6:00 A.M. Chuck and I yawned, stretched, and again riveted our attention to the house across the street. The radio had been fairly quiet and it was hard to keep awake. But we had to.

"The Dry Ridge boys are supposed to be back at seven," said Chuck.

"Yeah, but they'll probably use them to relieve the church team. I imagine we'll be here for a spell yet." I was right.

Four hours later we were still at the window when things began to happen. The command post managed to establish telephone contact with one of the hostages after ascertaining by the sounds coming from the microphone that Lucas seemed to have fallen asleep. Heavy breathing could be heard over the monitor, quite a change in sound over his previous actions. Lucas had been up, ranting and raving and stomping about for over thirty-one hours since the incident began. We had no way of knowing how long he had been going before the police were first called at 3:00 A.M. the day before. Maybe exhaustion had caught up with him and he had finally collapsed.

Sixteen-year-old Robert Wordlow answered the telephone at ten o'clock. "He's asleep, kind of. He's on the couch and he's bein' real quiet. He looks asleep to me."

"Where's your brother?" asked the hostage negotiator.

"He's in the back bedroom. He's handcuffed to the bed."

After a hurried discussion of what to do next, a decision was made. Two things could now be tried: get the lady and her two children out of the upstairs apartment and move them to safety, and try to rescue at least Robert.

Members of the Post 6 team, now rested and back on duty, were selected for the rescue mission. At a little after 10:00 A.M., they approached the back of the house, crept up the stairs, talked the lady out, and whisked her and the two children to safety. It went off without a hitch. We all breathed a sigh of relief. Phase one had been satisfactorily accomplished. Next came Robert Wordlow.

Robert, still on the telephone, received instructions. "Go to the back door," instructed Sergeant Hankins. "Be real quiet when you do. Then when you get there, open it. We'll have someone there to meet you. He'll be a state trooper, so don't be afraid."

Robert quietly cradled the receiver and did as instructed. When he unlocked and eased the door open he was greeted by Trooper Brumfield, covered a few feet away by Muravchick. Brumfield grabbed Robert and raced toward the alley behind the house. Three minutes later the boy, and the rescue team, were safely inside the command post.

But fourteen-year-old Larkin was still inside, handcuffed to the bed. There was no way to predict how Lucas would take the fact that he had lost a hostage when he woke up. But it didn't take long to find out. Ten minutes later, at 10:30 A.M., he awoke in a rage. Chuck and I didn't need a microphone or telephone to hear him. He could be heard from all the way across the street.

"Bobby! Where's Bobby?" he screamed, racing from one end of the apartment to the other. We could occasionally see his form behind the plate glass window as he crossed the living room, shouting curses and kicking furniture about. "Where's Bobby?"

He was really freaking out, working himself up into an extreme rage. It was frightening. The whole scene was quickly deteriorating far beyond anything that had transpired over the past twenty-four hours. The command post, along with everyone else, immediately saw the gravity of the situation. They called both sniper teams.

Command post to marksmen. Be vigilant. Subject is becoming very irate. He's likely to try and kill the other boy. Whenever you've got a chance, take him out!

As I watched, Lucas came to the window and pulled the curtain back. I could see his bald head and skull-like face. It was true. He *had* shaved off his eyebrows. I wanted to take a shot but remembered the orders on not shooting through the glass. Besides, we couldn't tell if he had the remaining Wordlow boy nearby or behind him.

Lucas closed the curtains and retreated back into the

room. His questions became threats—or promises. "He's going to die!" he screamed, referring to young Larkin. "He's going to *die!* I'm gonna *kill* him!"

The command post could hear even more as he moved toward the back of the apartment. He began to chant: "Larkin dies. Larkin dies. Larkin *dies!*"

Then he went to the phone. Sergeant Hankins tried to calm him, telling him that we had to get Robert out, that he was ill and had to go to the hospital. Lucas only responded with: "You've cost Larkin his life. Larkin dies. Larkin *dies!*"

My radio came to life. It was Lieutenant Evans. *Command post to all marksmen. Take the first opportunity you have and kill Lucas.* That was all. It was enough.[4]

I drew my rifle to my shoulder, easing the stock to my cheek. I had a clear, unobstructed view of the front door. I watched it intently. I would only get a shot if he came to the door and there was no telling how long he would stay there. I had to be ready. I let the crosshairs settle on the small broken window and waited.

Behind the window I could see something blue. I wasn't sure what it was at the time, but later found out that Lucas had upended a couch and jammed it behind the door to brace it against entry from the outside. Lucas could still stand in between the couch and the door, but anyone trying to open the door would have to fight the weight of the couch.

And then I saw Lucas. His face appeared in the window, turned slightly down the street diagonally away from me. I could see his mouth move as he shouted threats and warnings to anyone who could hear them outside. Again he began to scream, "He's going to die. He's going to die. . . ."

---

[4]Captain Fortner's report reflects what had happened in the command post: "At this point it was very apparent to me and all those in the command post that Larking's [sic] life was in immediate danger. I at this time instructed Lt. Terry Evans to alert the snipers to take the first opportunity to kill Lucas."

I eased the crosshairs down slightly, dropping down his face to just about his cheekbone. This would compensate for the cold temperature, the angle of the shot, and the fact that the rifle was zeroed for a standard reference range of a hundred yards. Any shot that varied from the standard setting could be compensated for with the mental arithmetic of "Kentucky windage," or in this case "Kentucky elevation." I shifted a bit to the left, as close as I could get to the window frame, to get as much solid head-mass as possible. Since his face was turned sideways, the main portion of his head—the part most critical to a sniper—was still behind the door.

Then I took up the slack on the trigger.

"He's going to die. . . ."

I squeezed.

The Steyr recoiled with a loud *crack.*

"Yow!" Chuck exclaimed. He wasn't ready for the shot, and had been so intent on observing the house with his binoculars that he had moved fairly close to the window— and the muzzle. He jumped in surprise at the discharge, and at the pain of concussion to his eardrums.

I quickly worked the bolt, ejecting the empty casing across the room and chambering a fresh round. I wanted to be ready in case the shot wasn't fatal, or worse, if I had missed. But I didn't think I had. Yet, if the round didn't strike anything fatal, such as just going through his sinus cavities or something, a guy this mental, so pumped up on adrenaline and who knows what else, just might continue to be a danger factor. I quickly locked the scope to my eye again.

I could instantly see a large splotch of red on the blue cushion of the couch. It was blood. Mixed with it were some other objects that looked like splinters of some kind. The quarter round on the edge of the small frame of the window had been nicked by the bullet, sending some of the splinters against the couch along with part of his face. It was a gruesome sight.

Chuck got on the radio. "We've taken the shot. Suspect appears to have been hit."

We waited to see what would happen next. I prayed that I would not hear gunshots. If I did, then the Wordlow boy would be dead. The seconds ticked by. Finally, about three minutes later, the entry team hit the back door.

Brumfield and a sergeant from the Dry Ridge team raced into the house. They moved from room to room clearing each as they went. Finally we got the signal. The house was clear, the hostage freed.[5]

Lucas was dead. In police language, 10-7. His body lay on the floor just inside the door. He was probably dead before he hit the floor. The bullet had entered his cheek just above his lip, crossed through his skull, and exited the opposite side, carrying everything in between with it. This was the debris that we could plainly see on the couch from over sixty yards away.

I had taken the shot at 10:55 A.M. By 11:03 the scene had been cleared and secured. Eight minutes from start to finish. Eight minutes that I will never forget.

• • •

Kentucky State Police Trooper Jim White's actions on that cold winter day are summed up in a single entry in a report written by Sergeant Robert Milligan.

> Tpr. White's performance and composure was exemplary during the situation considering the fact that he

---

[5]Brumfield later said that when the shot was fired, another officer blurted, "The suspect's shooting again." But Brumfield, knowing the sound of the shot, said, ". . . that ain't no handgun. This old boy is ten-seven. That's White shooting up there." He also stated that he knew the suspect had to be dead before entry was even made. He knew what White could do with a rifle after watching him on the range.

had been up all night and had to move his point of aim and sight in on target in less than five (5) seconds. Tpr. White is to be commended.

Sometimes just a mention in the report is all you get. But sometimes, when you realize that your single shot saved someone's life, it's all you need.

19

Forcing the Issue in Suburbia

Nestled in the forested green hills of northeastern Oklahoma is the city of Tulsa, the second largest metropolitan area of the state. Established as an Indian trading post when the land was known as Indian Territory, Tulsa straddles the muddy Arkansas River just as it bends south on a winding trail that eventually empties into the Mississippi. It was just southwest of Tulsa in 1901 that the Oklahoma oil boom began when the first well came in on the Redfork Field.

Prior to the discovery of oil, Oklahoma was known for two things: Indian reservations and criminals. The Indians, uprooted from various homelands around the country, were transplanted to lands within the open plains and rugged hills of the primitive territory west of Arkansas and north of Texas—a land the government felt held little value to white settlers. The criminals, also recognizing the territory as a "no-man's land" took advantage of the lack of civilization and government control. Indian Territory became a refuge for some of the worst outlaws in American history. Names such as John Wesley Hardin, the Dalton brothers, Bill Doolin, and "Tulsa Jack" Blake, along with their female counterparts like Belle Starr, "Cattle Annie" McDougal, and Jennie "Little Britches" Stevens found their way into Oklahoma history by means of gunsmoke and blood.

Few U.S. Army outposts existed within the territory, and other than Indian Tribal Police that patrolled the reservations, there was virtually no law enforcement in this rugged land. It was an ideal haven for robbers, gunslingers, and other assorted villains. Bands of outlaws that plundered towns and robbed trains and banks in neighboring states routinely fled to Indian Territory to escape apprehension. Few lawmen followed.

The nearest point of civilization, and the jumping-off point for anyone heading into Indian Territory, was Fort Smith, Arkansas. It was here that the famous "Hanging" Judge Isaac Parker established his courtroom and gallows. And it was here that his U.S. Marshals sallied forth to track down and bring back—or kill—the outlaws that burned their names into Western lore with six-guns, shotguns, and dynamite.

The Land Rush of April 22, 1889, brought fifty thousand settlers into Indian lands bought back by the government. At the sound of a pistol shot, "boomers" raced into Indian territory. Those who sneaked across the border before the official opening were dubbed "sooners." With the settlers came a semblance of civilization. Boomtowns sprang up around trading posts that did business with both Indians and settlers, and large tracts of land were granted to thousands of people who rushed on horseback and in wagons to claim it.

The towns had little, if any, law enforcement. Often the sheriff or town marshal was little more than the town bully or the fastest gun that could be hired for the money available. And there was little money to be had. Taxes were unheard of, and the majority of money that could be accounted for was that of the gambling tables and saloons frequented by every manner of crook, thief, and gunman. There is little doubt where the loyalties of the local lawman lay. When criminals *were* brought to justice, it was usually due to the efforts of the deputy U.S. Marshals from Fort Smith.

It was in these days of single law enforcement officers tracking down bands of armed desperadoes that the roots of the police sniper can be traced. Contrary to Hollywood depictions of the intrepid lawman facing down his quarry on a dusty street at high noon, confrontations were actually quite the opposite. Gunfights were seldom quick-draw contests. Instead, one man usually attempted to ambush, or "bushwhack," his opponent from a hidden position. And if he shot him in the back, so much the better—and safer. Outlaws and marshals alike adopted similar tactics. When a wanted poster stated, WANTED: DEAD OR ALIVE, it meant just that. Either way the criminal was brought in was satisfactory. As long as his career was ended. If two or more lawmen confronted a desperado or outlaw gang, one normally stayed hidden and covered his partner with a rifle.

Each marshal adopted his own tactics, but almost all used a rifle—preferably a Winchester lever-action—to address his prey from the longest range possible. A vocal demand to surrender, if given at all, was normally issued one time. If not complied with, it was followed by a bullet. It was a foolish lawman who waded into an armed encampment with six-guns or shotgun blazing. Such foolhardy individuals normally had very short careers.

As the towns grew into cities, law enforcement grew with them. By statehood in 1907, many of the town marshals were replaced by police departments, leaving the rural areas to the county sheriff and his deputies. When the Roaring Twenties and the following Depression brought forth the big name bank robbers and gangsters, Oklahoma once again became a haven for outlaws. Pretty Boy Floyd, Ma Barker, and Bonnie and Clyde are but a few of the notorious individuals that left their mark on Oklahoma history.

By the 1960s, police officers, state troopers, and most of

the larger sheriff's officers had developed into some of the finest and most professional law enforcement agencies in the country. It was a profession born in blood and tradition that continued to improve and grow to this day.

Leading the municipal law enforcement organizations of the state are the two largest police departments, those of Oklahoma City and Tulsa. Both cities, situated on major interstate highways, are subject to the flow of criminals that transit the state from all directions. With Kansas City to the northeast, Dallas to the south, Denver to the northwest, and Amarillo to the west, Oklahoma becomes the hub of criminal activity in the central midwest. Because of this, organized crime, drugs, interstate transportation of stolen property, transport of illegal aliens, and other forms of major crime transits the state.

And there is plenty of homegrown crime as well. As in any major city, Tulsa has its share of domestic crimes. Murders, armed robberies, burglaries, auto thefts, drugs, and every other category of crime found in other cities is faced on a daily basis by the six hundred members of the Tulsa Police Department.

The city itself covers two hundred square miles, divided into three police substation areas. Each substation, known as a Uniform Division, can handle almost any police matter within their area of responsibility. Though the police lab and the Detective Division is housed in the downtown Police-Courts Building, each Uniform Division has everything else it needs for day-to-day operations. Criminal activity, field investigations, street crimes (vice), traffic investigations and enforcement, and routine patrol operations are all conducted within the division. Only when something happens that exceeds the limitations of the uniformed officers does the division require assistance from without.

Such as when they need SWAT.

In Tulsa, because of a perceived stigma of violent reaction

attached to the word SWAT, the tactical unit is called the "Special Operations Team," or SOT. It began in 1971 as the Tactical Squad, or TAC. At that time, when the Vietnam War still ensued and such organizations as the Black Panthers, the radical Students for a Democratic Society, and the Black Muslims surfaced in communities around the country—including Tulsa—a special unit was formed that consisted of two squads of one sergeant and five men each. The TAC squad, supervised by a lieutenant, was a multipurpose unit of specialists that were cross-trained in such fields as rifle, pistol, and shotgun marksmanship, surveillance, working undercover, handling high-risk arrests, and a catchall list of tasks that included bomb disposal and riot control. Each squad consisted of a team leader, three officers armed with either submachine guns or shotguns, and a sniper/observer team. During their period of service they established themselves as the final word in police action. Before they were disbanded in 1973, only two years after their inception, they had participated in numerous arrests, armed and barricaded assailant calls, shootouts, and even a major prison riot.[1] But as so often happens to a good idea—and elite organizations—politics intervened and the unit was deactivated, its members sent back to field assignments.

---

[1] On a hot July day in 1973, the Oklahoma State Prison at McAlester came under siege by hard-core prison inmates. Fifteen guards were taken hostage, the majority of the prison was seized by the inmates, and the Highway Patrol Tactical Team was summoned. The Tulsa TAC squad was called in to relieve the OHP team at midnight of the day of the riot. By 0715 the next morning, after the sun had risen to illuminate the line of Tulsa TAC squad officers clad in riot gear, the inmates released the hostages and surrendered. They had already heard of the Tulsa team's legendary reputation—and the orders issued by the warden for the squad to assault the inmates' fortifications to rescue the hostages at 0730, and kill every inmate who offered resistance.

It wasn't until 1979 that a replacement organization was formed. Established for many of the same purposes and much along the same lines, the Special Operations Team came into being under a chief that believed in its existence and supported it much more than the previous administration. But because of manpower shortages within the department, SOT, like the majority of its SWAT team counterparts throughout the nation, became a part-time assignment. Each member kept his weapons and tactical equipment in his patrol car and responded as needed when the call to arms arose.

The mission of SOT also changed from that of the TAC squad days. No longer would they perform a hodgepodge of diverse tasks. Instead, they would specialize in missions that fell more into line with that of SWAT: armed and barricaded gunmen and hostage situations. They didn't stop there, but these two items became the mainstay of training since they comprised the majority of call-outs.

They were also better equipped. Old World War II Reising guns[2] and Thompson submachine guns were replaced with H&K MP-5s. Vietnam-era Model 70 Winchester sniper rifles were replaced by Steyr SSG .308 sniper rifles. A special equipment and command post van was added to the team's arsenal, and training was enhanced with more training days that included the use of the department's two turbine-powered McDonnell-Douglas MD-500 helicopters for aerial insertion capability. They now had personal body armor and ballistics shields, two items unavailable to the old TAC squad members. And instead of developing mission capability and training on the ground-breaking experimental basis of the early TAC squad, they subscribed to national standards of well-proven tactics and techniques. By 1982 Tulsa

---

[2]The Reising submachine gun was a .45 caliber weapon issued to the marines in WWII. Because of its full wooden stock, it resembled a carbine with a long magazine.

prided itself on having one of the finest teams in the country. And one of the most successful. For since its inception, the Tulsa SOT team has satisfactorily ended each hostage engagement without loss of life to a single hostage.

The same does not hold true for the gunmen they have come up against.

Kevin Young should not have been home on that hot fall day in 1991. He should have been safely locked away in the state mental hospital in Vinita, instead of being released to a halfway house in Tulsa. But he wasn't. The twenty-one-year-old had been diagnosed as a manic-depressive and had been undergoing treatment at the hospital when someone determined that it was safe for him to return to Tulsa to be near his family. They were wrong. Instead of reporting to the halfway house, Young showed up at his mother's home.

On the morning of September 11, 1991, after only one day at home, Kevin began causing problems. He was despondent, irrational, restless, and, as time wore on, increasingly combative. Even his mother became a target for his rage, and sometime during the early morning hours he attacked her with a walking stick. It rapidly became apparent that the family could not handle him, and by 10:30 A.M. they gave up and called the police.

The first car to arrive was E-201, Officer Bill Lee. Lee, an easygoing veteran officer, pulled up to the single-story ranch-style residence in an affluent part of south Tulsa only ten minutes after the call came in to dispatch. After stopping at the curb, Lee exited his black-and-white and carefully approached the front door. As he started to knock, Young's mother pulled into the driveway. Because of her son's threatening actions, she had left to call the police from a neighbor's house.

She quickly explained to Lee what her son had done during the morning, and that he was on leave from the state mental hospital, where he had been committed by the court.

She also told Lee that he had been released to Tulsa's Parkside mental health clinic, but instead had shown up at home. She went on to explain that he was not released with any medications, and that he was "worse since he got home than when he entered the hospital," and further, "worse today than he had ever been."

Lee entered the house in an attempt to talk to Young and judge for himself what condition the man was in. But as Lee began searching the house, Young, dressed in an olive drab shirt and black pants, ran out the back door, crawled over the back fence, and . . . disappeared. Lee, realizing that other officers would be needed to search for, and contain the suspect, returned to his black-and-white, called for backup, and put out a physical and clothing description. This done, he put the car in gear and began cruising slowly through the neighborhood searching for Young.

Officers Charles Ryan, F-264, and Mike Warrick, E-202, copied the description and joined in the hunt. As they drove independently toward the address of the call, Ryan spotted Young walking down the street southbound away from his mother's house. He followed him for a moment, then pulled up behind Young and attempted to stop him by calling out to him. But the man ignored Ryan as if he didn't exist and continued to walk away from the officer.

Ryan grabbed his microphone and summoned Lee and Warrick. It was obvious that more than words would have to be used to subdue the distraught young man. Ryan continued to follow in his car, transmitting updates on his position as he went, but before help could arrive Young doubled back behind some houses and disappeared. But not for long. He reappeared from between two houses, then, as Ryan again began trailing him, ran back toward his mother's house.

Bill Lee, just entering his patrol car to respond to Ryan's call for backup, spotted Young running toward him.

"Stop!" yelled Lee. "Stop right there, fella!"

The commands were futile. Young was beyond reasoning

with anyone, or respecting any kind of authority. Instead, in an act of defiance, he sprang up onto the trunk lid of Lee's car, ran up the back window, across the roof, then jumped down onto the hood. He then leaped to the pavement to make a dash on down the street to once again disappear. Lee stood there, incredulous.

The search resumed. Within minutes, Young was once again located by Warrick and Lee. This time the officers, though separated from Young by a chain link fence and a small open field, stayed abreast of him and attempted to calm him by talking as he walked. Young would have none of it. Instead, he worked his way back to the house and ran inside before any action could be taken. When he re-emerged, it was into the fenced backyard. In his hands he now grasped a driver-type golf club as if it were a weapon.

He walked to the fence in the direction of Lee, Warrick, and Ryan, who stood outside. Young climbed halfway up, leaned over the top, and challenged the officers. Brandishing the club menacingly, he yelled, "Come on, motherfuckers, come and get me. I'll kill you! I'll knock your goddamn head off!"

That said, he jumped over the fence and rushed directly toward Ryan and Lee, swinging the club as he came. The officers backed up to give him room. Though Young could severely injure—possibly kill—someone with the club, he had to be close enough to do it. By increasing the "critical distance" between themselves and Young, the officers reduced the threat sufficiently to buy time for more help to arrive. Hopefully there would be enough help to overpower the suspect in the shortest time possible without an extended fight, or the possibility of injury to him or an officer. No need to rush things if Young didn't press the issue too far.

Young turned away and again began walking around the neighborhood, Lee and Warrick trailing in their cars and giving updates on his location over the radio as they waited for more officers to arrive. The neighborhood was void of pedestrian traffic—most people were at work—so there was no danger to innocent civilians. And as long as Young could not reach an officer with his club, there was no immediate threat to the officers. Unless the situation changed, it would only be a matter of time before Young could be overwhelmed.

For ten minutes, he wandered aimlessly, stopping occasionally to brandish the golf club menacingly toward his followers. At one point he halted, faced Warrick, and began walking toward him. Warrick, exiting his car, once again tried to talk him down.

"Come on, talk to us. Put the club down and we can work things out."

The words had no visible effect on Young. Instead of dropping the club, he began advancing on Warrick, swinging it viciously over his head. Warrick, refusing to give ground at this point, drew his service revolver. "Don't come any closer!" he commanded. "Drop the club! Now!"

"Fuck you!" screamed Young. "I'll knock your fucking head off!" But he did stop. The sight of the gun evidently triggered something in his confused mind, something that told him that he was entering the danger zone.

Lee and Warrick separated and continued to keep their distance. Neither felt that deadly force was needed against such a weapon of limited range, but at this point their job was to attempt to contain the suspect until help could arrive—and the sight of the pistol seemed to work.

Young, obviously realizing that to challenge the gun would be futile, turned away and again returned to his mother's house. He paused briefly on the front porch, glared defiantly at the officers, then walked inside and locked the door.

Mrs. Young, who had meanwhile taken advantage of her son's absence, had gone back into her home. When he returned she attempted to beat a hasty retreat out the back door. But Kevin stopped her. He was going to stay inside now, and so was she. Whether she wanted to or not.

By this time supervisors began arriving at the scene. Corporal Sam King established a command post; Lieutenants John Bowman and Steve Steele, the area commanders, rolled up and were quickly apprised of the situation, then in turn instructed the dispatcher to telephone the house and try to make contact with Young. Foremost on their minds was the safety of Mrs. Young. Experience had proven that people with mental problems had little regard or loyalty to anyone—including relatives.

The dispatcher called back with disturbing news: *Frank 50, I've made contact with the subject, but he won't let his mother talk on the telephone.*

"Frank fifty, ten-four."

Also be advised that while he was on the phone we could hear a woman screaming in the background.

"Ten-four." Bowman's fears seemed to be proving true. He evaluated what information they had and quickly came to a conclusion. He picked up his microphone. "Frank fifty."

Frank 50, go ahead.

"Frank fifty . . . call out SOT. We may have a hostage situation here."

10-4, Frank 50. We'll try to contact Lieutenant York.[3]

While Bowman made arrangements with dispatch for SOT, Lieutenant Steele organized an evacuation of the surrounding houses, then directed the additional officers that were arriving to establish a containment perimeter until the Special Operations Team could arrive.

As these things were transpiring, Young's mother managed to escape from the house through the back door.

---

[3]Lieutenant Burney York was the commander of the Special Operations Team.

Almost immediately she was spotted by an officer on the perimeter who quickly took her to the command post. Her escape was a fortunate turn of events, but what she had to report was not.

There were firearms in the house. Kevin Young had access to them all. And he wasn't going to surrender.

20

Master Police Officer Rick Phillips, Tulsa Police Department
September 11, 1991

It never seems to happen on duty. It's when you're off, when you really don't want to be disturbed, that your pager begins that incessant beeping. So it was on this hot September day. And for me, it usually means one thing.

I pressed the digital readout button and confirmed my reaction. The numbers on the narrow LCD window read 911, the call-out code for SOT. I called in on my police radio on frequency "K," the seldom used channel assigned to the team to report in to dispatch. The response was immediate.

Young 517, we've got a barricaded subject holding a hostage at 7005 East 89th Place. Subject is supposed to be mental.

"Young five-seventeen to dispatch, have we confirmed that the subject *is* armed yet?" I asked. There was a slight pause as the dispatcher tried to get more information. I could hear computer keys clacking in the background as she searched her terminal for more information that might have come in to the complaint takers.

Young 517, so far there's no reference to weapons.

"Young five-seventeen, ten-four. I'll be en route."

Young 517, it's 1136 hours.

As I drove toward the scene, bits and pieces of information came over the radio that began to build a picture of what had happened and what was going on. But it wasn't until I arrived at the CP, which had been established in a neighbor's house, that I got the main synopsis of the story and what my assignment would be.

"Rick, this guy is going to be unpredictable. He's got some mental problems and he's already caused quite a bit of trouble in the neighborhood this morning. Now he's locked himself in the house and won't come out. He'd kept his mother inside for a while, but she's out now. The bad news is that he has a variety of firearms inside that he has access to," explained Lieutenant York, our team commander.

That was the first reference I had that there might be guns involved. "Have we got the scene contained?" I asked.

"Pretty much. We're filling in the perimeter and relieving the patrol officers as our guys arrive. Where I need you is on the east side to cover the balcony on the second story. He's come out a couple of times there and made several threats. My main concern is that from up there he has the high ground and can command the whole area on that side of the house. Take Spitler with you and see if you can set up someplace where you can get a clear view of the balcony. Report in on the radio when you're set up and give us your ten-twenty."[1]

I pulled my SWAT equipment vest on, grabbed my gear bag and my rifle, a Steyr SSG Model 69 P-2, then linked up with my spotter, Officer Joel Spitler. Together, we cautiously made our way to our assigned area.

As we walked, I couldn't help but think about the irony of where all of this was taking place. This wasn't some low-class slum of seedy buildings and high crime rate. It was an expensive neighborhood in south-central Tulsa where the homes were in the $100,000 price range and above. Not

---

[1] 10-20 is the ten-code reference for "location."

exactly an area where one would expect a SWAT team to be needed. And to make it a bit more bizarre to me, it was also my patrol district. I had cruised this very street many times and not once thought I'd ever work a SOT mission here.

As we neared our assigned area, I could see that there were few, if any, good positions that afforded both cover and concealment. The only place I could find that offered a clear shot of the balcony was a hedge bush at the corner of the house across the street. It wouldn't stop a bullet, but at least the suspect wouldn't be able to see us to acquire us as a target. He had a much more advantageous position, and if he *did* see us, he could take a shot from inside the room and there was nothing solid to protect us. But because of the layout of the area, we had no alternative. I got into the prone position, extended my bipods, chambered a round, and began the waiting.

As I was settling in, Spitler reported in on the radio. I noted that he had some difficulty doing this, as this particular part of town is hilly which creates "dead spots" the radio repeater tower can't reach. This could prove problematic if the situation came to a head and demanded rapid communications with split-second timing. This would be particularly critical if the command post gave a green light and none of the sniper teams heard the message. If that happened, it would be up to the individual snipers to determine that circumstances demanded a shot. I hoped it wouldn't come to that. But if the suspect threatened another officer with deadly force, I knew what I would have to do, green light or not.

I looked at my watch. 12:30 P.M. Fifty-eight minutes had passed since the original call-up. By now all of the field patrol officers had been relieved by the containment team, the negotiation team had arrived and was attempting to contact the suspect, and three sniper teams had been deployed and were in position. Not bad.

I thought about the other snipers. Any one of us might be the one that had to end the situation. Sniper Team 1, Chris

Claramunt, working solo, covered the south side of the house from approximately two-hundred meters away; Sniper Team 2, Kenny Vaughn and his partner, Joey Bayles, watched the back of the residence from a second-story window of a house on the next street behind the suspect's house; and I, from my position, covered the front yard, balcony, and porch area. And I was the closest. I estimated the range at approximately seventy to seventy-five yards.

Things remained fairly quiet for the next twenty minutes, but then, at 12:50, the negotiators were finally able to make contact with the suspect, Kevin Young. For the next hour, various exchanges between Young and the negotiators transpired. On the first call, he stated that "Mom wants to take me to Ireland, and she's trying to push Nancy off on me." None of this made sense to the negotiators, but they played along, buying time. The call lasted sixty-nine minutes, and during that time, Young made statements such as, "This conversation is going nowhere," and when asked to come out and give up, screamed, "No! No! I said 'no' five fucking times!" At 1:59 P.M. he hung up.

It was time to begin the next phase of operations. We had to begin subtle actions that would make staying in the house more difficult while at the same time make Young feel more isolated. Eight minutes after Young hung up the telephone, two of our SOT members crept up to the house and succeeded in pulling the circuit breakers to the air-conditioning system. The temperature outside was over eighty degrees, and on such a cloudless day, the temperature inside the house would build rapidly. Especially in the stifling humidity of Oklahoma. At the same time, the telephone company rendered the phone useless for making outgoing calls. Young could then only talk to the command post, and those calls could only be initiated by the negotiators. Twenty minutes later contact was reestablished and Young, perhaps feeling the discomfort of no air-conditioning and the isolation, stated that he would come out.

I breathed a sigh of relief. If Young came out and

surrendered, it would be one of the shortest call-outs I had ever been involved in. I didn't know then how close this was to the truth timewise, but the ending would be much different.

The suspect did come out. But only for a few seconds. He paused outside long enough to scan the area, paying particular attention to one of our containment teams, Sergeant Dave Walker and Officer Joe Gho, who were behind the cover of a Subaru located north of my position in a driveway. Gho, seeing Young staring in his direction, immediately took the initiative.

"Put your hands up! Do it! Come on! Put your hands up, now!"

Instead of doing as told, Young turned and ran back in the house. Three minutes later the front door opened again. Young stuck his head out, and to one and all, yelled, "Fuck you guys!" Then the door slammed shut.

"I don't think this guy wants to give up," I said to Spitler. "Seems to be content with dragging this out."

To be a police sniper, you have to have a very patient nature. You have no control over the chain of events that take place during an incident, and for the most part, you have to relegate yourself to sitting and watching, waiting for something to happen, then going home afterward without ever participating beyond reporting what you see to the command post.

But occasionally, even when you're in a position of cover and concealment and the suspect has no idea you are there, things turn to shit. Things that directly affect you, as a sniper. Such an event transpired five months before during a call-out for another armed and barricaded assailant. It was a call I would never forget.

Mahlon "Butch" Bastion was a badass. He was wanted for a double homicide, and when the detectives went to his grandmother's apartment to question her as to his whereabouts, they spotted him standing behind some drapes with a 9mm automatic in his hand. Realizing that an armed confrontation at that time would put the elderly lady—who was confined to a wheelchair—in jeopardy, they decided to discretely withdraw from the apartment and call SOT. By the time we arrived, he had barricaded both himself and his grandmother inside and stubbornly refused to surrender. The apartment in question was located on the ground level of a two-story building in a middle-class neighborhood in south Tulsa.

Bastion was not going to give up, or be taken out without a fight. Within minutes of our arrival gunshots rang out. It was like he was establishing his turf by marking out the kill zones with bullets.

No one knows how many shots he eventually fired, but he didn't worry about conserving ammo. He shot from the windows in the front, the side, and the rear of the apartment, and from the front doorway on occasion just to break the pattern. The perimeter teams couldn't approach the apartment without drawing fire, and because of his positioning inside the building when he fired, and the fact that the drapes were closed, the snipers couldn't get a clear shot to reply in kind. To add an even greater obstacle to our dilemma, his grandmother refused to come out even if he let her. She was afraid that if she left him alone inside, we wouldn't hesitate to storm the apartment and kill him. This made it difficult on us, because if we did have to do an entry, the prospect of her being hit in a close-quarters exchange of gunfire was very real. Obviously that was something we did not want.

It became apparent as time wore on that it would probably take a sniper to end the confrontation. A sniper who fired one well-aimed shot. But first, Bastion would have to expose himself in a window or doorway. And he wasn't doing that. Instead, he worked the angles. He stayed well back from the openings and fired across the windows, through the curtains and drapes, instead of directly out to the front. It was like he was a well-trained soldier who knew how to fight in urban areas.

Drawing the front of the apartment as my area of responsibility, I selected a spot in an adjacent upstairs apartment that had a good down-angle view of the front of his place. From my window, I could see both his front door and all of the windows on my side. Feeling confident that this was the best location, I settled in for what might be a long wait. I placed my walkie-talkie on a coffee table, set the Steyr up on its bipods, then laid my Benelli shotgun to one side. This done, I assumed a comfortable position, reported in to the CP, and began my observations.

It was one of the better locations I had drawn as a sniper. I was inside, comfortable, and relatively safe. Or so I thought.

As soon as I was set up, a scout team consisting of Corporal Mark McCrory and Sergeants Jim Clark and Rob Cartner tried to see how close they could get to the apartment, and if possible, use a pole hook to pull the drapes down. Using a large black ballistics shield as cover, they left the safety of a nearby apartment and began crawling along the wall toward Bastion's apartment. Just as they reached one of his windows and hooked the curtains, Bastion spotted them. He immediately opened fire. Several of his rounds struck the shield, and Clark, Cartner, and McCrory, forced back under a hail of bullets, made a rapid withdrawal.

Eventually we managed to get rid of the drapes on the windows by blowing them away with "Kinetic Batons"[2] fired by an Arwin. But even then I couldn't see anything inside. Because we had cut off the electricity, the interior of

---

[2]A Kinetic Baton is a large plastic slug that is shot from a large-bore weapon. It can knock a suspect down without causing permanent damage. In this case, an "Arwin" gun was used, which resembles a grenade launcher.

the apartment was pitch-dark. Bastion used this to his advantage by staying well back from the windows, making it almost impossible to locate him with my scope.

As I tried desperately to make out something—anything—in the shadows, Bastion opened up again with another volley of shots. Though I couldn't spot the muzzle blasts, I could see where the rounds hit. It was the first break I had. By triangulating, I formed a mental picture of where the shooter was. I suspected he was down the hallway of his apartment, firing across the living room, through the window, to the kill zone beyond. I decided to "work the angle" by inching my body slowly sideways, keeping my eye to the scope as I searched for a target through one of his windows. About every couple of inches I would stop and study what was in my field of view. If nothing happened, I moved again. And again. All I needed were some muzzle flashes, and with all of the shooting coming from the apartment I should at least be able to spot some sparkling somewhere inside that would give him away.

As I slowly moved sideways, keeping a door facing between myself and the open window as cover, I heard a sharp *crack!* At that instant I caught a sudden brightness in my peripheral vision. I took my eye from the rifle just in time to see an aerosol spray can of lacquer, which had been on a nearby table, spinning around and spitting flames. A tracer bullet, fired at random by Bastion, had come in through the window and punctured the can, igniting the flammable liquid inside. As it flipped through the air it spit streams of flaming liquid in an arc across the apartment. Before I could react, the can landed next to me and sent a blast of fire across my body, covering both of my hands and the Steyr in burning liquid.

I rolled away from the edge of the doorway and beat the flames out on my hands. Then I crawled to my rifle, grabbed it, and rolled it across the carpet to extinguish the burning lacquer.

But the hissing can had started other, larger fires around the room and smoke began filling the apartment. There was nothing I could do to put the fire out except radio the command post and request the fire department. Even if I had a means of fighting the blaze, my hands were by now in extreme pain from the burns I had received and I found it extremely difficult to grip anything. I managed to call the CP and tell them my position was on fire and that I was going to have to evacuate, but there was little else I could do except to try and get out before I was cut off from the rear window—my only means of escape. By this time the drapes had become fully involved and flames were licking up the wall. I had to get out of there. I painfully grabbed my gear bag and rifle and started to beat a hasty retreat to the window, but noticed as I turned that my extra box of .308 ammunition was on the table—and on fire. I debated trying to put it out and to attempt to salvage the rounds, but the fire in the room was spreading too rapidly. I abandoned the thought and turned to crawl toward the window.

But before I could reach it the rounds began cooking off. It sounded like a firefight had broken out in the room with me. I wasn't sure how much velocity exploding bullets might have since they weren't being propelled by expanding gasses in a barrel, but the fact that they were going off was frightening.

I managed to make the window just in time to be met by some of my team members who had come up the ladder I had used to gain entry to the apartment. Seeing my condition, they immediately grabbed my gear and helped me out the window and down the ladder. By the time my feet hit the ground the entire living room was engulfed in flames.

Our SWAT medics examined my burns and because of the seriousness, decided that I needed to be evacuated to the nearest emergency room for treatment. They began dressing my hands prior to being transported, and as they did I noticed a strange sickening smell. It was then that I found that my hair had also been scorched by the fire. Because I had my head down on the scope when the paint can was hit, my face had been saved.

The fire department responded, but because two sides of the building were in the kill zone, could not position their equipment to attack the blazing building effectively. They found it difficult to even contain the blaze to the one apartment. In an attempt to help out by working within the kill zone, Clark, McCrory, and Cartner once again ventured out. They were the only men available that might be able to get another fire hose into action. McCrory kicked out a slat in a fence and brought the hose through, but one hose just wasn't enough. The flames were horrendous by this time, swirling in a vortex in the alley over Cartner to the point that Clark had to pull him out under the cover of a ballistics shield. Without being able to contain the blaze effectively, it didn't take long for the apartment to burn to the ground.

While the fire burned furiously I was taken to the hospital ER where my burns were judged to be second-degree, and were treated accordingly. As soon as the doctor had finished wrapping me up, I returned to the scene. I couldn't stand being away from my guys when shit was hitting the fan. And I was mad. I wanted that bastard taken out. Though I couldn't hold a rifle, or even a pistol now, maybe one of our other snipers could get a shot and blow Bastion away.

When I arrived back at the scene I found that nothing remained of the apartment building I had been in but smoking rubble. Because the fire department could not surround the building the fire had broken out of the apartment I had been in and had progressed through each apartment, reducing the complex to ashes.

Since I could no longer participate in the action, I relegated myself to hanging around the command post. At least there I could keep up with what was going on around the perimeter and stay abreast of the action. I arrived there just in time to witness a bizarre and somewhat humorous series of events.

One of our deputy chiefs decided to try something innovative. With negotiations at a standstill, and Bastion still cranking shots out the windows at random, he decided to send our department's bomb robot into the apartment to scout around. His intention was to try and locate Bastion, and to ascertain the condition of the grandmother. With all of the shooting going on, we feared that Bastion might have killed her.

The team leaders disagreed with this tactic. They felt that the robot would be of little value, and worse, be damaged or destroyed by the gunman. But the deputy chief was adamant. He would send the robot in, and with the aid of its TV camera, check the place out.

But first we had to figure out how to open the front door. The robot, with its tank-tread-type tracks, could climb up the stairs and cross the porch—all under remote control of its operator who guided it with control handles, navigating by TV monitor. But it couldn't open doors. Then someone thought about the fire department. Maybe a stream of high-pressure water would knock the door open. It was worth a try.

One of our officers located a district chief and explained our plan. He made a call on his walkie-talkie, and a couple of minutes later a large snorkel truck that had responded to the apartment fire drove up.

"Can you blast the front door open with that thing?" asked our officer of the fireman on the truck.

"Son, I can cut the whole goddamned building in half with this baby. Just let me know what to do and I'll crank up the pressure."

"Just get the door open and that'll be enough for now."

Within minutes the truck was in position and the snorkel was extended. The fireman, perched behind the controls at the top of the gantry, rotated the long arm of the snorkel toward the apartment as the pressure built up. As it moved, the engine roared to a high crescendo, the needles on the pressure gauges rose to peak, and the lines stiffened in anticipation. Then, with a gigantic *whoosh,* a stream of water as straight as a pool cue blasted toward the door.

The door didn't just open, it almost exploded. It blew inward, taking the hinges with it as it disappeared from view. We were impressed.

Then it was time for the robot. Moving slowly, the white metal machine lurched its way forward looking like something out of the movie *Short Circuit.* Its head was a television camera, and on one side of its framelike body was a twelve-gauge shotgun that is normally used to open suspicious packages. It would probably be of little use in this situation due to its lack of rapid maneuverability and accuracy, but it was impressive nonetheless.

After negotiating the steps, it crossed the porch and entered the apartment. Once inside, it turned left into the darkness of the front room.

Then we heard the shot.

The officer working the controls, concentrating on the monitor, froze as the gunshot reverberated from the apartment and the monitor went white with snow. One second there was a dim picture of the interior of the apartment, the next nothing but static. Jim Clark later stated, "It looked like an ant fight." The operator's expression was one of "Aw shit."

"He's killed my robot! He's killed my goddamned robot!" Everyone looked at the deputy chief. "Well, at least we tried." He shrugged and that was that. Needless to say, the bomb squad guys were pissed.

After twenty-six hours of standoff, numerous applications of tear gas and flash-bangs, Bastion had had enough. But instead of giving up, he placed a pistol to his head and blew his brains out. When his body was examined later, we found that he was wearing a ballistic body armor vest previously stolen from a Tulsa police car. It might have helped him if someone came at him with a pistol, but had it come down to it, against my Federal .308 168 grain match bullets, it was worthless.

The mission, as a whole, was costly. An entire apartment building was destroyed; numerous bullet holes marked the surrounding buildings, trees, and vehicles; our expensive bomb robot was seriously damaged; and my Benelli shotgun was missing in action. But only temporarily. The fire department, after sifting through the burned rubble later, found it and gave it back to the SOT team. All that was left was the aluminum receiver melted around the steel bolt like the petals of a black flower.

In retrospect, the whole scenario was a disaster in the events that transpired. But we did our job as well as we could. Bastion's grandmother was safe, and other than our pride, there were no serious injuries to the good guys—except to the robot, who had bravely sallied forth without question to certain destruction.

This day would be different. I wasn't in a building that could catch fire, and if I had to leave my position in a hurry, it wouldn't be through a smoke-filled room. If we took fire from Young, Spitler and I could just abandon the hedge and withdraw between the houses to the backyard. Provided he didn't hit one of us first. I shifted my body position to relieve the tautness in my muscles that were growing sore from being too long immobile, readjusted my scope to my eye, and continued to concentrate on the house.

At 2:28 P.M., Young slipped out of the rear door of the house into the backyard—clutching a weapon. Kenny Vaughn came on the radio.

Sniper two, I have a visual on the suspect. He's armed with a long gun. Clothing is a black jacket and black pants. He's now looking around the backyard as if he's searching for targets!

Damn! This wasn't going to be as easy as I thought. If this guy started shooting, Vaughn would have to take him out. If he decided to climb the fence, the containment team would have to deal with him. And if he came around the end of the house, he would either come into my field of view or into

Claramunt's. It appeared like the whole issue was about to come to a head. I tensed and waited.

Sniper two, he's going back inside.

Young reentered the house, but as he did I heard the crack of a large-bore weapon echo from somewhere out back.

Sniper two, he's just fired a shot!

Command post to all officers, is anyone hit?

The replies came back in turn. Negative.

"That sounded like a shotgun," I said to Spitler. "I wonder if he's shot himself."

"I don't know. If he's as mental as they say, he just might have."

We continued to wait and watch.

A few minutes later the front door opened. I couldn't see it from where I was, but I heard it and could identify the sound. That's how close I was. Then I saw him. For a fleeting instant I saw part of his clothing at the corner of the garage. But that was all. Then I heard Gho, from his position behind the Subaru to my right, yell, "Put your hands up!"

There was no mistake in his response: "Go fuck yourselves!" He then retreated into the house.

A few minutes went by and the front door opened again. This time, a large black Labrador retriever bolted from the house and ambled out across the yard in my direction. I returned my attention to the porch, and at that moment saw something black behind some foliage. It moved.

I squinted through the scope. Behind a large square stone pillar I could see what appeared to be the edge of a person—and the barrel of a long gun. I couldn't tell exactly what type of weapon it was, but it appeared at first to be a shotgun. I was wrong.

As I watched, I saw the barrel move slightly, triangulating toward the containment team of Walker and Gho. Young had obviously used his first foray from the house to check out their position, and now he had returned ready to do damage.

I fixed my crosshairs right on the barrel of his weapon. It was all I could get at the moment. I felt that if he moved forward, I would be leveled and ready. Then I noted that his barrel looked just like mine. It was a rifle. A high-powered rifle. Walker and Gho would not be safe behind that little car—or anywhere else with the cover that they had available.

I watched the barrel move. It was as if Young were looking for a target. For four minutes he remained in place, searching, seeking, patient. Then the barrel retracted back out of my sight.

I felt that he would either go back into the house, or come out on my side of the pillar to get another position. But instead, the rifle barrel again came out on the opposite side of the pillar, this time moving more briskly as it swung around. It then began to move forward. As it did, I saw the scope. By the size of the gun, I could tell that it was definitely a large bore hunting rifle. Such a weapon could penetrate clean through the Subaru. The officers on the other side would not stand a chance against such a weapon.

Though it happened in milliseconds, my mind took in what my eye was seeing as if it were in slow motion. The rifle kept extending beyond the pillar until I could see his left hand on the fore end, then his right hand around the comb of the stock and his finger on the trigger. Then I saw his face. He had a look of cold determination. It was a look that was unmistakable. This was not a guy who was coming out to give up.

Finally his body appeared. He began to walk. Slowly at first, then increasing his pace as he crouched into a very defensive position quite similar to someone in combat who is walking point.

He was stalking prey. And I knew who his prey would be.

I no longer felt the heat. I no longer felt the discomfort of remaining in the prone position for so long. I only felt apprehension. The gunman was in *my* area of responsibility, and I was the only one who could effectively do anything to stop him from killing one or more of our officers. He had the advantage in range over Walker and Gho, and now the arrest team led by Sergeant Jim Clark who had moved up into close proximity. Their MP-5s and shotguns simply didn't have the range to be effective against Young's rifle.

Young held the rifle to his shoulder as he moved. All he had to do was acquire a target and pull the trigger. It was as if he'd gone to the same schools we had. Tactically, he appeared to move as if he'd been trained by professionals.

My mind computed what had happened in the past few minutes. He had scouted out Walker and Gho the first time he came out the front door, he had already fired one shot in the backyard, he had come out the front armed, and now he was stalking across the yard with the rifle at the ready.

Someone had already reported the latest turn of events to the command post. As I centered my crosshairs on the suspect's head, one inch in front of his ear in the no-reflex zone, Burney York's voice burst from my radio.

Command post to all sniper teams. You have the green light. I repeat, you have the green light.

I squeezed the trigger. I'm not sure if hearing the command had any bearing on my decision. I had already determined that at least one officer's life was in danger. That was all the justification I needed. But Burney's words cinched it.

It was the damndest thing I ever saw. Young's head virtually exploded, but instead of the cloud of pink that erupts from the exit wound, his entire brain came out of the *top* of his head *intact!* His entire brain! It just spiraled straight up into the air, hovered for an instant, then fell back to the ground next to his crumpled body. It was incredible.[3]

---

[3]The medical examiner later called Phillips and stated that he could not find an entrance wound. He asked Phillips where he had placed the shot. Phillips replied, "In the temple, just in front of the

I couldn't see him after he dropped below some vegetation that obstructed my lower view. I was sure that he was dead, but not wanting to take any chances, I immediately bolted in another round and stood up where I could see. By using the corner of the house as a rest, I reacquired his still form with my scope and prepared for another shot. But it appeared obvious that no further action would be required on my part. He wasn't moving.

I continued to survey the scene with the scope as the arrest team closed in. With them went one of our SOT medics.

I couldn't hear what was said from where I was at. But I found out later that one of our arrest team guys approached the body, then in the warped sense of humor that often follows the release of tension inherent with a traumatic incident, pointed at the lawn and said in parody of an often seen antidrug commercial: "This is your brain. This is your brain on grass. Any questions?"

The medic examined Young, then turned toward me and drew his hand across his throat. It was the signal that he was 10-7, or "out of service."

I had no desire to get any closer or to view the body. I'd seen enough from where I was at. I didn't even look at the photographs later. The memory of the incident alone was enough.

Sergeant Clark and my team leader, Sergeant Bob Cotton, came up to me. "You all right?" asked Jim.

---

ear." The surgeon said that he could not find any point where there was a mark where the bullet entered. But after detailed study after dissection, he found that the bullet had entered directly into the ear canal, severing the brain stem, which permitted the brain to be driven by hydrostatic pressure out of the skull cavity. Phillips's shot had struck one inch from his aim point, fired from a distance of seventy-five yards. This difference might be attributed to Young's movement forward at the time of the shot.

"Yeah."

"Okay. Remember that this is a crime scene and we have to protect the evidence."

"I'll take care of it," I replied. As Clark returned to the front yard where the body rested, I unloaded the Steyr, removed the next live round from the chamber, and put it in my pocket. I removed the magazine and laid the rifle down, bolt open. It was now time to go through the drill with the homicide investigators. I hated that part. It was almost like you were a criminal. There's nothing worse on a cop than being read the Miranda Warning before making a statement. There's something chilling about the part where it goes: "You have the right to remain silent, and anything that you say may be held against you in a court of law." And when that's followed by, "You have the right to an attorney and to have him present during questioning," you think, *Christ. Do I need a lawyer now?* Hearing these words gives a police officer a definite sinking feeling. It's like that's what we're supposed to say to the bad guys, not what we're supposed to hear from our own.

Then I had to go to the Deadly Force Review Committee. This added further irony to the situation as I am normally a member of the committee. This time I sat on the opposite side of the table and went through all the questioning on the receiving end. But the bottom line was that the shooting was justified and the committee determined that I had adhered to our very strict departmental policy on the use of deadly force. After the mandatory three days off they give you to get your thoughts together I returned to duty.

I've driven down that street several times since then. Each time, the events of that day flash through my mind. I'll always wish that there had been another solution to that problem, but I didn't make that final decision, he did. And the thing I'll always remember are the two guys on the containment team that ran over after it was over and gave me a big bear hug and thanked me for saving their lives.

That's what I dwell on and I think that this show of emotion really helped me through it.

I don't relive the incident in a negative sense. Life goes on, and I never know when I might be called again to take a shot.

But when I am, I'll be ready.

21

A Rough Town to Work In

It's been called the "Murder Capital of the Country." That may not be a fair, or accurate statement, but Houston, Texas, certainly ranks high in the various homicide-per-capita studies that have been done in the past ten years. And for good reason. Houston, according to the police officers who work there, is one tough town.

"We've always had a lot of crime here," explained one Houston police sergeant. "It's a blue-collar town, and unlike some of the other, more cosmopolitan Texas cities that have a lot of high-tech industry with a large population of middle- and upper-class people, Houston has more of what you would call working class individuals that have migrated in to search for jobs. We therefore have more of the basic inner-city type street crimes and altercations that end up in gun or knife play. Because of our geographic location we get a lot of transients, many of whom are illegal immigrants that have come up from Mexico, that bring a different set of values and their own version of criminal activities with them. And to make matters worse, we've become the dumping ground for the Texas prison system. Busloads of criminals are brought in from Huntsville Prison on an almost daily basis and just put out on the streets here. It makes for a crime rate that far exceeds that of any other city our size."

Also influencing Houston's crime rate is its proximity to the Gulf of Mexico. Galveston Bay, a huge inlet that extends thirty miles from the eastern borders of the city to Galveston, permits water traffic an almost unlimited access to over forty miles of sheltered interior coastline on the Houston side of the bay alone. From Galveston, running northeast to southwest along the Gulf Coast, are hundreds of miles of remote beaches, inlets, and islets, in many cases isolated from civilization by marshlands, that permit clandestine landings by smugglers that are essentially undetectable. Small boats often travel north from Mexico bringing in loads of marijuana, heroin, and cocaine. Supplementing these beach landing sites are the numerous small airports that dot the coastline for a hundred miles in either direction. It is more than the limited resources of the Coast Guard, U.S. Customs, the Border Patrol, and the DEA can handle. A great deal of the illegal cargo brought in by plane and boat finds its way to the streets of Houston, contraband that by its very nature swells the number of violent crimes in this Texas city over that of other, more stable American municipalities.

To handle the inordinate number of crimes-in-progress involving deadly force[1], the Houston Police Department, unlike most cities, has a full-time SWAT team. Instead of officers who serve in other functions, such as patrol or detective, and respond to tactical situations in an on-call capacity, Houston SWAT keeps a team ready to roll at all times.

First established as a small experimental unit in 1975, Houston SWAT has grown into one of the most professional, well-trained, and equipped teams in the world. Each officer

---

[1] As an example, in the two-year period leading up to the incident related in the following chapter, three Houston police officers were killed in the line of duty and a further thirteen were wounded. Houston police, during the same time frame, killed twenty-three suspects and wounded forty-four others.

undergoes a rigorous and varying daily training schedule involving physical training, tactical deployment, weapons proficiency, rappeling from both buildings and helicopters, surveillance, and other tactical subjects. Any time not dedicated to training is consumed with equipment maintenance, and serving high-risk warrants. The sniper team schedules at least one day on the range every week, assuring both a high skill level and a constant check on the accuracy of their weapons.

Equipped with the latest in hi-tech equipment—most of which was provided by local citizens groups—Houston SWAT is capable of handling virtually any type of violent activity call that might occur. A motor-home-size equipment van/command post vehicle contains every possible item necessary to run any type of SWAT operation. The aft section of this huge vehicle is a self-contained command post filled with computer systems, map panels, radios, and monitoring systems. The forward section is the equipment storage area consisting of metal lockers neatly housing miscellaneous items of equipment that range from basic rappeling gear to sophisticated surveillance devices. The van itself is completely self-contained, having its own generator, air-conditioning, and heating systems.

For a base of operations, Houston SWAT shares a large, unmarked building with two other specialist units: the Bomb Squad and the Hostage Negotiation Team. Resembling more a fire station than a police station in appearance, this modern complex contains drive-in bays large enough to house the SWAT van, the Bomb Squad vehicles, and a workout area complete with weights and exercise machines. Behind the vehicle bays are offices, a kitchen, a squad room, showers, and radio room. It is indeed an impressive facility.[2]

Most SWAT call-outs are handled in a fashion typical of

------

[2]For security reasons, the size of the Houston SWAT team cannot be published. Suffice it to say that they are capable of handling any situation that should occur.

that of the rest of the country. On scene, the normal response elements may consist of up to four assault teams and two or more sniper teams. Each assault team is positioned strategically to contain the inner perimeter, and may be called upon to "make entry" depending on the flow of events. Each of these officers is trained in all aspects of tactical operations, ranging from the use of gas and explosives to the rescuing of hostages in confined areas.

The sniper teams, armed with custom-modified Remington Model 700 .308 sniper rifles, remain in a constant state of readiness. Sergeant Rodney Hill, a ten-year member of SWAT and a sniper since the 1980s, elaborates: "We shoot every week. Because we devote so much time to training on a regular basis, we have a great degree of confidence in our skills and our equipment. Personally, this allows me to concentrate on one thing in my mind when I'm out on the scene of an operation: Am I right in taking this man's life? That's the only thing I have to worry about. Once I settle that in my mind, then my automatic reactions take over. I don't want to have to worry about whether or not I can hit the target, or whether my equipment is going to work. I only have to determine if I'm right when it comes time to take the shot. If we didn't have excellent training and confidence in our equipment and our abilities, there'd just be too much to think about that might confuse the issue and delay what must be done when seconds count. In this job, hesitation at the wrong moment can cost an innocent life. We can't have that. When it comes time to take the shot, the shot must be taken. Your mind must be on the job at hand, not worrying about other things. That's why we spend so much time training and working with our weapons and equipment. In this job, there is no room for error.

"When it comes time to take the shot, we operate on a very personal basis. No one orders you to take a shot here. They can give you permission, but that's all. After that it's up to you. And if time allows, they usually try to come over and tell you in person that you have permission to fire. If not, they do it over the air. And here we don't use a code system. We talk in plain language. It's like 'We've called the DA's office and we're cleared to take action. The next time you see the suspect you've got authorization to shoot him.' That's it. Plain and simple.

"In other cases, we have to make up our own minds if we need to take a shot when there's no time to get clearance. By Texas law, we can use deadly force whenever our own lives, or the life of someone else, is in danger. Then it's up to you. You have to determine in your own mind and heart that it's the best thing to do. And you better be right. Every shooting goes before a grand jury for deliberation. You have to be ready to answer for your actions. You really have to make sure that you're right in what you do."

In Houston SWAT's seventeen-year history, they have proven themselves "right" on every incident. And there have been several. But in the eight years leading up to the following story, there were only two fatal shootings by SWAT team members. That changed dramatically on April 28, 1983. For on that rainy Thursday night, two armed suspects, in two separate incidents, fell from bullets fired by the Houston SWAT team.

22

Officer Rodney Hill, Houston Police Department
April 28, 1983

When the phone rings at my house late at night, it means one thing. Work. At the time of this incident I was the only Houston SWAT sniper that lived within the city limits, and being a full-time SWAT team member, I know what the call concerns before I even pick up the phone. With all of the other snipers living outside the city, it doesn't take a rocket scientist to figure out who gets called first when things go down and SWAT is called out in the middle of the night.

Even when I'm sound asleep, I've conditioned myself to become instantly alert when the telephone rings. I have to be. In the few seconds that I have my team leader, who is responsible for notifying his officers, on the line, I have to be mentally prepared to accurately write down the address of the call and any details he might be able to provide. There's no time to waste in trying to wake up and ask questions. I have to be able to get it all the first time, then quickly dress and rush out the door. It's not like a nine-to-five job where you can have a cup of coffee, take a hot shower to wake up, then casually drive to work. It's more like the fire department, where when the alarm bell rings, you just jump out of bed, pull your boots on, and go. If for some reason someone

225

has dialed my number by mistake, I find myself up and full of adrenaline from the instant anticipation that brought me to full consciousness. I hate it when that happens.

On this night I found it doubly difficult to pull myself out of a sound sleep when the phone rang. I had already worked one call-out earlier in the evening, and had come home afterward physically and emotionally drained. Now, just a few hours later, the phone was ringing again.

I looked at the clock. 4:00 A.M. I thought, *Great. This is all I need right now.* I picked up the receiver and forced myself awake.

"Rodney, we've got a call-up. There's a guy with a gun who has beaten a woman half to death, and now he's holding her and some kids hostage. They've got the scene cordoned off, but that's all they can do until we get there. It's in the 6900 block of Ashburn."

I wrote down the address and hung up. Five minutes later I was dressed and on my way to the scene, a quiet and sleepy affluent section of Houston north of Hobby Airport.

As I drove I listened to the citywide channel on my police radio. The voices of the patrol officers at the scene were tense, describing things that gave me clues to the seriousness of the situation. One particular statement really caught my attention: "I can see blood in there." That sent chills up my spine. I could envision the worst, especially since I'd been informed that the suspect was holding kids as hostages. Had he already done something to them? I pressed the gas pedal down.

As I wove through light early morning traffic I thought about my earlier call. On the preceding morning some psycho had gone off the deep end and had started shooting up the neighborhood around a town house apartment complex on High Star Drive on the west side of Houston. Someone had complained to him about loud music coming from his place, and an altercation ensued. His solution was to get a handgun, go outside, and fire several shots into the neighboring town homes. Then he went back inside his place and locked the door.

It was 4:30 A.M. when we received the call, "Discharging firearms, barricaded suspect." Not much to go on, but still, it pretty much says it all. It was enough for us.

By 5:00 A.M. we were on the scene, a semirural part of west Houston that was still under development. Many of the sections that had been built up were next to open fields that had not yet been developed. And as it turned out, one large field bordered the back of the suspect's apartment.

When I arrived at this particular scene, I braked to a stop on a north-south street near two patrol cars that guarded the northwest corner of the perimeter. To the southeast, across the field, was the town home complex. The building, which contained five homes in a linear block-type structure, ran at a ninety-degree angle, extending left from my position. I estimated the range at between sixty-five and seventy yards. Behind the two patrol cars several officers milled about, keeping their units between themselves and the suspect. It was a good thing, because as soon as I got out and started getting my gear out of the trunk, the suspect came outside and began cranking shots off at random. Some of the bullets whizzed dangerously overhead, forcing the officers to take cover.

I had a clear view from where I was and could see in the available light that he appeared to be armed with a chrome or nickel-plated revolver, which to me resembled a Smith & Wesson .38. As it turned out later, I was right. That's how good I could see.

I immediately came on the air and told the command post that I had the suspect, and that he was moving around on our side of the building shooting a handgun. This concerned everyone, as the complex had not yet been evacuated. If he entered another town home, there was a good possibility that he would take hostages. We couldn't allow this. If he tried to get into a neighbor's house, I would have to tactically neutralize him.

As I watched, he walked to one corner of his backyard and looked around. Mentally, I picked two reference points that I would permit him to stay inside without engaging him. One was a light pole on one side, and the other was the back gate of his neighbor's apartment. As long as he stayed inside that area, I would hold my fire. But if he got out, I would have no choice.

"See that pole on the left and the gate to the right?" I asked the officers I was with, who were now leaning on their cars to get a better look at the suspect. "Those are his limits. If he gets out of there, we lose control of him. So this is the area I have to cover. If he gets out of it, I'm going to have to shoot him." It was a simple statement of fact. We just couldn't take a chance of him getting into another apartment and taking a hostage. It was the only way we had of stopping him.

I moved to the patrol car closest to the objective to set up. "You guys get off of the car so I can use it as a rest. I don't want anyone shaking the car while I'm trying to set up on this guy." The officers stood back as I worked the bolt of my Remington 700 to chamber a 158 grain soft nose and took up a rest on the trunk lid. Satisfied that I could make a shot from here, I locked the scope on the suspect. As I did, he began walking toward the corner of the fence—to the edge of my predetermined limit for his movement. Once he reached that point there was no way I could let him go any farther. I squeezed the slack out of the trigger and held my breath, following him with the crosshairs as he moved. But before he reached the limit, he stumbled and fell. I had noted that as he walked he was somewhat unsteady. I guessed that he was probably drunk, which might explain some of his bizarre behavior. I relaxed for a second to see what would happen next.

He got up almost immediately and resumed walking toward the edge of the fence. Again I prepared to shoot. I took a breath and began concentrating on the mechanics of the shot.

He walked right up to the edge of his "limit" and stopped, almost as if he knew exactly where it was. Then, instead of crossing the boundary to meet his fate, he turned, walked back to his yard, opened the gate, and went back inside his apartment.

By this time my adrenaline had really pumped me up and my pulse was racing a hundred miles an hour. I had psychologically braced myself twice within the last minute to kill this guy, and now I was hanging there on the edge of extreme mental acuteness, ready to shoot, and it all just stopped. It was as if my metabolism were on an emotional roller coaster, pushing me up to the point of terminal action, then dropping me down when I didn't have to pull the trigger.

I relaxed my grip on the rifle and began to breathe evenly, slowly, composing myself for the next time he came out. But for now, he was out of sight and there was nothing I could do but wait.

While all of this was happening on my side of the perimeter, other SWAT officers were still in the process of establishing positions at the front of the building. The sniper that was assigned to that side was geared up, but was still trying to work his way up to the roof of the building across from the suspect's apartment. Below him, one of our team leaders, armed with a CAR-15,[1] had positioned himself inside the apartment directly across from the suspect's front door. Only a narrow courtyard separated the two structures.

As I concentrated my attention on the suspect's back door, waiting for him to reappear, I heard gunfire erupt from the opposite side of the building. I could tell by the sound that it was the .38 pistol, and I knew that we had officers stationed at each end of the courtyard to keep him from escaping in that direction. Had he shot one of them? I

---

[1]A short-barreled version of the 5.56mm M-16 with a collapsible stock.

couldn't help thinking that I should have taken him out when I had the chance.

Then I heard another shot. One that sounded different. Then there was silence.

The suspect, instead of exiting the apartment on my side for another sojourn along the back fences, had gone out his front door into the courtyard. He stopped at the walkway, and spotting the officers that blocked the ends of the courtyard that led to the parking lot, opened fire on them. As they dove for cover, a sergeant who knew that there was a team leader not fifteen yards away from the shooter, keyed his radio and said, "Take him now!"

But there was a problem. The team leader had not been able to get the window at the front of the apartment open. It had been built with security in mind and was locked shut, with burglar bars covering the outside like a jail house door. The only choice he had would be to shoot through the window glass and take a chance that his light .223 bullet would not deflect to the point that it missed the target. He elected to take a shot by placing the muzzle of the CAR-15 right up to the window and, because of the close range, hope the glass would not greatly influence the trajectory of the bullet.

There was nothing else he could do. He had to at least try. Shoving the muzzle up to the glass, he lined up the form in the walkway and pulled the trigger.

The glass blew out in a spray of crystal shards, scattering pieces across the courtyard. The bullet, though not deflected, began to tumble as soon as it cleared the barrier. It struck the man in the side, tore through his torso, and destroyed his liver. He died on the spot.

It was over. But I felt like I was the one who had taken the shot. I had come so close to shooting him myself that I was emotionally and physically drained. I had spent so much time hanging on the edge of anticipation, mentally prepared to eliminate the threat, that when I came back down I felt like I had been in position, with my eye to the scope, for hours. But when it ended, and I finally looked at the time, I saw that we had been there just under an hour. The fatal shot was fired at 6:00 A.M.

After homicide, IAD, and the DA's investigators showed up and took over the scene, we all went downtown for debriefing. By the time we finished the critique, it was time to report for another day of duty. I felt like I hadn't slept all night.

I went for a run to try and relieve the stress of the night's activities, then after completing the rest of the day's schedule, went home to relax. After dinner I caught the news, and all they were talking about was the guy who had been shot by the Houston police out on High Star. According to the commentator, the suspects name was William Manuel Tryan, an unemployed sixty-one-year-old Columbian who had moved to the States in the mid-1960s. Though married, he was evidently separated and had been living alone.

I was exhausted when I went to bed. I felt like I'd really been put through the wringer in the past sixteen hours and was looking forward to a full night's sleep. Then, almost exactly twenty-four hours after the call-out, the phone rang again. When I answered it, I felt like I'd hardly had any sleep at all.

As I drove toward Ashburn, listening to the anxious voices of the patrol officers on the radio, my fatigue gave way to a reserve of energy. The closer I got to Ashburn, the more pumped up I became.

As I rolled up on the scene, I could see the area had been cordoned off. Police cars blocked streets and officers were denying entry to everyone who wasn't a police officer and didn't have an immediate reason to be inside the perimeter. Even the paramedics were held back because of all the shooting that had been going on.

I parked the car, grabbed my gear, and reported my arrival by radio to the CP. They acknowledged immediately and gave me my area of operations. I was to cover the frontal approaches to the house where the gunman was holed up from a house across the street. From what I had picked up on the radio and from officers at the scene, the house he was in was not his residence, but was his ex-wife's place. He had come over during the night and had gotten into a fight with her over custody of their two children. He had become enraged and had pistol-whipped her, then fired three shots at her—missing all three times. Her sister-in-law, who was also in the house at the time, managed to escape during the fracas to call the police.

While we were responding to the call, the assailant called the *Houston Chronicle* and stated that he had barricaded himself in the house and wanted to "tell his story" before he killed himself. He said that he also wanted to see a doctor from Methodist Hospital psychiatric ward who had treated him for mental problems in the past. He also called the doctor's office and left a message on his answering machine: "I'm at 6980 Ashburn at my ex-wife's place, and I'm sitting here with Katy with a gun in my hand." Katy was the two-year-old daughter.

As information filtered in, we established that the man's name was Michael Thomas George, and that he was a thirty-two-year-old unemployed plumber. He had driven over in his pickup truck, which was now parked in the driveway, and, according to a friend, had taken a gun "for protection." Now he was sitting inside with the two children, Katy and four-year-old Michael, Jr., and their badly beaten mother, Irma.

When I reached the house across the street, I found that all of the windows were barred and had been painted shut. No matter how much I tried, I couldn't budge them open to gain entry. My only other choice was to find a suitable spot in front of the house where I could get a good visual on the objective.

I found a carport at one side of the front of the house with a car parked inside. By using the bumper of the car as a rest for my rifle, I could scan the front yard of the suspect's house with my scope. Though the lots in this addition were quite large, approximately an acre each, and there were several trees in the yards, I had a fairly good view of the house. I reported in to the command post.

"Paddlefoot to CP. I'm in position across from the suspect's house." "Paddlefoot" is my nickname, which doubles as my code name for SWAT operations.

Okay, Paddlefoot. Can you see anything?

I looked at the house through my scope. "Paddlefoot to CP, the front door is open and the interior is lighted. I can see blood on the walls, and I can see the suspect. He's sitting on the sofa with the two kids—and he's got a pistol in his hand."

Understand he's got the kids and a gun. Anything else?

"Negative at this time. I'll keep you informed." I released the mike button and reevaluated my position. I wasn't totally happy with it. It was pitch-dark outside, limiting visibility in every area that wasn't directly illuminated by a light, and I didn't like the range factor. But to move meant that I had to have someplace to go. And there wasn't much to work with out there.

Then I had an idea. I picked up my radio. "Paddlefoot to CP, how about getting the armored van over here? If we parked it in the street I could get inside and have a better position, and if the suspect tries to leave, we can use it to block him."

We'll see what we can do, Paddlefoot.

Given enough time to bring the armored van in, I could decrease the range by fifty percent. If something happened before then, I'd just have to work with what I had. I would feel a lot better about the situation if the van could be brought in. But for now, I had to just wait and see what happened.

As I waited the dispatcher made contact with George and talked him into releasing his ex-wife to get medical attention. But he wouldn't let the kids go. Instead, after she came out to be met by SWAT officers who hustled her away, he came to the front door with both of the children and stood there yelling things like "Go ahead, blow me away!" to anyone in earshot. As he was doing this, I put the crosshairs on him and thought, *I've got a good clean shot right now. Should I do it? Should I take him out right now? If he kills one of the kids later, I'm going to have a really hard time living with that.* But as I watched, it appeared that he was not threatening the children yet. I decided to hold my fire and see what developed.

He went back inside, then a few minutes later, he came out with both kids and walked over to his truck with the attitude "Well, I'm done and I'm getting out of here." I followed him with the scope as they approached the truck, but I couldn't take a shot because he was moving and the children were right beside him. There was nothing I could do as he climbed into the cab with the kids and started the motor. But unknown to him, some of our SWAT officers had managed to get to the truck and had flattened the tires.

He put the truck in gear and started to back up, but it bogged down and quit. As I reported these latest actions to the command post, he exited the vehicle and took the kids back inside the house. Now it seemed he was saying, "Well, that didn't work. I'll have to do something else."

In just a few minutes he reappeared at the door with a child cradled in each arm. He looked around for a moment, then began walking across the yard toward an inner perimeter patrol car parked in the street between my spot and his front door. Crouched behind the police car, two SWAT officers gripped their M-16s in apprehension as he approached. Then through the scope I caught something else. In his right hand he held the pistol.

I keyed my mike button. "Paddlefoot to CP, he's coming out again. This time he's carrying both of the kids and he's got the gun in his hand. He's walking toward one of our patrol units."

Okay, Paddlefoot. Watch him. The suspect will NOT leave

our inner perimeter! This was the CP's way of telling me to shoot if I thought it necessary.

I kept him in my scope as he crossed the yard and walked out into the street. As he neared the car, the two officers became very nervous and tried to reason with him. One of the officers was keying his mike, and as George approached, he unknowingly held the transmit button down. I could hear them pleading through my headset. "Please, mister, put those babies down. Don't do this. *Please* put those babies down!"

But George didn't stop, and he refused to release the children. Instead, he started walking around the car toward the officers. It appeared to me that if he got close enough he intended to shoot them. The two SWAT officers, moving around the car to keep it between them and George, continued to beg him to drop the kids. Though they held their guns on him, they couldn't shoot for fear of hitting one of the children.

Finally, after circling the car twice, George stopped on my side of the car, his back to me. The two officers, still pleading with him to let the kids go, stood opposite him on the other side of the car. Though the range for me was now down to about forty yards, due to the darkness all I could see was his silhouette from the waist up and the head of each child over his shoulders.

I was now faced with a dilemma. If I had to take a shot, the two officers were crouched behind the car in my line of fire; the two kids' heads were within inches of his; and I couldn't tell exactly where their little bodies were on the other side of his torso. The only thing that I had in my favor was the excellent light-gathering capabilities of my 3.5x10 Leupold scope. Even though it was hard to hold the crosshairs on the target's head because of movement, at least I could make them out. Barely.

I decided to get as low as I could to get an up-angle shot. I didn't want to take a shot, then have one of the officers end up catching it if they decided to stand up to shoot him at the same time I fired. I also had to concentrate on trying to keep his head centered in the crosshairs. But I was finding this difficult to do. He was talking to the officers, saying things like "I'm not going to hurt you. Why are you running from me," and moving his head all of the time he's saying this stuff. I just couldn't take a chance on squeezing off a round, then having him move where one of the babies' heads entered the path of the bullet. Instead, I elected to drop the crosshairs down the center of his back, between the two kids, and set up for a heart shot through his spine. I estimated about where the body of each child would be, then split the difference. The darkness made the crosshairs barely visible, but there was enough there to judge where the center of impact would be with a fair degree of accuracy. It was less than an ideal situation and I didn't like it, but I had no other choice.

At that moment the man made his move. He bent over to drop the child that he held in his gun arm. I had to make a split-second decision right then. I couldn't take a chance on him coming back up and getting a round off at one of the officers. I had to neutralize him.

Because of the way he leaned over, I had to move the crosshairs over to the right about three inches to ensure missing both of the children at the point of exit. This final adjustment made, I held my breath, steadied my aim, and took up the slack on the trigger.

I squeezed off the shot.

He crumpled on the spot, releasing both children as he fell. Both officers ran around the car and gathered the kids up. I held my breath waiting to see if I had missed them. After a few seconds one of the officers came on the radio.

CP, the suspect is down. Both kids are okay.

I exhaled a great sigh of relief, then crawled to my feet. As paramedics rushed in to check on the suspect, I sat on the back of the car and waited for the investigators. A few minutes later some of my guys brought me a Coke. As I sat there drinking it, running the events over in my mind, I heard a helicopter approach. A couple of minutes later Life Flight landed and evacuated the body. Even though the paramedics did what they could, he died before the chopper could land.

I was off for the next three days and took the time to drive to Shreveport to visit my parents. When I returned, a stack of newspapers awaited me. I hadn't seen any of the news accounts since the incident and hadn't heard any of the press reactions over the past few days. When I opened one of the newspapers, a big picture of George, drinking water with one of his kids from a drinking fountain in a park, stared at me. Here was this nice looking guy, with this beautiful kid, enjoying a day in the park. It was like the perfect dad with the perfect family, and I had torn that apart. It was kind of rough dealing with that. But it would have been tougher to deal with the prospect of him shooting one of our officers if I hadn't taken action when I did.

After returning to work, I discovered that George had forced our hand on purpose. He was bent on committing suicide and used us to do it for him. When the first officers had rolled up to the scene, he had stood in the doorway of the house and demanded that they call SWAT. Even the newspapers printed in one article that he yelled, "I want SWAT. I just want SWAT!" This, coupled with a few other statements he made during the ordeal, including the one he made on the phone at 4:15 A.M. to the *Chronicle* when he said he wanted to talk to someone before he killed himself, pretty much summed up his intentions.

The grand jury deliberated the shooting and came back with a "no bill," which is a way of saying that I was cleared of any criminal wrongdoing. They didn't even call me in. They called all the witnesses and my sergeant in, but all they asked was "Who gave permission to shoot?" I sat out in the hall until the jury foreman came out and told me that I had been cleared and the case was closed. There were tears in his eyes as he gave me the final decision. He said that he never realized how hard it was to be a SWAT officer.

But even after the grand jury decision the incident wasn't finished. Not until over a year later. George's family filed a lawsuit against me through the Justice Department, and several months went by before I received word of the disposition of the case in the form of a letter. The context went something like: "Dear Fellow Law Enforcement Officer, we have decided not to indict you for shooting this guy. We consider it justified. If we can ever be of service . . . " That was it.

Finally it was over. All wrapped up nice and neat with a form letter. For the court system, the whole matter was filed away to become a forgotten part of history. But for me, even though I know that we had no choice in actions and that George dictated the turn of events, it was one night I will never forget.

23

Cop Stalker on the Potomac

It is said within the police tactical community that there are three schools of thought regarding the proper way to handle armed and barricaded gunmen and hostage situations: The West Coast doctrine; the East Coast doctrine; and the Mid-West meld.

The "West Coast doctrine," as we have seen, is one of predictable reaction. Though no "time limit" exists in handling a situation, the amount of time spent before deadly force might be used is often limited. It is felt that an incident, once contained, should be ended as soon as practically possible. If it appears that negotiations are breaking down or not progressing satisfactorily, and that danger to innocent people is increasing, there usually is little hesitation in giving the "go" signal to an entry team, or a "green light" to the snipers.

The "East Coast doctrine," for those cities that ascribe to it, is totally different. In this school of thought the weight of reaction to an incident is given to the negotiators. Time is no factor. It is felt that the police can always outwait the bad guys—no matter how long it takes. The problem with this tactic is that it can be dangerous. There always exists the possibility that waiting *too* long will put a hostage's life in jeopardy. Especially in cases where terrorists are involved.

New York City is perhaps the best example of the "East Coast doctrine." The NYPD teams, according to sources within and outside of the tactical community, "never shoot anyone. They just talk them to death." This persistence in negotiations is not totally accepted by the officers of the team itself. Most feel that they are restricted in action by higher echelon administrators and inflexible policies and procedures. One officer explained: "Hell, we don't shoot nobody. They won't let us. Even if they start shooting hostages we can't do anything but hope they quit. It's like if the bad guys are shooting the hostages, it's their fault. Not ours. We don't like it, but right now there's nothing we can do about it. It's bullshit."

The "Mid-West meld" is not a basic doctrine. Instead, the tactical teams use a flexible combination of West Coast and East Coast philosophies. If negotiation teams can do the job, fine. Even if it takes hours or days. If not, or if at any time a hostage is subject to danger, an escalating reaction that can instantly change to maximum deadly force is used.

Because basic doctrine in most cases is a reflection of past experiences, local sensibilities, and politics, there are always exceptions to the rule. Contrary to the generalizations above, some departments in the West may lean heavily on negotiators, while some Eastern organizations may not hesitate to use the marksman's bullet. This last held true in the case of the Arlington cop stalker.

Straddling the mouth of the Chesapeake Bay is perhaps the most historic of all the fifty states. Located almost exactly halfway between Florida and Maine is Virginia, the state known as "The Mother of Presidents" for the eight presidents born there. It is named for Queen Elizabeth I, the "Virgin Queen," of England, and can trace its history back to 1584 when Elizabeth gave Sir Walter Raleigh permission to colonize the region. In 1607 the first permanent English settlement in the New World, Jamestown, was established on the James River about forty miles southeast of what is now Richmond.

Virginia played a key part in the War of Independence. Not only were such notables as George Washington, Thomas Jefferson, "Light-Horse" Harry Lee, and Daniel Morgan from Virginia, but the colony provided the greatest number of soldiers per capita of any Southern colony for Washington's Continental Army. And it was in Virginia that Cornwallis surrendered, ending the war.

During the Civil War, Virginia was the center of the South's activities in what became known as "The War in the East."[1] From the Delmarva Peninsula, shared with Maryland and Delaware, to the jagged shoreline of Tidewater, to the Appalachian Mountains, bloody battles fought on Virginia soil burned their names into American history. From 1861 to 1865, the sound of bugles, the shouts of soldiers, and the roar of cannon fire echoed in such places as Chancellorsville, Fredericksburg, Spotsylvania, and Cold Harbor.

Though the first engagement between military forces occurred in South Carolina when Fort Sumter was bombarded, the first actual large scale land forces battle between the Union Army and the Confederacy occurred in northern Virginia. On Sunday morning, July 21, 1861, thirty-four thousand Federal troops under General Irvine McDowell engaged thirty-one thousand Confederates under General P.G.T. Beauregard near a town called Manassas, just twenty-five miles southwest of Washington, D.C.[2] McDow-

---

[1]The Appalachian Mountains, which form Virginia's western border, divided the Civil War into two geographic areas: the War in the East, and the War in the West.

[2]Civil War battles often have two names. The Confederates named them after the nearest settlement, while the Northerners usually named them after the nearest body of water. Therefore, the "Battle of Bull Run" is also known as the "Battle of Manassas."

ell, confident that his "regulars" could route the ragtag rebels in a few hours, quickly found that his poorly trained volunteers were not superior in any manner to the brigades of Southern volunteers.

McDowell, forming ranks on the west side of Bull Run Creek facing south, launched several assaults on the Rebel lines. But each was doomed to failure. The Rebels held firm. During one of these attacks one of Beauregard's generals, Thomas J. Jackson, received the nickname "Stonewall" for his resolute defense.

Finally Beauregard saw an opportunity to counterattack. In the ensuing melee the loose formations of Union volunteers broke ranks and ran for Washington in wild retreat. The North realized for the first time that it faced a long and determined fight.

On August 29-30, 1862, the Second Battle of Manassas (Bull Run) took place in the same vicinity. The results were similar, with Robert E. Lee routing Union general John Pope in a daring counterattack.

Since the end of the Civil War the northern Virginia region near Washington, D.C., has grown into a metropolitan area of vast proportions. Like spokes on a wheel, four major highways exit Washington into the Virginia countryside, linking Alexandria, Arlington, Annandale, Fairfax, Woodbridge, and Manassas to the nation's capital in a fashion that virtually makes them suburban residential areas.

It also makes the communities subject to not only the crime that plagues Washington, D.C., but that imported by transient criminals who use the "Route One Corridor," the highway that parallels Interstate 95. Because of I-95, the "Restless Ribbon" that runs along the eastern seaboard from Florida to Maine, the placid countryside of northern Virginia is no stranger to criminal activities that transit the motorway from Miami to New York City.

To handle the criminal elements, both homegrown and transient, there are two local levels of law enforcement. Each township has its own police department, and each county has a county police organization that not only patrols the county proper but can assist the townships when matters exceed the capabilities of the smaller departments. For this reason, many of the county police departments have a SWAT or emergency reaction team. There is also a county sheriff's department in each county, but its main function is serving court process and handling civil matters. Criminal law enforcement at the county level is the responsibility of the county police.

But on the night of November 21–22, 1990, in a multijurisdictional area of northern Virginia, a lone gunman suffering from delusions of persecution tragically involved both organizations in a bloody confrontation that would bring one department its first officer killed in the line of duty.

To Captain Daryl F. LaClair of the Arlington County Sheriff's Department, it looked like just another routine "motorist's assist." At least it appeared as such when the driver of the gold Buick Century pulled alongside his cruiser and motioned him over as he motored west on Route 29. It was 11:55 P.M., and LaClair was on his way home. Hopefully this would be the last official action he would have to take that night.

LaClair flipped on his emergency flashers and fell in behind the Buick. Almost immediately the car pulled over to the shoulder of the road and stopped. LaClair, still feeling that he was encountering a lost motorist or someone with car trouble, exited his cruiser and approached the Buick. But before he could completely close the distance the driver turned around in the seat, leaned out the driver's side window, and opened fire with a .25 caliber automatic pistol.

LaClair was struck three times. Two bullets hit both of his elbows, and a third round punched into his face next to his right eye. Even though partially blinded and seriously wounded in the arms, LaClair managed to drop to the ground, pull his pistol from its holster, and return fire. As the gunman's car sped away, LaClair's desperate fire shattered the rear window.

Unable to drive, LaClair called for help on his radio. At the same time, some college students who had been nearby when the shooting took place and had witnessed the event wrote down the license tag number of the assailant's car.

As LaClair was being transported to Arlington Hospital, a make was run on the Buick. It checked to a Michael Francis Arban of Dale City, a small community on Interstate 95 between Alexandria and Quantico. At about the same time it was discovered that whoever was driving the car had been spotted earlier in the evening in Alexandria, writing down the license tag numbers of police cars in the parking lot of a Denny's restaurant. It appeared that he had been stalking cops all evening.

Dale City was only twenty-two miles from Washington, but it was two counties—and two jurisdictions away. Tiny Arlington County is surrounded by Fairfax County, which gives way to Prince William County to the south at the snakelike boundary line formed by Bull Run Creek and the Occoquan Reservoir.

Prince William County Police, now alerted to look for Arban's car in Dale City, dispatched patrol units. Within minutes the car was found, backed into the driveway of his house at 14764 Dodson Drive. It was obvious to the officers driving by that whoever parked the car had made an effort to hide the rear window from view from the street. They would have to get closer to see if it had been damaged.

But even if it had, the officers had no way of knowing exactly who had driven the car when LaClair was shot. It could have been Arban, or he may simply have let someone else use his car. The only description they had received was that the gunman was a white male, approximately thirty years old, who had a thin mustache.

The patrol officers parked their car out of sight and crept up to the dark house. Easing their way around the car, they came to the back window. Or what was left of it. It appeared as if two bullets had shattered the glass, leaving a spiderweb of crystalline fragments suspended in clear plastic lamination. It was the right car.

Withdrawing silently from the driveway, the officers reported in. Almost immediately backup officers, who had been enroute for some time, began arriving and establishing a loose perimeter. No one wanted to wake up any of the residents and create a commotion until they knew exactly what they were dealing with, and they didn't want to alert the suspect until they were ready to move in on him.

But the information they had to work with was sketchy at best. The car matched perfectly, but the suspect description was vague. It was determined that the best way to proceed would be to get a search warrant and search the house and car for the gun used in the shooting of LaClair—keeping an eye out for someone with a thin mustache in the process.

And because the suspect had already shot one officer, it was decided to use SWAT to serve the warrant.

24

Corporal Ben Fravel, Prince William County Police

November 22, 1990

I hadn't been home very long when the call came. I had spent the evening at a Capitols' game and had barely got in bed when the phone rang. Fortunately, the only thing they sold in the way of alcohol at the game was beer and I'm not much of a beer drinker. I had stuck with soft drinks throughout the game and when I got the word about the call-out I was glad I did.

I immediately got dressed in my black SWAT uniform and drove to the Gar-Field substation in Woodbridge, fifteen miles east of my home in Manassas.

The briefing was short and sweet. We got the rundown on the shooting of the Arlington deputy, the suspect vehicle, and how it was now parked in the driveway of a house down in Dale City. It was pretty apparent that we had the right vehicle, but no one was sure that the registered owner was the shooter. It would take entering the residence to find out if he matched the description.

As for the owner, we had little on him. His name was Mark Francis Arban, a white male, thirty-one years old, who had only been arrested one time in the past by one of our investigators for carrying concealed "numbchucks."[1] He was the right race and about the approximate age as the shooter on Route 29, but it would take someone to physically check him out to see if he matched the description of the suspect. For that, we'd have to go inside. If he didn't want to let us in, we'd need a search warrant. That was already being taken care of. By the time we reached the staging area a warrant should be in hand.

As soon as the briefing was finished we decided to stage at the telephone company building on Cloverdale Road, about three-quarters of a mile away from Arban's residence. My older brother works for the telephone company, and I knew that I could get him out of bed to open the building up. This would give us an instant command post well situated to the scene. With the details worked out, we loaded our gear and drove toward Dale City, five miles south on Route One.

As I drove I ran a few scenarios through my mind, trying to anticipate in advance what actions and reactions would take place if things got bad. If this Arban was indeed the shooter, and he was the same guy who had deliberately stalked police officers up in Alexandria and had written their tag numbers down, there was no way to tell what was going on in his mind. Was he mentally unbalanced? Was he out for some type of revenge? We had no way of knowing. We would just have to stay flexible and see how it went. First we'd try to talk—explain that we had a search warrant and wanted to look around his house. If he got difficult, we'd have to force entry. Since we didn't have a typical armed and barricaded situation, and there was no mention of any other people that might be hostages, it would basically be a

---

[1] Actual spelling *nunchaka*. Nunchaka is an oriental marshal arts weapon that resembles two short clubs connected by a chain. In many jurisdictions they are considered deadly weapons and treated accordingly.

simple search warrant. Simple, that is, except for the fact that this guy was probably armed—we had to assume as much—and would most likely not hesitate to shoot at us.

As the sniper team leader my job would be to recon the scene and locate positions for my sniper teams. This night I only had myself and one two-man team. My observer, Mike Bennett, had been diagnosed with cancer just before we were supposed to go to Gunny Hathcock's SWAT sniper training down in Virginia Beach a few weeks before. He decided to go ahead and postpone treatment until we completed the school, and was now going through chemotherapy. With him temporarily out of action I would have to work this one alone. I still had my other two-man team, Steve Collins and Bob Bowen, which I could use on one side of the house, but I would have to cover the opposite side solo.

After arrival at the telephone building and initiating the command post operation, it was time to do the first recon of the scene. Our standard procedure is to do a "drive-by," wherein we simply drive by the scene and take a look at the layout. I took one of the entry team guys and cruised by the house, giving it a good look to see where I could spot my snipers. I decided to deploy my two-man team to cover the rear of the house—the most likely avenue of escape. And since it was the darkest area I wanted two sets of eyes back there in case the suspect fled in that direction. I would have to cover the front solo.

After delivering my plan to the entry team leader, Pat Finnigan, I sent Collins and Bowen toward the back of Arban's house and began making my way toward the house across the street. It was early in the morning and the street was dark and quiet. It would remain so for a few hours yet, especially since it was Thanksgiving Day and people would not be getting up to go to work. As I moved I noted the lighting conditions. They were poor, to say the least. The only illumination on the street came from the streetlights and a few yard lights scattered up and down the block. The street itself belonged to a typical middle-class neighborhood with one- and two-story houses built on medium-size wooded lots. There was little remarkable about the neighborhood; it was typical of the middle income suburbs scattered along Route One and Interstate 95.

Most of the yards were fenced, and I was sure most of the people had dogs. I had to move through the shadows along the shrubbery in front of most of the houses to reach my position to keep from causing a commotion that might wake the neighbors. We didn't want to alert anyone until we had all of our people in position, and we had found in the past that even if we decided to try to evacuate the neighbors, they resisted leaving their homes. Most people wanted to stay inside their houses during an operation, so when it came time to look out for their safety, we normally just had them move into a basement or to the rear of the house.

When I arrived at my preselected area at the front of the house across the street from Arban's, I examined the yard for a suitable spot to set up. The most advantageous location was the northeast corner of the house, which put me facing east toward the front door of the suspect's residence. I estimated the range at about seventy yards. Here, I had some large shrubbery to provide concealment, and because of the slight angle, I might be able to use the brick wall of the house as cover by retreating behind the corner of the building if needed. At first I thought I had a straight shot at the front door, but as it turned out when the sky finally began to lighten a few hours later with the coming of dawn, I was at a slight angle which put me off center to the left. Still, it was almost an even flat trajectory shot and appeared to be the best position available on this side of the perimeter.

I pulled myself up under the bushes and positioned my bag for a shooting rest. I laid my Remington 700 BDL on the bag and established communications with the command post on my portable radio. These preliminaries completed, I began a visual observation of the target area, transmitting intel reports over the radio as I noted any details that might influence a course of action.

Scanning the house itself, I began working on my priority of shot. I had determined in my mind that this would probably be a confrontational situation, a scenario where the suspect might try to fight it out instead of attempting to escape. If I was right, the most likely places he could shoot from would become my priority target areas. I decided that the front door was the number one priority since that was where entry would occur. This would make it the most likely spot for an initial confrontation. I then began dividing up the rest of the front elevation of the house into target areas of descending priority, each where I thought he would have a probable area of vision to the outside approaches. If he could see an area, he could shoot into it.

The house itself was a two story, but the way it was built resembled kind of a split-level in elevation. The front door stood framed on a high front porch about five feet above the ground with steps leading up to the door. To the right of the door was a large picture window. Beyond that was the south corner of the house and the driveway below where the gold Buick sat backed in.

To the left of the door were two smaller windows, both of which were partly obscured by a tree and several tall shrubs. I made the picture window my second priority of engagement, and the two smaller windows my last area of concern. From the prone position, I shouldered my Remington and began establishing my body position for each shot. I did this by sighting in on a target, such as the shoulder-high area of the front door, then scooting my butt a certain number of "clicks" to the right or left and counting the movements until my crosshairs rested on the next target area. This way I could memorize how many "clicks" I had to move to acquire a target to the right or left of the front door.

I looked at my watch. It was 0215 hours—2:15 A.M. The

entry team was in the planning stage, deciding on the best way to approach the house and what to do when they got there, and a discussion at the command post was in progress on whether we should try to negotiate. But for me and my other sniper team, it was now just a waiting game.

This was not the first time I'd been called into this part of the county on a SWAT call-out. Only a year before, on July 19, 1989, I had to deal with a situation involving a very dangerous individual which ended in a terrifying confrontation between myself and the suspect. In fact, the '89 incident occurred only a mile and a half from Arban's house.

Abdur-Rasheed Ali Muslin, a twenty-five-year-old drug dealer and enforcer, was wanted for murder in Greensboro, North Carolina. He, along with another dealer named Kenneth James Jones, had murdered a man in a vicious execution-style slaying the previous January. They had led a man out into the middle of the street in a tough Greensboro area known as "The Hill," made him kneel where all could see, then shot him point-blank through the head. It was a terrorist-style object lesson intended to coerce the community into doing exactly as they bid. Muslin's strong-arm tactics also included shoving someone who owed him drug money into a filled bathtub, then dangling live electric wires just over the water, threatening electrocution, until a friend of the victim returned with the money.

Jones was eventually captured in New Jersey, but Muslin —considered armed and extremely dangerous—remained at large. At least until the evening of July 19, 1989.

On that day, an investigator in Fairfax County received a tip from an informant that Muslin was staying in a home in Dale City. He relayed the information to our department, along with the particulars of the North Carolina case concerning the homicide. He also stated that an informant had given them information that Muslin had stated that he would not be taken alive, and that he was supposed to have several weapons, including a .45 automatic pistol and a high-powered rifle.

There was enough information to secure a search warrant. This, along with the fugitive warrant, would give us what we needed to go after Muslin. And with the danger elements involved, considering what a bad actor Muslin had proven himself to be in the past, both investigators and the SWAT team were assigned to the case. Though I was the supervisor in charge of motorcycles, I looked forward to these diversions to break the monotony of traffic enforcement. I loaded my gear and headed for Dale City.

Because of the summer vacation schedule, we could only field about half of our team. This would give us about seven men, including myself. It would have to be enough.

I conducted a drive-by of the house, which had already been under surveillance by our investigators for a couple of hours. After looking the place over, I returned to the command post and reported what I had seen to the team leader, Ron Christofano. After a bit of a discussion, the decision was made that entry would be made at the front door. Initially, there was going to be no one put in the back, but after further discussion between myself and Christofano, we decided that it would be best if I covered the rear. After all, it would be real embarrassing if we went in the front door and a dangerous fugitive bailed out the back and ran away. Especially if we didn't even have anyone there to cover the exit point.

Covering the rear would be difficult at best. There were no fields of fire for a sniper—at least none with any range to speak of. The area behind the house was extremely wooded and covered with brush and vegetation. Within ten feet of the back wall of the house the slant of the ground went up at about a thirty percent grade. It was a fairly steep embankment, and because of the dense foliage, would not be conducive to a sniper with a precision long-range rifle. Instead of the Remington, I would take my 9mm H&K 94 mounted with an Aimpoint scope. It was an ideal combination for working up close.

I worked my way down behind the houses as the entry team was getting into place two doors down. As I drew near to the suspect's house, I stopped and notified the entry team that I was almost in position. This way, if Muslin spotted my approach and decided to bust out of the front door, he wouldn't catch the entry team flat-footed.

I moved about ten feet closer and set into position. From there, I could see the back of the house at an angle and also part of the front yard between the houses. Almost immediately I could see the entry team begin to move in, disappearing from view as they passed the corner of the house. Because of my location behind the house I never heard the standard announcement, "Police; we have a warrant!" But a couple of seconds after they reached the front door I heard the unmistakable sound of two sharp cracks of the battering ram against the door.

I shifted my attention to my area of responsibility. I began to pan across the back of the house, taking in the windows and bushes as my eyes moved continuously, searching for movement or any possible avenue of escape. I had visually searched all the way to the end of the building and had just started panning back when I caught some motion at one of the basement windows. I locked onto it. The window was about twenty inches square, enough for a man to get out, and was located almost at ground level.

I no sooner had determined that it could be used as an escape point when a man virtually exploded from the opening. Diving out Superman style, hands in front of him, was a black male with extremely short hair. In his hand he held a weapon. My mind raced in recognition, registering the weapon to be a firearm. There was no time to think, only react. The elements of the situation had already been filed into my consciousness: the fugitive was a known felon, a drug dealer; he was wanted for murder; he was to be considered armed and dangerous; and he was attempting to escape—in *my* direction! And I could see that he was armed.

I had already come to bear with the H&K, locking it onto the man as soon as he dove out of the window. As I took up the trigger he began to close the distance. I fired three shots in rapid succession. The first shot hit him dead center in the top of his head, knocking him instantly to the ground. The second two shots missed and hit the house above and behind him. The force of the first round caused him to make one quick gasp before he dropped. That was it.

I stood there for a moment and, as I covered him with my rifle, ran over what had just happened in my mind. I knew I was right, but you are always trying to second-guess yourself. Always trying to mentally make sure all the pieces fit after all the action was over. The bottom line was that this guy was a fugitive, a wanted murderer, and that he had come at me and was armed. He left me with no choice.

That's when the entry team scared the hell out of me. Over the radio came the message: "We've got him in the back bedroom."

Immediately a spasm of fear hit me in the pit of my stomach. If they've got him in the back bedroom, then *who is this?*

It seemed like an eternity before my teammates appeared to take over the scene. It was then that I found out what had happened inside the house. As the entry team was approaching the front, Muslin had parted the blinds and spotted them. He had already set up an escape plan and immediately put it in motion. As the entry team busted through the front door—which was on the basement level—Muslin ran toward the rear of the house. Sprinting as fast as he could, he dashed through a bedroom, jumped up onto a bed, and using it as a springboard, dove out the rear window. It had almost worked.

When I fired, the entry team thought they were being fired upon. They took cover, held their position inside the house, and relayed on the radio: "We've got him in the back bedroom."

The last they had seen of Muslin was when he disappeared into the bedroom, where they now thought they had him cornered. This held them up for a moment, but then they quickly determined that the shots had not come from within the house, but from outside, toward the rear of the house. Then they thought about me.

As I stood there covering the body, it was like a mental roller coaster ride. The information that was pouring into my brain tore me in two directions. First the guy tried to rabbit, and he was armed, and I shot. Then it wasn't the right guy—Muslin was cornered in the back bedroom. Then it *was* the right guy.

And then he wasn't armed.

The officers that surrounded me began working the scene. But they couldn't find a weapon. It had disappeared. But I *knew* what I had seen. The guy had a gun. It was a pistol, shiny and long. And he would have used it to kill me.

One of our SWAT team EMTs began checking the body for vital signs. There were none. The shot had entered right at the top of his head and taken him out immediately. The EMT rolled him over to check his front. It was only then that they found the weapon. It had fallen under him.

But it wasn't a gun. It was a large hunting knife.

I didn't dwell on whether I was right or wrong in taking the shots. It doesn't matter what kind of weapon it is when you're only a few feet away from each other. Whether it's a gun or a knife, if you hesitate too long, you're a dead man. Besides, it didn't really matter whether or not he was armed anyway. I could not let him escape my perimeter. That fact was the final deciding element of the whole scenario. He made his choice and forced me into mine.

The bottom line was that I had done exactly as I had been trained to do. It had been an automatic reaction, and later in court it was found to be a justified shooting. Though a civil action transpired, initiated by Muslin's relatives who claimed that he was a good father and that the kids would suffer and so on—all the normal lawsuit stuff—the investigation conducted by the Commonwealth's Attorney's office cleared me. Later, the Justice Department also investigated the case on civil rights grounds. In their letter, their findings were summed up with: ". . . we concluded that this matter should be closed and that no further action is warranted."

And now, only a few months later, I was back in the same neighborhood. On an almost identical scenario.

By 0330 we had established some contact with some of the neighbors and had begun building a picture of Arban. He was somewhat of a recluse, who normally only came out at night. He'd had some confrontations with neighbors in the past, and was suspected of slashing some of the tires on their cars. They complained that he never cut his lawn, and that he would sometimes back up and down his driveway all night long. They believed he lived alone since they had never seen anyone else living in the house since he had been there. Though the neighbors appeared to be scared of him, none of them had bothered to call the police to intervene in any of the confrontations or activities. One lady who lived two doors away said that she ". . . knew he was a little strange. He never came out during the day. He only came out at night. He ordered pizzas, morning, noon, and night . . . he never did anything to the house. He was sort of an eyesore."

We began evacuating the homes to the right and left of Arban's at about 0400. This was done in order to tighten the perimeter in preparation to moving the entry team in. I concentrated my attention on the house, trying to note anything that I had not yet seen, getting mentally into what Gunny Hathcock says is "the bubble," a state of mind wherein neither heat, cold, rain, snow, nor any other outside influence affects you. Your concentration on your target area and mission is total. But thirty minutes later my concentration was interrupted in a blaze of light.

At 0430 the window above my head blinked bright as someone inside turned the light on. I could hear voices and people opening and closing doors. A few minutes later a man came out of the front door not ten feet away—*carrying two rifles!* I hunkered up under my bush and waited silently, hoping that he would not see me and become startled. I assumed that since there was no way of him knowing about the police activity happening just outside his bedroom, he was obviously getting up early to go hunting. If he looked to his left, he just might see a man dressed in black, tucked up under his bushes, with a scoped rifle pulled to his shoulder. There was no telling what his reaction would be to that.

But he didn't look. Apparently he was still half asleep and not very aware of his surroundings. After all, who would expect a police SWAT team action to be happening in your front yard on such a quiet holiday morning? A few more trips inside to retrieve more gear and he drove off. Thirty minutes later his wife did the same.

By 0500 there had still been no movement whatsoever in Arban's house. For someone who normally was nocturnal, this guy had been strangely silent all night long. It was as if he were hiding out for some reason—and I felt confident that we knew exactly what that reason was.

The decision was made to abstain from making any advance contact with him. Instead, we would follow procedure for a "knock" search warrant. A knock warrant meant that we would have to knock and announce ourselves prior to entry. A "no-knock" warrant means that you can just bust in and go for it. This time we would have to knock, announce, and then if he didn't open up, force our way in. At 0530 the entry team moved up onto the front porch. I trained my scope on the door.

I could see my friends across the street, lined up behind a ballistics shield as they waited for the word to go. Mike Pennington, an eleven-year veteran of the force who was married and had a six-year-old son, led at the number one position. Behind him was Bobby Arnold, followed closely by Bobby Williams. Each man was a well-trained, dedicated officer who would know exactly what to do. All they had to do was get in the house.

I watched as they climbed the stairs to the porch. Seeing the activity clearly through my scope, I had a good view of the knock and announcement. Immediately Steve Collins, one of the snipers I had positioned behind the house, came on the radio and stated that a light had come on in the basement. Almost simultaneously Bobby Arnold, who crouched behind a ballistics shield with a halogen light mounted on it, and had turned it on to illuminate the living room through the picture window, announced that he could see a subject coming up the living room stairs toward the front door. The way the house was designed, the family room was downstairs, with the stairs leading down from directly behind the front door while the living room itself was on the same level as the door.

The description of the man given by Arnold matched that provided by the Arlington deputy. The man climbing the stairs was a white male with a thin mustache, wearing a white sweater-type shirt. As he came up the stairs, Arnold checked what he could see and announced that the suspect's hands "were clear."

I could only discern tidbits of the conversation from my position. But I distinctly heard, "He's unarmed." Then, before anyone could get through the door, "He's trying to barricade the door!"

The entry team sprang into action instantly. Using a battering ram, they began pounding on the door. But after the ram had struck the door several times, they realized that something was wrong. It should have broken the door wide open by then. It took the combined body weight of two officers to force the door open. After they got inside they found that Arban had dragged a home safe up to the door to use as a barricade. The heavy metal box was about two feet square and had effectively slowed the entry team's progress enough to permit Arban to retreat to the bottom of the stairs and duck inside the open doorway of a room to the right of the stairway.

The first two officers, Pennington and Arnold, pushed their way through the door. An instant later I heard the report of a gunshot.

Arban had pulled the .25 automatic that he had used to shoot LaClair, and had reappeared to brandish it at Arnold. Bobby, instantly recognizing the threat, had fired a quick shot. But his bullet had stuck dead center on an upright of the metal handrail mounted on one side of the staircase. The bullet disintegrated, sending a fragment of the metal jacket into Arban's back. The wound was superficial, but was enough to force him back down the stairs. At the bottom he once again disappeared into the room.

Pennington and Arnold, knowing their ballistics shield would provide sufficient cover against the small pistol, backed up to the front door to afford them the best vantage point for viewing the area at the bottom of the stairs. Mike figured that there was still a chance to negotiate and, determined not to give up any ground if possible, began talking.

Arban, hidden from view in a room at the bottom of the stairs, asked, "Who are you?"

"We're the police," explained Pennington.

"Well, I'm the KGB and you can't arrest me! Only the FBI can arrest me!" It quickly became obvious that this guy was not all there. But it would not be until much later that we would find that he had been medically diagnosed as a paranoid schizophrenic.

Mike continued to try to negotiate with Arban for twenty minutes. Arban would exit the room at the bottom of the stairs briefly, then go back inside. Almost like he was pacing. Even though he was armed, carrying the pistol down at his side, he seemed to be passive. No real problem so far.

By this time the entry team leader, Pat Finnigan, had withdrawn from the house and had returned to the SWAT commander to discuss the next step. It was quickly decided to pull the entry team back and use tear gas to force Arban from the house. As this planning session was going on Pennington whispered to his teammates on the front porch behind him that he had a shot. By looking through the little window in the ballistics shield, he would see Arban clearly each time he came out of the doorway. He repeated this information each time Arban showed himself. But the statements were more along the line of capability than a request for permission to shoot. The decision on whether to shoot or not at that point was totally Mike's. Though an order to shoot could have been given after the point where Arban had fired, it was Mike's ball game. He held his fire.

Then Bobby Arnold heard something ominous: the sound of a slide working on a large caliber weapon and a bolt slamming home. To him, it sounded like some type of automatic weapon much heavier than a pistol. In actuality, it was a 7.62mm x 39 Poly-Tech AKM, a clone of the AK-47 assault rifle. Without realizing it at the time, Mike and Bobby were outgunned.

Bobby, realizing the shield would not stop a heavier round, announced, "He's got an automatic rifle!" Immediately the team began to scoot backward toward the front porch. But before they could escape the line of fire, the muzzle of the stubby rifle swung around the corner and came to bear on the team.

From my position, I had no way of knowing exactly what was happening inside. I could only go by what I could see, hear, or what came over the radio. The first indication I had that something had gone desperately wrong was when I heard the chilling sound of someone screaming. I never heard the shot.

Bobby Williams, now dragging Mike out of the doorway, was screaming, "Oh no! Not again!" As he yelled this, three or four other officers who had moved up to the front porch to back them up, began falling back from the doorway. It was obvious to all that Mike had been hurt. As Mike's body cleared the storm door, it slammed shut. Simultaneously, another officer ran around to the front of the porch to get aligned with the door. For a second I was concerned that he might be a problem by getting between me and my priority one target, but since he was lower than the porch, he remained out of my line of fire.

Meanwhile, Arban, who had watched Pennington and Arnold disappear through the door, ran up the steps and looked out through the picture window to see what was happening outside. Seeing all the police officers, he decided to open fire through the glass. There was no need to wait for orders to shoot. We were now in a firefight.

Instead of approaching the picture window—my priority two target—he stopped in a spot that he must have considered safe where he could shoot out through the glass at an angle. But, unknown to him, his choice of position put him directly in line with the front door—and me.

I had guessed right. He was in my priority one engagement area—and I was ready. As Bobby was dragging Mike away, I concentrated on my crosshairs.

Arban got off one shot. The muzzle flash illuminated his face like a brilliant strobe light, briefly showing me his thin mustache in detail through my scope. My mind assimilated every detail at once: the face, the mustache, the fact that he had not shouldered and aimed the weapon because his cheek was not down on the stock, and the fact that he had opened fire on my teammates.

I squeezed the trigger.

When I worked the bolt and came back on target he was gone. I felt confident that I had got him, but there was no way to confirm it. I could see the bullet hole in the glass right where his face had been, and I knew in my mind that I had hit him. But was he dead? Had the threat been eliminated?

In front of the house the scene could best be described as "organized pandemonium." Officers were trying to get reorganized and reestablish the perimeter. Meanwhile, Bobby Williams had dragged Mike down the stairs to the front yard and had pulled a ballistics shield over him to provide protection. But it was too late. Mike was dead.

Arban hadn't even aimed. He had just shoved the assault rifle around the corner and fired a shot. The bullet went through the top of Mike's ballistics shield like butter and struck him in the temple area directly below his helmet. He was killed instantly. There is no way a ballistics shield, even backed up by a ballistics helmet, will stop a rifle bullet. Mike hadn't stood a chance.

The team was finally pulled back up into a safe position and everybody began organizing another tight perimeter. Positions were being adjusted, and as all of this was going on, I grabbed my radio to let everyone know that I had fired a shot and I thought the guy was down. Since I had not heard Arban's shot inside the house, or the one when he shot out of the window, I felt that the rest of the team may not have heard my shot.

The damned radio didn't work! I couldn't get through to them that I thought the threat had been neutralized. I had, at that moment, what one might call a minor flash of temper. I chucked the radio down the street. I finally got the word to the rest of the team by shouting out to them. This accomplished, I continued to watch the house.

Dawn came like someone had thrown a switch. It seemed that one minute it was completely dark, then the next it was bright sunlight. At the time I had taken the shot it was pitch-dark. It seemed like it was just a moment ago. I looked at my watch: 0630. It was as though I had just gone through a time warp. I couldn't believe that we had been on the scene for six hours. All I could remember were the few minutes of gunfire in the dark—and then it was daylight.

They were taking Mike away. The ambulance attendants

were talking to the hospital, and I could hear the radio coming through the vehicle's PA system. Stuff about them having a victim with a gunshot wound to the head—that it doesn't look good and so on. I didn't like what I heard, but I still had to try to concentrate on the house. I was sure that I had hit Arban. I knew in my heart that I did, but we couldn't take a chance that he had not been neutralized. If he hadn't, the possibility existed that he could become offensive again.

As I continued to watch the house, another tragedy almost occurred. A mix-up sent a notification team to Bobby Arnold's house to tell his wife that he had been killed. But fortunately, before they could arrive, they were turned around and sent to Mike Pennington's house instead. A traumatic scene had been barely averted.

The team began mustering for an assault on the house. It was time to end the situation and, if tear gas didn't force him out, go in after him. They brought up the 37mm gas launcher and began to deploy CS. And as Murphy's Law of SWAT operations says, if something is going to go wrong, this is when. No one wanted to expose themselves by approaching close, so the gunners tried to lob the shells into the house from almost the same range I had fired from. The rounds, designed for a much shorter flight path, fell short and began skittering around on the yard spewing white clouds of tear gas into the morning breeze. And as luck would have it, the wind was blowing in my direction. As a sniper, I never carried gas equipment—not even a mask. It's almost impossible to shoot through a scope with an M-17 gas mask on. Knowing this, one of our guys threw a mask at me just before they fired the gas, but it hit me on the back of the head and bounced away to roll down the incline toward the street. I hadn't bothered to retrieve it.

It only took a couple of seconds for the gas to roll up to my position. At first I only got a few light wisps, and I thought *I can handle this. Keep concentrating.* If the gas got to Arban and he came out shooting, I wanted to be ready.

Then it was like someone brought a fist around the corner of the house and hit me. This huge white cloud came out of nowhere, and the next thing I knew I was in the backyard, choking and hacking in the morning air. My lungs and sinus passages were on fire, my eyes burning and clenched shut streaming tears, and I could hardly suck in a breath.

They had to stop the operation until I could get back into position. Without me, there was not enough coverage in the front of the house for the reconstituted entry team. I was mad at myself. My job was to be up there to cover them and I didn't hold my position. But anyone who's been there will know that it's ridiculous to blame yourself for succumbing to gas. It doesn't matter how tough you are, if gas gets to you, that's all she wrote. You're out of the fight until you get over the chemicals.

It took about fifteen minutes for me to regain my senses enough to get back into position. During this time they managed to pepper the house with gas rounds and get a few inside. Still, there was no motion, no movement from within. This being the case, the entry team rushed the place.

Arban was inside, but not where I had expected him to be. My shot had knocked him back down the stairs to the spot where he had fired the shot at Pennington. His body lay crumpled on the floor, a single bullet hole marking his right cheek just above his jawline. It had traveled across his neck, exiting the opposite side, blowing two vertebrae across the living room where they, and my round, still remained. Like Pennington, he had died instantly. It seemed fitting.

My greatest fear had been assuaged. I was afraid that if my shot had not done what I wanted it to do there would be another confrontation inside and maybe another officer would get shot.

It was a great relief to find that Arban was no longer a threat to my friends. I only regretted that he had managed to get that one shot off at Mike Pennington.

After things calmed down and we had time to sort out what had happened, I thought about Mike's wife and son.

It was a hell of a way to start Thanksgiving.

25

Major E. J. Land, Jr., USMC (Ret), Sniper Instructor

The Psychological Aftermath

Sniper. The very word conjures up a host of images, most of which are negative. To those of us who have spent years in the precision marksmanship community, the word has held a connotation by others of someone who "bushwhacks" from concealment, and therefore doesn't fight fair. It is probably the most misused and misunderstood word in the English language.

Even more misunderstood are the men who were snipers during war. They bore the enmity of both sides—the enemy and their allies alike. They plied their deadly trade alone, or with a single partner. They hunted and they killed methodically. Each move—the fix of the scope on a prey's vitals, the gentle pull of the trigger—was slow and deliberate. There was no heat of battle, no rapid flow of events running almost out of control, tempered by shouted orders from superiors to rationalize the task. It was a different type of combat. It was a simple matter of kill, or be killed. The sniper's target, ending the flight of a .30 caliber bullet fired from distant shadows, rarely knew what hit him.

The men who fought in squads, platoons, and companies rarely understood the sniper. Those few who did showed silent respect. Still, when the fighting stopped, even they joined the ranks of the majority who thought it best to closet the sniper, disband his small units and training schools, shelve his equipment, and return him to a regular unit—or to civilian life. It was as if the world turned suddenly ashamed and scurried to erase every trace of the man and his job.

If military men could not understand the sniper, civilians certainly fared no better—and the media worse. Every random shooting by the criminal or the violently deranged was the work of a "sniper." The political assassin, the crackpot, the drug-crazed junkie shooting passers-by from a tenement window, were all "snipers." Cops hated the word, decent law-abiding folk feared it, and such misuse of the word was inevitably followed by misunderstanding. Mention "sniper," and the conditioned reflex is one of revulsion. "Police sniper" therefore sounds like a contradiction in terms.

To the men who are snipers, the term means a special fraternity—a brotherhood of men skilled in the art and science of precision shooting. The true sniper is a man not given to the swagger and bragging of regular troops. Snipers are quiet men, professional men, patient men. They are strong individuals of conviction, ethics, and morals. For military snipers, like those in civilian life who have donned the badge and baton, are protectors. They strive to keep their colleagues out of harm's way and at the same time to keep the enemy at bay. They are also lone investigators, intelligence gatherers who can quickly learn the habits and characteristics of the enemy—or the criminal.

In many ways, the lessons learned and practiced by the military sniper are directly applicable to law enforcement. The basics of their missions are quite similar: to perform under impossible conditions in a professional, dispassionate manner—and to protect and preserve life. The irony, of course, is that often a life must be taken so that others might live.

In the law enforcement role, I personally prefer the term "precision rifle shooter" in lieu of "police sniper." This designation breaks away from the emotional connotation historically presented by the term "sniper," and at the same time casts a different light on the job when referred to by the media. But whatever the correct clinical term, the principles are the same. The precision rifle shooter must master the principles of marksmanship, tactics, fieldcraft—and more.

I can say that a precision rifle shooter shouldn't wear glasses, should be right-handed, shouldn't smoke, and should not be exceptionally large. But those are physical attributes. There's much more to being able to do the job than technical skill or understanding the mechanics. There is much more to being a police marksman than being able to punch holes in paper targets with consistent accuracy on the rifle range. There is the mental aspect—the mind-set of the precision rifleman—that is every bit as important as the above subjects, if not more so.

A person's mind-set is normally based on upbringing. We are all products of our environment. That's why in Vietnam, when Carlos Hathcock and I put the 1st Marine Division Sniper School together, we mainly had country boys. Men who grew up in a rural community with its closeness to nature. They had hunted and killed, they had seen farm animals and pets die, and they psychologically accepted death in a different perspective than most people in today's society. Death was a fact of life that they learned in the natural surroundings of the simple country life. The people we selected as members of our sniper team who had this background made our jobs somewhat easier. We could devote more time to training them on the mechanics of producing a center hit and less on the mental preparation of taking someone's life.

Police departments often do not have a similar pool to

draw from. Most police officers grow up in the cities, and to them, death is something that is remote. They have far less exposure to it than their country cousins. Yet, when it comes time to fill the role of precision rifle shooter and be ready to shoot without hesitation, someone has to do it. Someone has to have the training and mental discipline to shoulder a rifle, line up the crosshairs on a human being, and drop the hammer.

When this happens, when the marksman takes that shot, he changes. He changes in the eyes of his family, and he changes in the eyes of his friends. Even his peers view him as somewhat different, even though he might be regarded as a hero for doing his job under the degree of stress only they can identify with. But to everyone else, he's a guy who has killed someone. He'll never be the same guy you knew before—and he has to live with that.

Another thing police precision marksmen must deal with psychologically is the lack of the defensive mechanism normally used by other officers. It's not like the marksman, shooting from outside of the zone of action, is defending himself. He can't say, "I did it because he was going to hurt me." He can say it was the bad guy's fault, because he was going to hurt the hostage, or he was going to hurt his fellow officers. But these, in the marksman's mind, are different, abstract reasons in comparison to simple self-defense.

To prepare for the emotions and aftermath of taking the shot—taking someone's life—a police precision rifle shooter must mentally prepare in advance. He does this by rehearsing in his mind individual scenarios all the way through the entire flow of events. He takes a typical scenario and thoughtfully goes over the call-out, the set-up, the waiting, the "green light," the shot, the following police investigation, the court proceedings—every event that occurs through and after dropping the hammer. He must continually, religiously, mentally rehearse in advance the flow of events encountered in a typical call-out. When the events actually do go down, his mind is prepared to accept the results. The shock effect is reduced because now it is not like it's the first time.

An equally important part of mental preparation is knowing that you are the best man for the job. Not just thinking it, but *knowing* it. This is accomplished by proper training that builds confidence in one's equipment and in oneself. The police marksman must *know*, within himself, that no one on the team can do his job better than he.

And he must know that when he drops the hammer, he's taking down a threat to society that must be neutralized. Even though his target may be the worst scum bag in the city, when it is later presented in the newspapers and on TV it will be different. The guy he just shot was the nicest neighbor anyone could ever want, the best father in history, with the greatest kids in the world—an absolute Mr. Wonderful. With the proper training and mental preparation, the police marksman should be psychologically capable of handling it when people ask, "How could you do it?"

He has to be prepared to accept the aftermath. He can only do it by mentally rehearsing every detail, knowing and feeling almost exactly what will happen and be ready for it. Then, at the most critical emotional period, it comes as no surprise.

Most important, he must be prepared to survive the consequences of the simple pull of the trigger—the emotional and social consequences that often come from fellow officers, loved ones, the media, and the public. After the hammer has dropped, the police precision rifle shooter may find himself treated as someone different and apart from the rest of the department, the community—and humanity itself.

No matter what he is called, whether it be "sniper," "countersniper," "rifleman," or "precision rifle shooter," accomplishing the mission of the police marksman is not an easy task. But it is a very necessary one. And the thing that must be remembered above all else when the time comes for him to drop the hammer is that all the training and skill he has must be summoned for one reason: to provide the only means left to save a life. For when it comes time for him to squeeze that trigger, every other alternative solution has already been tried.

He is, by necessity, the final option.

In 1991 sixty-two American police officers were killed in the line of duty. Of these, fourteen were killed in disturbance calls, fourteen while attempting arrests, twelve during traffic stops, nine on suspicious persons calls, and five while transporting prisoners. The remaining eight were killed in ambushes.

Of the sixty-two cases, fifty-seven have been cleared by arrest—or by a single well-aimed shot.

About the Author

CRAIG ROBERTS is a twenty-four-year veteran of the Tulsa Police Department, having served as an explosives expert with the TAC (SWAT) Team and now as a police helicopter pilot. He was awarded ten decorations for his Marine Corps service in Vietnam, where he served as a Marine sniper, and is now an Army Reserve Ground Liaison Officer attached to an Air National Guard F-16 fighter squadron. He has authored and coauthored numerous nonfiction books and articles. Roberts currently lives with his wife and three daughters in Tulsa.

IN THEIR OWN WORDS, THE INSIDE STORY OF THE HIGHWAY PATROL

TROOPER DOWN!

LIFE AND DEATH IN ONE OF THE NATION'S MOST ELITE LAW ENFORCEMENT AGENCIES

MARIE BARLETT

Foreword by JAMES J. KILPATRICK

POCKET BOOKS   AVAILABLE FROM POCKET BOOKS   761